MEDITERRANEAN MAELSTROM

By the same author

FIGHTING DESTROYER
  The story of HMS *Petard*.
VALIANT QUARTET
  His Majesty's anti-aircraft cruisers *Curlew*,
  Cairo, *Calcutta* and *Coventry*.
ARCTIC DESTROYERS
  The 17th Flotilla.
JACK'S WAR
  Lower-deck recollections from World War II.

MEDITERRANEAN MAELSTROM

HMS *Jervis* and the 14th Flotilla

First published in 1987 by
WILLIAM KIMBER & CO. LIMITED
100 Jermyn Street, London, SW1Y 6EE

© G. G. Connell, 1987
ISBN 0-7183-0643-0

Typeset by Ann Buchan (Typesetters)
and printed and bound in Great Britain by
Adlard & Son Ltd, The Garden City Press,
Letchworth, Herts

Dedicated
to the memory of
Ron Bone
whose idea prompted this book
and has since bravely 'crossed the bar',
and to
Lily and Bill Skilling,
founders of the J's and K's,
14th Flotilla Association.

Contents

List of Illustrations

Acknowledgements

It would have been difficult to have produced this book without the interest and support of many who had served in HMS *Jervis* and the 14th Flotilla. I am especially grateful for the help given by the following: Lieutenant-Commander Peter Aylwin who put me in touch with a number of ex-ship and flotilla staff officers and for his own recollections of the ship; Bernard Blowers for his illustrations and art work; Heather Bone who gave me access to her late father's research notes and correspondence; Captain R.D. Butt CBE FBIM who prepared photo-copies of his midshipman's journal. Lieutenant-Commander D.O. Dykes for loaning his cadet diaries; John Ellis who provided '*Jervis*' extracts from his war diary; Captain C.B. Featherstone-Dilke CB DL who put on tape extracts from his midshipman's journal; Lieutenant-Commander Patrick Fletcher DSC for his information, hospitality and arranging a gathering of ex-ship's officers; Commodore Daniel Geluychens, Belgian Navy, for travelling over from Belgium to attend a re-union; Geoffrey L. Green who sought out and loaned much research material; Captain M.A. Hemans DSC* who prepared a tape of his recollections; Lieutenant Commander Roger Hill DSO, DSC for permission to quote from his classic autobiographical book 'DESTROYER CAPTAIN'; George Morel for his taped memories; Commander J.P. Mosse DSC for his written recollections of some of the major events; Commander Hugh Mulleneux DSC for giving me unlimited access to his comprehensive and illustrated diary and for providing so many unique photographs; the special assistance given by the Naval Historical Section of MOD; the Public Record Office, the Keeper and his staff, for their assistance; Rear Admiral A.F. Pugsley CB, DSO** who has allowed quotations from his unique book 'DESTROYER MAN'; W. (Bill) Skilling for access to his 'Black book' diary and for the many addresses of ex-*Jervis* shipmates; Albert Stoker for his diary covering the period April 1942 to October 1943; to ex-Petty Officer L.F. Waters for his invaluable advice and his labours with my typescript drafts, and to Alex Wisely for extracts from his diary.

All contributors who were so generous with their time, interest and information are listed in the Sources Appendix.

G.G.C.

Preface

During 1938 on the river Tyne, in the same shipyard at Hebburn, two identical and powerful fleet destroyer flotilla leaders were launched. They fitted out and commissioned in 1939 within a few weeks of each other as leaders of the J and K class destroyers of the 7th and 5th Flotillas.

The first to be commissioned was the *Jervis* which survived the entire period of World War Two, and in the Mediterranean theatre achieved a fighting career of matchless quality yet is hardly known or remembered by the public at large or by the contemporary navy. *Jervis* and the destroyers she led inflicted immense damage on the enemy at sea and shore installations; she suffered very few casualties and no dead from enemy action, her record is second to none. She was commanded by a succession of highly professional, formidable and successful captains who led and inspired a ship's company of battle-hardened veterans.

In total contrast, her unfortunate sister flotilla leader, *Kelly*, was destined to survive only twenty-one months of the five years and nine months of the 1939/1945 war and to suffer in her short life grievous casualties: 148 dead and many wounded out of a complement of 223 officers and men. Because of four long repair and reconstruction periods in dockyard hands due to damage successively sustained from the weather, being mined, collision at sea and torpedo, *Kelly* was only able to give a bare nine months of active sea service before her final demise during an air attack south of Crete on 23rd May 1941. In retaliation for those who had died in her, *Kelly* was able to do very little to embarrass the enemy's war effort.

Despite *Kelly*'s less-than-effective nine months' sea service, a legend of a glamorous destroyer leader has been created from what was in actuality a minimal impact on the enemy. This legend has produced for the nation and public, the navy's best remembered warship of the Second World War British fleet. It is a strange paradox that while her brief damage-prone sea service is commemorated in the fact that many naval establishments, training classes and awards bear the name *Kelly*, the fighting successes of her distinguished sister destroyer flotilla leader, *Jervis*, remain virtually unhonoured.

It was only in late 1946 that *Jervis* concluded a long and active career after carrying out the unrewarding, frequently distressing and always dangerous task of intercepting and boarding ships crowded with Jewish refugees trying to break the naval blockade of Palestine.

Jervis was awarded thirteen battle honours, an achievement equalled by the destroyer *Nubian* and cruiser *Orion* and exceeded by only one ship in the entire British fleet, namely the battleship of two world wars *Warspite*, which was awarded fourteen battle honours.

This book is a belated endeavour to put on record the achievements of the men who served in *Jervis* and the 14th Destroyer Flotilla.

CHAPTER ONE

Creation of a Flotilla Leader

'My first destroyer – thought that I was dead lucky, a new ship and a Captain (D) Leader!' recorded a young stoker when he joined his first ship on 8th May 1939. 'There she was looking sleek and lovely outboard of the *Kelly*, over which we had to clamber with our gear.'

The ship was the brand new flotilla leader *Jervis*, leader of the J class fleet destroyers (also later the K class) and the 7th and 14th Flotillas.

The *Javelin* or J class destroyers were products of the 1936 programme of fleet destroyer construction, ordered in April 1937. They followed immediately after the 1935/36 programme which had produced sixteen large and powerful Tribal class destroyers in which the gun armament dominated a reduced torpedo capability.

The design of the Tribals had received by no means unanimous naval approval; there were many experienced destroyer officers who considered the double funnelled ships to be too large and inadequately equipped to deal with air attacks. The J class design contained a low single funnel profile and silhouette. They were the first destroyers given a graceful trawler and flared bow. The hull drawings would be the standard for the J and K class and for the first two emergency class flotillas ordered when the war was clearly imminent, the only difference being that the emergency destroyer hulls would have 3/16th inch plating instead of the J and K class 5/16th plating.

Arming of the J class was conditioned by Naval Staff thinking which had continued to be influenced by a concept of major encounters between fleets of capital ships. Consequently the factor of defence against air attacks was to take a very secondary role; 'No construction of high-angle(gun) fire can be countenanced which might prejudice low-angle(gun) performance until such time as aircraft threaten the accomplishment of the destroyer's main objective.'

So ran one of the 32 points set out in the Naval Staff requirements for the 1936 programme of destroyer construction.

There was initial stiff opposition, by the Director of Naval Ordnance, to the fitting of twin 4.7 inch mountings until further trials had been completed in the trials destroyer *Hereward*. It was proposed that the ships should carry four single gun mountings until this was overruled by the Director of Naval Construction who decided on six 4.7″ guns on three twin mountings, two forward a single mounting aft, leaving a quarter-deck area clear for delivery of anti-submarine depth charges.

The J and K class hull dimensions were: length overall, 356′6″ and beam 20′6″ with a draught of 13′8″. The standard displacement of the J and K class ships was 1690 tons except for the leaders, *Jervis* and *Kelly*, their displacement being 1760 tons. The engines fitted in the ships were Parsons, impulse reaction, single reduction turbines developing shaft horsepower of 40,000 and at 350 revolutions per minute capable of giving the destroyers a capability of 32 knots, deep-laden. Furnace fuel capacity was 484 tons which gave a range of 5500 nautical miles at 15 knots reducing to 3700 nautical miles when proceeding at 20 knots. *Jervis* actually achieved, on her sea trials, a speed of 33.813 knots with her turbines running at 345.1 rpm.

With the J class main armament decided upon, some consideration was given to anti-aircraft defence. The 4.7″ QF Mk XII guns could elevate only to 40 degrees which in some senior naval quarters was considered adequate defence against any aircraft likely to attack a destroyer, and for a destroyer barrage put up to defend the fleet from low-flying torpedo carrying biplanes. However, additional close range guns were authorised, one 2-pdr QF pom-pom 4 barrel Mk VIII mounted abaft the funnel, two 0.5″ 4 barrel machine guns Mk III and four .303″ Lewis guns.

When these proposals were made initially, the then Director of Plans expressed his misgivings and referred to the previous completions of the inter World War destroyer construction programmes '. . . our position with eight flotillas completed, none of which can produce any effective fire against aircraft, is one which is difficult to contemplate with equanimity. . .'. Six years after having written this observation the officer, later Admiral Sir T.S.V. Phillips, went down in his flagship when the battleship *Prince of Wales* and the battle-cruiser *Repulse* were sunk on 10th December 1941 by a massed attack of Japanese aircraft.

With the J class, the Naval staff returned to the true origins and purpose of the destroyer, namely its task to deliver a torpedo attack.

May 1939. HMS *Jervis,* leader of the 7th Flotilla, on her acceptance power trials.

Winter 1939/1940. East coast FN convoy, *Jervis* in right foreground.

(*Left*) Winter 1939/1940 Norway convoy and the air escort. (*Right*) September 1939. *Jervis* leads the 1st Division of the 7th Flotilla to sea from the Humber.

8th October 1939. *Jervis* pom-pom crew after their first action off the east coast.

(*Left*) Winter 1939/1940 on the east coast. Captain Philip Mack on his bridge. (*Right*) March 1940. Swan Hunter's yard, Tyne. *Jervis* in dry-dock with portside plating rolled back intact to No 2 mounting exposing upper and lower mess-decks.

19th March 1940. Neutral Swedish ship ss *Tor* which was in collision with *Jervis*.

The Tribal class had been reduced for the first time (for destroyers) to one set of quadruple mountings, whilst *Jervis* and her flotilla ships were fitted with two sets of 21" Pentad mountings and ten torpedoes Mk IX and IX*. For anti-submarine attack, the destroyers were equipped with two depth charge throwers and two sets of double rails for delivery of charges over the stern.

Jervis, launched on 9th September 1938 by the Hon Mrs Hilda Maud St Leger Jervis in the shipyard of Hawthorn Leslie at Hebburn on Tyne, was named after John Jervis, Earl of St Vincent; the flotilla leader was the first ship, and to date the only ship, of the fleet to be named after the distinguished and formidable Admiral. Several weeks later, *Kelly* was launched from the adjoining slipway.

Alongside the fitting out berth, gun mountings, two sets of quintuple torpedo tubes, boilers and engines, boat davits, capstan, the 44" stabilised search-light, pom-pom mounting and the elegant tripod and foremast were hoisted inboard. In the bowels of the ship, wiring and cabling to connect propelling, gun and navigational control gear were installed. At the same time living accommodation was being created and furnished. This followed a standard and long established format, ratings living in the fore part of the ship with the officers separate, aft and remote, a practice not suited to modern ships and warfare.

Crews of the armament located amidships and aft, therefore, lived forward away from their action stations. This same remoteness affected the officers living aft with most having their fighting stations on or near the bridge area. At night and especially in bad weather, closing up for action could be a hazardous evolution with searchlight, torpedo tube, gun and depth charge crews rushing aft over wave-swept iron decks, crashing into officers moving forward to their battle stations. Only the captain had a sea cabin immediately under the bridge and the navigator a settee-bunk in the chart-house.

The after-guards accommodation was spacious and comfortable, the furnishings in all cabins, the wardroom and pantry were surprisingly luxurious and constructed from polished wood. Most cabins doubled as offices and, as *Jervis* was a flotilla leader, she would carry more officers than a private ship. Because of this, some cabins were fitted out with two berths for the ship's own junior officers, the larger cabins were earmarked for heads of departments and the flotilla specialist staff officers, navigation, engine-room, signals, gunnery, torpedo and supply/secretariat. The after superstructure which supported the twin No 3 gun mounting contained the wardroom galley, a couple of cabins, the officers' heads and bathrooms. The captain had his own heads and bathroom attached to his day and sleeping cabin suite situated at the after end of the main cabin and ship's office flat. The luxurious cabin suite surprised one commanding officer when he arrived to take over. After *Jervis* became a 'private' destroyer following her serious damage off the Anzio landing beaches in 1944, Captain (D) Henderson and his staff transferred to *Grenville*, while Lieutenant-Commander Roger Hill, who had relinquished his command of *Grenville*, surveyed his new quarters.

> . . . The size and quietness after the war-built cabins of the *Ledbury* and *Grenville* which were amidships, were marvellous. There was a big mahogany dining table, a large writing desk, a settee the length of the wall along the ship's side, a deep blue armchair which was so comfortable I went to sleep whenever I sat in it and all sorts of lights and radiators. The bunk was almost a double bed and the bathroom led off the sleeping cabin. . .
>
> *Jervis* was the flotilla leader of the J class and was the sister ship to the *Kelly*, leader of the K's. When she was being built it was not known which ship Lord Louis Mountbatten was going to command, hence the luxurious captain's quarters.

In marked contrast the mess-decks were crowded, cluttered with ammunition winches, hoists and chutes, noisy with fans and auxiliary machinery, claustrophobic when battened down in bad weather or in war zones, running with condensation in northern and Arctic seas, stinking after long periods at sea, stifling and unlivable in tropical waters. Bathrooms for both senior and junior rates were primitive, containing only a few galvanised basins, one hot water tap and buckets for overall ablutions. The seamen, stoker and miscellaneous mess-decks were short of slinging berths for hammocks, so locker seat tops, mess-table stools, the mess-tables, on and below, became prime sites for bedding that could not be slung. The ship's company galley was located at the base of the tripod mast so that access to deliver victuals for cooking and collecting of mess meals had to be made over an open deck, exposed to the hazard of seas sweeping the iron deck in heavy weather.

Senior ratings, the chief and petty officers, had separate but cramped quarters located inside the No 2 gun mounting superstructure forward and under the bridge. The accommodation consisted of two messes and their associated pantries, one for the chief and petty

Forward and lower Miscellaneous messdeck (signalmen, telegraphists, cooks, stewards, supply and writer ratings) looking aft to the bulkhead separating the stokers' messdeck. Both messes were opened up to the sea and flooded after collision with the ss Tor, *19th March 1940.*

officers of the seamen, stoker and miscellaneous branches, presided over by the ship's coxswain as president of the mess. The second mess was for the engine-room artificers, all of chief and petty officer rate. Both messes were staffed by a seaman and stoker messman.

The junior rating's messes of all branches centred on individual scrubbed mess tables ranged along the ship's sides in the spaces allotted for seamen, stokers and miscellaneous ratings. Twelve to fourteen men lived in numbered messes presided over by a leading rating or the longest serving and senior hand. The leading or senior hand of the mess usually marked his status by reserving the privileged slinging berth over the mess table for his hammock. Each mess had a simple steel structure of shelves for storing plates, cups, condiment containers and cutlery drawer, welded or bolted to the ship side or adjacent bulkhead. The messes were provided with an oak bread barrel that served as an extra seat and a large polished tin-plate box with a hinged lid and two compartments for storing the weekly issue of tea and sugar ration. The messes were fed by the canteen messing system which required from the ship's victualling store and refrigeration plant a weekly issue of basics to the nominated caterer for each mess including the wardroom.

The caterers received from the galley, bread daily, when it was possible to bake, fresh or tinned meat, then weekly from official (pusser) sources, tea, sugar, flour, tinned milk and condiments, the issues being based on the numbers victualled in each mess. The mess caterers were also credited with 2/- (10p) per day for each mess member for the purchase from the ship's NAAFI canteen, of fresh vegetables, fruit, butter, cheese, baking powder and other necessities as decided by the caterer to meet his plans for feeding his messmates. Purchases were made by the 'chit system' which the civilian canteen manager and his assistant converted into invoices to be submitted monthly to the ship's paymaster if one was carried, but more usually to the supply petty officer for payment.

If a mess incurred a debt balance, the caterer had the responsibility for collecting the cash from his mess members to reimburse the 'pusser'. Credit balances were paid out in cash and shared out by the caterer as mess savings unless they were very small when they would be used to purchase mess extras. Mess caterers who achieved a balance between well fed mess-mates and a modest monthly payout of mess savings were highly popular especially if the ship was enjoying a period of giving night leave at ports of call. On the other hand some caterers developed a fixation for large and regular mess savings which could be obtained only by forcing the mess to live off basic ration issues and a near starvation diet. Most caterers of this persuasion were eventually removed and replaced at the will of their enriched but ungrateful and ill-fed messmates.

In all ships, with the canteen messing system, when the morning muster of hands for work took place, two members of each mess 'stood fast' as cooks with duties to clean their mess and mess space, at the same time to prepare the main meal planned by their mess caterer and to deliver it to the ship's galley staff for 'cooking'. The quality of the meal submitted to the galley depended upon what the mess caterer had supplied and planned plus the individual ability of the cook of the day to prepare pastry, roasts, cakes and sweets capable of being cooked by the galley staff. At sea in heavy weather when mess-decks became noisome spaces of swilling vomit, sea water and other flotsam, the best that any mess cook could produce was limited to an item known as 'pot mess' – tins of meat, tomatoes, Bisto and other edible ingredients. These were tipped into a mess fanny, stirred and offered to the galley for heating and subsequently hung by cod-line from hammock bar or hook over the mess table so that members struggling off watch or during action breaks could dip a cup into the glutinous mixture to survive, supplemented by a hunk of bread or if the galley had been incapacitated – the ship's emergency biscuit issue.

The great advantage of the 'pot mess' was that the mess cooks could prepare it in the frantic minutes of intervals between action assaults or when the ship was writhing and plunging during bad weather and high seas.

One destroyer sailor wrote of his experience of a mess caterer:

> In our mess, the leading hand said that he would take over as mess caterer for three months. In that period the only second vegetable that we ever had was issue dried 'pussers' peas, very cheap 2p per lb. The peas had to be soaked in a fanny overnight with added a small piece of soda and a spoonful of sugar to make them edible. On Sundays sometimes our caterer became generous and added a couple of Naafi canteen tins of carrots to the 'straight rush' – issue meat roasted on the top of potatoes and no sweet to follow. The evening supper could be just bread and tinned sardines. After a couple of months of this the leading hand was invited to stuff his 'pussers' peas and a new caterer was elected, one who encouraged the mess cooks to produce duffs, chinese wedding cakes, clackers and so on.

Before *Jervis* had been launched she was then known only as 'Job number 614' – a small office within the Hebburn shipbuilders' yard had been allocated to an advance naval party of uniformed specialists, appointed to serve eventually in the ship, to check, inspect and approve technical progress of the ship's construction to final completion. First to come were artificers led by Chief Engine-room Artificer T. Hathaway, until the arrival in July 1938 of the officer who was to be the flotilla engineer, Engineer Commander J.A. Ruddy.

The numbers joining the office space allocated to the ship's company of Job Number 614 grew gradually to include experts in gunnery, torpedo, asdics, communications, naval and victualling stores. These arrivals in their order of appointment and appearance at Hawthorn Leslie's yard included in September Mr G.P. Packman, the torpedo gunner, and a few days later Lieutenant V.D. Ravenscroft, the ship's first lieutenant, executive officer and second-in-command. In December the group was joined by Lieutenant (T) C.R.L. Argles, the flotilla specialist torpedo and electrical officer.

It was only a few days before commissioning day in May that the advance party moved from the office in the yard and took up residence in the ship and assisted the contractor's staff clean up the living spaces in preparation for the arrival of the main draft of the ship's company from Chatham barracks, HMS Pembroke. Before this event and in March, Captain (D) designate of the 7th Flotilla and commanding officer of the *Jervis* arrived in Hebburn to oversee the final completion of his ship and to draft his flotilla orders and policy as well as the ship's work-up programme. He was to be the first of *Jervis*'s six wartime commanding officers. Forty-six years of age and a captain with five years' seniority, Captain Philip John Mack had commanded his first ship in 1916 while still a lieutenant and subsequently had commanded eight other ships, seven being destroyers. For the three years prior to his appointment as Captain (D) he had been naval attaché serving in HM embassies in South America.

Captain Mack came to command *Jervis* as a highly experienced destroyer commanding officer. Events would prove that his professionalism and strong personality set the high standard of effectiveness and morale which would survive intact despite the vicissitudes of a long and brutal war and many changes of command.

Captain Mack's arrival had been preceded a few days earlier by four more of his flotilla staff officers, the navigator Lieutenant (N) J.

Cochrane, his gunnery specialist Lieutenant (G) H.H.H. Mulleneux, signal expert and flotilla 'Flags' Lieutenant (S) R.F. Wells and the anti-submarine warfare professional Lieutenant (AS) G.O. Symonds. In the succeeding weeks, one or two at a time, other officers appointed to serve either as ship or flotilla staff officers continued to arrive. Lieutenant J.B. King-Church joined as the ship's second lieutenant, Warrant Telegraphist Mr G.I.R. Long and Warrant Ordnance Officer Mr C.A. Simms came as flotilla staff. Earlier in the year, in January, Warrant Engineer Mr N.H. Card had arrived to be Engineer Commander Ruddy's right hand man and to be head of *Jervis*'s boiler and engine-room department. Paymaster Lieutenant J.R.S. Engledue came as Captain (D)'s secretary and later before the destroyer left the Tyne, the ship's sub-lieutenant joined, Sub-Lieutenant P. Aylwin.

The First World War practice of storing and ammunitioning newly constructed ships before their departure from the shipyard had not as yet been reintroduced. In the case of *Jervis* however, the Director of Victualling had decreed that all victualling stores must be stowed before the main body of the ship's company arrived and that the galleys should be ready in all respects.

Amongst the advance party who had been standing by the ship was the captain's writer, Petty Officer Writer Lewis Waters who had previously served with J.R.S. Engledue in the battleship *Malaya* in 1932; the Paymaster Lieutenant had then been a Paymaster Midshipman and Waters a boy writer. Mr Lew Waters now recalls:

> Just before commissioning day, we who had been standing by the ship while building had to transfer our gear and records to *Jervis*. I was last to leave, 'Jimmy', 'Torps' and 'Navi' officers having had their things moved by a working party, of course. I took a last glance round the office that we had used and peeked into the cupboards. There, on a shelf, stood a big, shiny torch in splendid isolation, so I took it inboard and checked the ownership with the first lieutenant and the navigating officer, both giving negative replies. Lieutenant Argles (Torps) on the other hand expressed interest and – while not actually claiming ownership of this fine, large, impressive torch with its focussing ability and very strong beam – instructed me to 'Put it in my cabin', 'Like hell I thought' and kept it.

Throughout the two weeks preceding its closure the shoreside office had been the scene of intense activity and concentration led by First Lieutenant Ravenscroft and assisted by the coxswain, Chief Petty

Officer Mortimer, the Chief Gunner's Mate Bowyer and, drawn into the task, Petty Officer Writer Waters. The task was the preparation of *Jervis*'s Watch and Quarter Bill, requiring long hours of transcribing names, rates, experience and qualifications from the nominal lists as they arrived from the manning depot at Chatham and allocating men to the multiplicity of duties. For every rating a card had to be prepared, giving each individual the particulars of his mess, part of ship, division, watch and part of the watch plus his duty at cruising, defence and action stations. In addition the card gave him his station for damage control, collision at sea and abandon ship. The Watch and Quarter Bill cards had to be ready for the arrival of the main draft of the ship's company from barracks.

The draft arrived at the local railway station in mid-afternoon of Monday, 8th May. The men were quickly formed up in a column of threes under the crisp direction of the Chief Gunner's Mate, booted and gaitered, with his whistle in place. He was on the platform to greet the train. Then – preceded by two 3-ton lorries bearing the drafts bag and hammocks – the column of blue jackets marched off with the characteristic relaxed gait that all sailors acquire, folded oilskins over the left arm and chests crossed by the canvas sling of their gasmask containers. This was a common sight, a swinging column of sailors entering a shipyard to man their ship, yet it never failed to stir the emotions of even the most hard bitten 'yardie' who had shared in the building of a new warship. These were regular, long serving seamen and it showed when they were received, standing at the fitting out berth, by Captain Mack flanked by his first lieutenant, most of the officers, the coxswain, the chief bosun's mate, the petty officer Captains of the Top and a curious group from the advance party searching the ranks of the draft for faces of old shipmates. Carrying their bags and hammocks the draft filed past Coxswain Mortimer, who was sitting at a table handing out their watch and quarter-bill cards and then guided by members of their advance party shipmates they found their messes to settle in and ate their first meal aboard.

One of the marching men in the draft was the young stoker quoted earlier, Stoker Second Class George Morel:

> I went up to Hebburn with the draft in a 'lump', marched from station to
> the yard and my first destroyer – thought that I was dead lucky, a new
> ship and type and a Captain (D) leader. There she was looking sleek and
> lovely, lying outboard of the *Kelly* over which we had to clamber with our
> gear.

Jervis indeed looked a beautiful greyhound of a ship, immaculate in her Home Fleet grey livery, a single funnel topped by a broad black band distinguished her as a flotilla leader. 14.6 tons of paint was the allocation to paint each ship of the J and K Class, red lead, bottom anti-fouling, undercoats, inside and outer colours – a costly item especially in the case of the *Kelly*, due for completion in August. This sister flotilla leader had had the first of many coats of high quality light Mediterranean grey enamel paint that would give her a yacht-like, glass-finish. Other unusual 'extras' set this ship apart from her supposedly identical sister destroyer. The captain's bathroom and heads were panelled and supplied with bath, bidet and other fittings more appropriate to a private suite in a luxury passenger liner or exclusive hotel. The day and night cabins were furnished and fitted in similar lavish scale.

Those from *Jervis* who pondered on this extravagance when it seemed that a war with Germany would be inevitable, were informed that *Kelly* in the Mediterranean would have to act as host to her captain's many Royal relatives and heads of state.

Jervis successfully concluded her sea and acceptance trials and sailed on Friday 12th May for Chatham. Second class stoker George Morel: 'We had two days at sea on power and acceptance trials, then sailed for Chatham, had my first watch in the engine-room, the ship was very light and lively, only partially fuelled – no naval stores or ammunition – very many of us sea-sick.'

On arrival at Chatham the ship berthed on the NE wall, No 3 basin. Over the next few days the ship's full war outfit of naval stores was embarked and at the same time outstanding members of the complement joined, totalling 63 senior and junior ratings including ten additional for Captain (D)'s communication department plus, rather surprisingly, sixteen boy seamen.

The ship remained alongside while the gun, torpedo and anti-submarine crews went daily into the depot for training in their respective training schools. On 7th June the ship moved to Sheerness to the mid-stream buoys and commenced to embark ammunition, torpedoes and depth charges from several lighters. The J class ammunition specification was as follows:

SAP. 1140 rounds of 4.7" semi-armour piercing projectiles and fixed charges.
HEDA. 60 rounds of 4.7" high explosive direct action and fixed charges.
HETE. 300 rounds of 4.7" high explosive timed fuse and fixed charges.
    50 rounds of 4.7" star shell and fixed charges.

In addition the ship embarked 195 practice projectiles for surface fire and 69 rounds of fused high angle ammunition for anti-aircraft practice. There was 2-pdr ammunition for the four barrelled pom-pom also 0.5" and .303" embarked. Ten torpedoes were hoisted inboard and slid into the tubes of the 21" Pentad mountings while war and practice warheads were struck below into a magazine shared with 30 depth charges. *Jervis* was now very nearly ready to depart to Portland base and to commence her month long work-up period.

It is interesting to note that the average cost of a J class destroyer, fully stored and ammunitioned was £596,197! This price included the fitting of HF/DF set Type FH3 and MF/DF Type FM7. RDF sets would be fitted later.

Jervis sailed for Portland on 8th June and arrived next day soon after 0700 hours. From then onwards the ship sailed most days for gun practice, torpedo firings and anti-submarine hunting exercises. These progressed on to days and nights at sea to include evolutions designed to acquire seamanlike skills; towing, being towed, ramming stations, sea-boat drills, damage repair from action and collision causes, night encounters with other ships. The exercises and evolutions were repeated time and again but the weather was good and the new ship's company quickly found their sea legs and began to combine into an effective sea-going unit.

Captain Mack saw to it that there was time for relaxation; leave ashore was given whenever the programme would allow, and this frequently included all-night leave. A few officers and senior ratings had their wives installed in lodgings either in Weymouth or nearby villages. Very few junior ratings were married, for the Admiralty actively discouraged marriage by men less than 25 years of age and in fact no official recognition or payment of marriage allowance was permitted to officers or men below this age.

Captain Mack – the catalyst in the drive to achieve fighting efficiency – was an impressively handsome man who looked very much the sea captain. He was heavily tattooed with snakes that encircled his arms and chest, he smoked a large pipe and had an extensive command of naval invective. A stern disciplinarian within the contemporary context he was nevertheless an understanding and kindly man. He was prone to sea-sickness, but made no attempt to disguise the fact and was encouraging and supportive to others who suffered from the same scourge.

Many of the original ship's company look back with affection to this 'peacetime' work-up period: 'Lots of sea-time in good weather and happy banyan parties in the ship's boats under sail and oars – picnics and girls galore.'

By mid-July, four destroyers of the J class, including *Jervis* had been commissioned; in April *Jackal* (Commander T.M. Napier) and *Jersey* (Lieutenant-Commander A.M. McKillip) followed by *Javelin* (Commander A.F. Pugsley) in June. The flotilla specialist officers – especially those of the gunnery, torpedo and anti-submarine disciplines – had frequently been away from *Jervis* overseeing the progress of these skills in the new flotilla ships. Captain (D) in early July had the opportunity to exercise with some of his flotilla in company, on concentration shoots, day and night encounter exercises and flotilla manoeuvres. The 7th Flotilla numbers were made up with the E class (1931 programme) destroyers until they, one by one, were replaced by new J's commissioning and joining the flotilla, after completion of their individual work-up programmes.

Following a long day at sea exercising off Portland on 9th July, *Jervis* concluded her work-up period and sailed immediately for Chatham, arriving in the dockyard to berth the following morning. During that first morning back in Chatham, the first of her ship's company was punished by warrant, for misdemeanours committed while at Portland. Warrant No 1 was read in the presence of the entire ship's company, 'cleared from the lower-deck', then the culprit, under escort, and carrying his bag and hammock, was marched off ashore to the barrack cells.

New faces continued to arrive in the ship including the first reserve officer, Sub-Lieutenant G.N. Walker who joined to carry out his two weeks' annual training in a ship. On 3rd July before *Jervis* left Portland another new J class had commissioned – *Juno* (Commander W.E. Wilson).

While in Chatham, *Jervis* continued to carry out extra and intensive training for her officers and ratings, using all the facilities of the home base and depot. On 29th July she sailed to Rosyth and from there Captain (D) sailed daily with his fledgling flotilla to exercise with the cruisers *Southampton* and *Glasgow* of the 2nd Cruiser Squadron. While this was going on, *Jackal* (Commander Napier) joined the flotilla fresh from her work-up period at Portland. On the 12th, Captain Mack led the 7th Flotilla to Scapa Flow for exercises with the Home Fleet.

The situation vis-à-vis Germany was tense. Events in Europe were moving fast and looked hopelessly bad. Germany had mobilised and seemed determined to wrest the city of Danzig from Poland which, with the support of France and Britain, would resist. A German/Russian non-aggression pact had been signed. It contained the ominous undertone of an agreement to partition Poland between the two signatories. Unless Poland caved in to German demands and both France and Britain 'walked back' on their pledges, war was a certainty.

In this atmosphere of oppressive menace, units of the 7th Flotilla began to carry out anti-submarine patrols outside the entrances to the fleet anchorage at Scapa Flow. While in the Orkneys the seventh J Class ship, *Jaguar* (Lieutenant-Commander J.F.W. Hine), arrived to join the flotilla. After four consecutive days at sea on fleet exercises, Captain Mack led his flotilla away to Invergordon. Three days later he left with *Jervis, Jackal, Jupiter* and *Echo* bound for Dover where the ships berthed on 25th August.

War was imminent and a Royal Proclamation mobilised the entire fleet and called out the remaining reserves. At Dover, therefore, awaiting the arrival of the destroyers were some officers and men drafted to bring complements up to full war strength.

The inevitability of war had its effect on *Jervis*'s sister flotilla leader. *Kelly* had been commissioned on the 23rd but instead of sailing in the full glory of her immensely expensive livery of glass-like enamel of light Mediterranean grey, it had been obliterated, painted over and out, with standard Admiralty Home Fleet grey or – to use the sailor's vernacular – she was now covered with 'pusser's crab-fat'.

Immediately upon arrival at Dover the 7th Flotilla commenced patrols outside the harbour. The ships detailed for the first 24 hours of patrol, *Jackal* and *Echo*, found themselves enjoying pleasantly warm weather with light winds and calm seas. The flotilla gunnery staff officer, Lieutenant (G) Hugh Mulleneux made contact with the local Dover military to organise co-ordination of the harbour defences against air attack and to arrange for the RDF station to transmit air raid warnings to the ships in harbour.

One of the newcomers to the ship was acting Paymaster Sub-Lieutenant George Jago of the Royal Naval Volunteer Supplementary Reserve who, without prior naval training of any kind, came direct from his employment in the Bank of England:

> On the 25th I took leave of the bank, ordered my uniform and during the forenoon of the 26th travelled from my home in Middlesex to Dover, in plain clothes. Eventually I found that the Rear Admiral Dover was using

the Grand Hotel as a 'reporting centre'. His flag lieutenant appeared in the lounge and told me to report to Engledue in *Jervis*, which happened to be alongside, with *Jersey* outside her. As we were not yet at war no one seemed to worry about my plain clothes. . . Shortage of cabin space meant that from the beginning, and on and off for well over a year I slung a hammock in the wardroom flat. Occasionally for various reasons I had a cabin and altogether used five during my time in *Jervis*. Doc Hamilton used the sick-bay when he joined a couple of months later.

Two days later another junior officer joined but from totally different origins. An embryo naval officer joining his first fleet destroyer for his sea training, Cadet David O. Dykes reported to *Jervis*:

Joined Jervis soon after 1130 hours having been all the way up to Invergordon on Saturday to report to the King's harbour master. *Jervis* was alongside the Admiralty jetty outside the *Jersey*. It was rather a terrible moment as there were no gangways and I had to jump and scramble inboard. Gunner Dobson came up to me first and introduced me to No 1, Lieutenant Ravenscroft, who took me down to see the captain. I went to the wardroom next and then saw my billet. . . I shared a cabin with Lieutenant Argles, but my hammock was slung in the flat outside. . . . The captain's steward hung himself in his galley in the evening.

This death, the first of the commission and its circumstances, made a macabre and sombre ending for a young cadet's first day in *Jervis*. As events would prove, in the ship's long career of action no member of her ship's company would be killed by the enemy; her only casualties would be as the result of accident, misadventure or by the victim's own hand.

On 30th August, with *Javelin*, *Jupiter* and *Echo* in company, *Jervis* departed from Dover for Grimsby where they arrived the next day. The flotilla had been allocated to the Nore Command and was to be based on the Humber, and – to use Commander A.F. Pugsley's (*Javelin*) description – at the 'unappetising port of Immingham'. On arrival Captain Mack received the Admiralty's general signal: 'Prepare for war – ship torpedo war-heads and fuse all ammunition.'

The 1st Division of the 7th Destroyer Flotilla formed part of the Humber Force with cruisers of the 2nd Cruiser Squadron (CS2), *Southampton* and *Glasgow*, commanded by Vice Admiral Sir G.F.B. Edward Collins with his flag in the *Southampton*. The 1st Division (7th Flotilla) consisted of *Jervis*, *Jersey*, *Jupiter* and *Javelin* with *Jaguar* of the 2nd Division soon to join. The other ships of the 2nd Division were to be based on Plymouth as convoy escorts under the orders of Commander-in-Chief Western Approaches.

The Humber Force put to sea from Grimsby on 1st September, crossing the North Sea in a defensive sweep towards the entrance to the Skaggerak. Next morning the cruisers came across a small German merchant ship off the coast of Norway. The ship was stopped and boarded, then ordered to a British port with a naval escort embarked. Captain Mack led his destroyers in a sweep south along the Danish coast, across the entrance to the Elbe and the Dutch Friesian Islands looking for signs of German naval activity. That night, turning north again, his ships were darkened and ready for war. During the forenoon of the 3rd, Telegraphist D.W. Hague on watch in *Jervis*'s wireless office read the Admiralty General Message to the Fleet, Priority Most Immediate – 'Total Germany – repetition – Germany', which when decyphered became a more explicit directive with no ambiguities, addressed to 'All concerned – Home and Abroad: Commence hostilities at once with Germany'. The flotilla was steaming at speed in warm flat calm and foggy conditions in the vicinity of Heligoland.

Captain Mack ordered lower deck to be cleared of all those not on watch and, in a few short sentences, told his silent and subdued men that Great Britain and the Empire were at war with Germany; he then read the Articles of War. The Humber Force continued to patrol with every expectation that the German fleet would emerge to challenge their presence in the south-eastern corner of the North Sea. During the night Vice Admiral Sir Edward Collins moved his force towards the English east coast and the Home Fleet, with the intention of intercepting the German liner ss *Bremen*, which was reported to be making a run for a home port. Instead, at noon on the 4th, a small French coaster was sighted and sent on her way to a safe haven then, in mid afternoon, a second ship was sighted who, in reply to a challenge for identity claimed that she was Danish, the ss *Knud*. The *Knud* was recorded as being a vessel of 1944 tons. This ship was clearly much bigger, so she was ordered to heave to and *Jervis* sent over a boarding party. It was then quickly established that she was a German, ss *Johannes Molkenbuker* of 5294 tons; her name was still painted on the lifeboats. The ship was beginning to settle in the water; her master had ordered the seacocks to be opened and was burning the ship's papers.

Jervis took off the crew of 40 and three female passengers and Captain D ordered *Jersey* to hasten the demise of *Johannes Molkenbuker* by gunfire. Much to Captain Mack's annoyance, *Jersey* expended 61 rounds of 4.7″ semi-armour piercing ammunition before the merchantman sank. This was the end of any immediate excitement.

Over the next two weeks the flotilla ships all made abortive attacks on suspected U-boat contacts culminating on the 15th with the entire flotilla making a wild high speed dash into the teeth of a violent northerly gale to seek, unsuccessfully, a reported damaged enemy submarine. All the destroyers suffered in varying degrees, bridges swamped by waves, smashed upper-deck fittings, wrecked boats, davits and guardrails. Commander Pugsley in *Javelin* described the attitude of those who commanded these new and powerful fleet destroyers; 'In the early months we behaved like untrained puppies!'

The month of September, for the flotilla, finished somewhat ingloriously. *Jervis* had her first boiler clean of the war in Rosyth and because there was so much leave breaking and men returning to the ship drunk resulting in one case of a libertyman losing his life from drowning, Captain Mack withdrew the privilege of all night leave.

While *Jervis* remained alongside, Captain (D) attended many meetings in CS2's flagship *Southampton*, giving rise to rumours that a special operation was imminent, these reaching fever pitch when each destroyer was ordered to nominate and equip two armed ship-boarding parties. The 'buzzes' covered a wide range of possibilities when the Humber Force received reinforcements in the shape of the cruisers *Aurora* and *Belfast* with five Tribal class destroyers.

The force sailed at 0400 hours on Friday, 22nd September, to undertake Operation SK with the task of penetrating deep into the Skagerrak, further than any of the attempts made in the First World War. The objectives were to investigate reports that a boom had been laid across the entrance to the Kattegat, barring access to the Baltic, to stop and search all shipping, to sink German ships encountered and in particular any trawlers equipped with powerful W/T apparatus. The major objective was to lure the German High Seas Fleet out and towards the Home Fleet which would be at battle stations cruising over the Great Fisher Banks.

The raiding force sailed high on excitement and expectations of glory, setting off at high speed to cross the North Sea. Three and a half hours later the enterprise collapsed ignominiously when *Jersey* collided with *Javelin* causing deaths and damage which required the remaining destroyers to stand by to tow the crippled ships and to give anti-submarine and AA protection. The operation was abandoned still-born and the force returned to base, but with *Jervis* and *Jupiter* escorting *Javelin* to the Tyne where she remained for five weeks under repair at Hawthorn Leslie. *Jersey* dry-docked at Leith.

This collision was to be the first of several involving the 7th DF that occurred during this first calm autumn and then the stormy, freezing winter of the war along the east coast and North Sea. At Rosyth on 30th September, *Jervis* was roughly mauled by *Jupiter* trying to berth on her leader. *Jupiter* scraped along Captain (D)'s scuttles and sprang a large number of rivets which had to be repaired before *Jervis* could return to sea.

The weather remained calm, sunshine alternating with fog. It was an autumn which did not prepare those in the Humber Force for the harshness of the winter to follow. Captain Mack sailed on 8th October taking *Jupiter* with him to investigate a German naval vessel which was believed to be acting as a decoy to lure the Humber Force to sea and into the range of the Luftwaffe bombers. The patrol failed when *Jupiter* broke down and lay stopped, broached to in a heavy seaway. The situation became precarious when the disabled destroyer and *Jervis*, circling her consort on an anti-submarine patrol, were sighted by a German reconnaissance aircraft at about 1500 hours. Shortly after the sighting, *Jervis* was in action for the first time against enemy aircraft when three bombers dropped eight bombs in two groups, the nearest only 150 yards from the ship. Cadet David Dykes wrote in his diary:

> I have no HA action station so not wanting to miss the fun, I went up to the Director feeling rather helpless. They did not want me rather naturally as I would have been in the way. I then went to the after flat and joined up with No 3 gun supply party. The supply machines would not work, so all shells had to be sent up by hand.

Half an hour later three more aircraft dived out of the clouds, dropping their bombs rather closer this time. The fire in reply from *Jervis* and *Jupiter* was ragged and ineffective, fuses were incorrectly set or not at all and tracer ammunition for the close range weapons was not used. The weather had deteriorated and the ships were rolling badly, up to 45 degrees, as *Jervis* closed to take *Jupiter* in tow. With darkness hiding the ships from renewed attacks, lowerdeck was cleared in *Jervis* and a long, dangerous process began, hauling in by hand the towing pennant from *Jupiter*. After a dirty night with the ships suffering a certain amount of internal damage, in terms of broken crockery and fittings, the two ships arrived off the entrance

9th July 1940. *Nubian* (D14), *Mohawk*, *Janus* and *Juno* in pursuit of the Italian fleet off Calabria.

27th November 1940. *Jervis* and the 14th DF lead the 1st XI out of Suda Bay. *Warspite, Illustrious* and *Valiant.*

July 1940 — Captain Philip Mack in his day cabin after the arrival of *Jervis* from the United Kingdom.

December 1940. *Jervis* and *Janus* bombard Sollum and (*right*) fall of shot from the return fire.

22nd January 1941. Malta, *Illustrious* down by the stern after bomb damage.

25th January 1941. *Illustrious* escapes. Off Alexandria, photograph from *Jervis* while *Juno* patrols ahead.

boom gate to Scapa Flow at 1200 hours. *Jupiter*, whilst under tow, had managed to get one boiler going so entered the Flow under her own power.

Still in Scapa Flow on the 11th, Captain Mack had lowerdeck cleared so that he could talk to his ship's company. He first congratulated everyone on their efforts in carrying out a tough and dangerous task taking *Jupiter* in tow, then castigated his gunnery department for the appalling performance in the ship's first encounter with enemy aircraft, giving notice of his parameters for an immediate improvement.

The flotilla ships continued to suffer minor collision and stranding incidents, *Jaguar* put herself into dry-dock after striking a small islet above the Forth bridge. *Jersey* with her collision damage repaired tangled with the Rosyth boom and at Kirkwall, *Jackal* and *Janus* mauled each other as the two ships manoeuvred. In spite of these setbacks Captain Mack had all his flotilla – with the exception of *Jaguar* – patrolling with the CS2 cruisers off the Norwegian coast on 14th October seeking enemy shipping.

Jervis stopped two ships which her boarding parties identified as enemy ships and sent them into Kirkwall with prize crews embarked; they were the ss *Bonde* and a tanker, *Gustaf E. Reuter*. The tanker which was masquerading as a Swedish ship was unmasked by the fluent knowledge of German possessed by Captain (D)'s secretary, Ralph Engledue, who accompanied the boarding party. The first lieutenant, Ravenscroft, took command of the prize crew and the ship for her passage to Kirkwall.

The next day *Jervis* and the flotilla rounded up a mixed bag of neutral and Allied shipping, formed them into a convoy – with Lieutenant Symonds and two signalmen placed in the Polish ship ss *Ruhr IV* as convoy commodore – and sent the formation on course for Rosyth.

The autumn weather continued fair and the convoy made good progress; although found then shadowed by enemy reconnaissance aircraft, no attacks developed. The cruisers departed early in the morning of the 16th taking *Jersey*, *Jackal* and *Janus* with them, leaving *Jervis* alone with the merchantmen until the Tribal class destroyer *Mohawk* joined after mid morning.

As the convoy made its way past May island a German bomber was sighted, *Jervis* and *Mohawk* went to action stations but before the destroyers could open fire two Spitfires appeared out of the clouds and shot the bomber down to crash into the sea not far from *Jervis*.

This was the first enemy aircraft seen to be shot down by *Jervis*'s ship's company; a whaler, with the lifeboat's crew was ordered away, this time with the captain's secretary, Ralph Engledue, as cox'n. The two airmen, badly injured, had been picked by a small passing merchant ship so the whaler pulled in alongside to transfer the aircrew. The co-pilot was already dead and the pilot had bad facial injuries caused by the crash. He was still conscious when lifted inboard and carried to the sickbay. Interrogated in German by Ralph Engledue the pilot expressed surprise that he and his co-pilot had been picked up, and said that he was part of a squadron of bombers sent to attack the cruisers (2nd Cruiser Squadron) which had frequently been observed to lie below the Forth bridge, and to bomb HMS *Caledonia* (the depot) and the Forth bridge; he was aged 31 years and had fought in Spain. His co-pilot was only 17 years of age, and considered that his country was fighting the British but not the French; and that the war could last eight years.

At 30 knots *Jervis* chased after the convoy which had come to anchor in Largo Bay. *Jervis* closed the ss *Ruhr IV*, collected Lieutenant Symonds and the signalmen and proceeded to Rosyth from where sounds of bomb-blasts and heavy gunfire had been coming. By the time *Jervis* secured alongside an oiler to fuel, the bombing attack was over; *Mohawk*, while still with convoy, had been near-missed and strafed by machine gunfire, wounding everyone on the bridge; the first lieutenant had been killed and her captain, Commander R.F. Jolly, had been mortally wounded; he died as he brought his ship alongside 'Y' berth. The petty officer writer, in charge of an ammunition supply party, had been killed by a bomb splinter and twenty other men had been wounded by either splinters or machine gun fire. A near miss on the cruiser *Edinburgh* had killed one man and wounded several others. Vice Admiral Sir Edward Collins's (CS2) flagship *Southampton* was hit by one bomb which passed through her port hangar and the boys' messdeck below, then came out through the ship's side to explode underneath, destroying the Admiral's barge lying at the boom.

Jervis berthed on the *Mohawk* which was lying on and outside *Jupiter*. Here she landed the wounded German airman and the body of his crewman. Next morning, Tuesday 17th October, the First Lieutenant Ravenscroft, Mr Card and the boarding party from the tanker *Gustaf E. Reuter* returned to the ship from Kirkwall. They had had an uneventful passage in the prize ship but after spending a night in the *Iron Duke* at Scapa Flow they rejoined *Jervis* with grim reports of the heavy casualties suffered in the torpedoing of the *Royal Oak* by the U-boat *U-47* on the 14th.

There were two air raid warnings on Tuesday afternoon but no raids materialised. The captain's secretary Ralph Engledue visited the German pilot at Port Edgar hospital but found him heavily sedated with morphia in a ward crowded with the wounded from the air attack carried out by his bomber squadron.

Jervis was given no time to reflect upon the casualties inflicted on her Humber Force sister ships. She was sailed at 0300 hours on the 18th with *Jersey* and two Tribals (*Cossack* and *Maori*) screening the battle-cruiser *Repulse* on a high speed dash via the Pentland Firth toward the Faeroes in a bid to intercept an enemy blockade runner. It was to be an abortive operation memorable only for the westerly gale that turned the tortured waters of the Firth, with its whirlpools and tidal races of unimaginable power, into a hideous maelstrom of giant confused and roaring waves. Into this howling sea wilderness the destroyers twisted, writhed and plunged; there was no respite for bodies straining and battered by continuous movement. Men came off watch soaked, twitching with eyes raw from the wind and spray, and for a short period tried to sleep with only the top layer of soaked clothing removed or loosened, with the partially inflated lifebelt making a constant pressure point on an aching rib cage.

This torment from appalling sea conditions was to be an unforgettable feature of that first winter in Home Waters of what at times was to seem an endless and at times hopeless war. This was especially so for the destroyers and escort vessels protecting convoys in the Western Approaches, the Atlantic crossing to America and in later years of the conflict, on the North Atlantic and Arctic runs to Russian ports. For those escorts there would be no rest or respite from constant buffeting and dreadful living conditions for two or three weeks at a time. For the destroyers of the J and K class, their deployment on the east coast, and later into the Mediterranean, was to save them from enduring rarely more than four to five days at sea without a return to harbour, even if it was to be no more than an hour or so to refuel.

In the dash into northern waters, *Repulse* and her destroyers steamed clear into calmer conditions on the Thursday, which continued until the ships met up with the Commander-in-Chief Home Fleet on offensive patrol with his entire fleet SE of Iceland. They joined at 1630 on the Friday as fog closed down with the fleet at full alert to intercept a number of German merchant ships expected to try to break through the blockading of the North Sea.

Jervis remained with the fleet on the screen only until late evening of Saturday 21st October when she was detached with *Jersey* and ordered to return at speed to Sullom Voe in the Shetlands to refuel and then assume an immediate anti-submarine patrol to intercept a U-boat that was expected to pass Muckle Flugga on Sunday evening. After refuelling, a search was carried out in a worsening sea, showery and cold conditions without success until Monday afternoon when Captain D7 received orders to proceed with *Jersey* towards the Norwegian coastline and endeavour to stop an American merchant ship, the *City of Flint*. The American had been stopped in mid-Atlantic by the German ocean raider, pocket battleship *Deutschland*, who found that she was carrying a contraband cargo. A prize crew had been placed onboard who were now endeavouring to break through to a German or neutral port. The *City of Flint* had been sighted in the area of Tromso making for Germany.

One ship was sighted at 0730 on Thursday by *Jervis* but it proved to be British, bound for Bergen and, after a day and a night of fruitless patrolling the search was called off by a signal which reported that the *City of Flint* was at Murmansk with the German prize crew interned. 'The *City of Flint* had distinguished herself picking up survivors when the passenger liner *Athenia* was sunk south of the Rockall bank on the first day of the war. The American ship was herself sunk by *U-575* on 25th January 1943 when she was a straggler of convoy UGS 4, USA to Gibraltar, recorded Lieutenant Hugh Mulleneux.

Cadet David Dykes wrote in his diary recording the search made by *Jervis* for the *City of Flint*:

> I was at searchlight stations till daylight and then I closed up in the director. It was a terrible night on the bridge, waves coming in continuously.

In the tumultuous seas, late in the afternoon of the 23rd, *Jersey* had a stoker swept off the iron deck. At the same time the seas that buried the after part of the ship deep tore clear one of the depth charges set for shallow firing. The explosion in the sea astern removed any slim chance of recovering the unfortunate man. The two ships after a short search of the area turned for the United Kingdom, arriving at Rosyth at 1700 on 25th October. Here orders were waiting for Captain Mack to concentrate his flotilla in the Humber and prepare to set out on a special operation. On Saturday the 25th, six ships of the 7th Flotilla were together for the first time; only *Javelin* and *Jaguar* were missing, anchored off Immingham.

The flotilla departed to carry out operation AG, this was to be a sweep across the North sea to the Terschelling light vessel, then to proceed south through the night along the Dutch coastline seeking enemy coast convoys.

The destroyers at full action stations and in line ahead passed swiftly along the Dutch offshore islands and only found one inoffensive Dutch coaster. In the early dawn light the flotilla turned back towards the Dogger bank then shaped a course for the Humber. The ships were sighted and followed by two reconnaissance Heinkel seaplanes; a few ineffective rounds fired by the speeding destroyers did nothing to deter the seaplanes. One in fact slowly gained height until it was over the flotilla where, in slow and almost studied disdain it dropped two bombs which narrowly missed *Jersey*, then, ignoring the furious anti-aircraft barrage, turned away and rejoined its companion to disappear astern. The flotilla anchored in the Humber at 1700.

Captain Mack was charged to set up a destroyer flotilla base at Immingham for the east coast destroyers and given the following policy directive to implement:

(1) Carry out operations directed by the Admiralty or the C in C Rosyth.
(2) To give protection to the FS and FN convoys in support of the anti-aircraft cruisers based on the Humber.
(3) To provide anti-submarine patrols.
(4) To have two destroyers always at immediate notice for any small operations or excursions that may arise.

FN convoys were now established as a regular movement of formed groups of merchant ships between the Thames estuary and the Tyne. The FS convoys were the southbound equivalents. Similar convoys with the prefix TM ran between the Tyne and Methil (Firth of Forth) and MT in the reverse direction. These convoys steamed inside the British mine barrage that stretched from the North Foreland to Kinnairds Head. In spite of the constant efforts by the mine-sweeping force to maintain the channels swept free of enemy laid mines, the routes were becoming very hazardous. In October, 19 ships had been sunk and the enemy mining activities by aircraft, submarines and surface vessels were becoming more serious. East coast navigation lights had continued to burn since the outbreak of war; these helped the enemy destroyers and minelayers to place their mines accurately in the east coast swept channels. The situation continued to deteriorate as Germans began to lay magnetic mines. The coastal navigation lights were eventually extinguished on 21st November but 27 ships totalling 120,958 tons had been sunk and movement within the Thames estuary had practically come to a halt due to deprivations caused by the German laid magnetic mines.

As Captain D7 set about establishing his base ashore at Immingham, his flotilla gunnery staff officer wrote in his personal diary: 'At the moment there are practically no facilities at Immingham, we have got to build up a destroyer base on our own.'

Philip Mack put ashore his secretary, Paymaster Lieutenant Ralph Engledue with Lieutenant G.O. Symonds the flotilla anti-submarine warfare staff officer, Mr C.A. Simms Warrant Ordnance Officer, Mr N.H. Card, Warrant Engineer, Mr Long, Warrant Telegraphist, and Petty Officer Writer L.F. Waters. A support party of seamen, engine-room artificers and stokers was provided from the *Javelin* which was still under repair and would take several weeks before completion. Mr Lew Waters wrote later:

> Then came relief; we put into Immingham, the Secretary and I were put ashore to set up office in the dirty scruffy, unpainted Immingham dock office. A ship's working party soon made short shrift of the dirt and we got things in order, without the deck on a perpetual up and down and sideways motion beneath us. That was the winter of 1939 when the sea froze outside the dock gates at Immingham. Home was the old Union Castle liner hulk *Dunluce Castle* with shore side lighting laid on but no heat – no heating at all. It was purgatorial for the lads but my wife joined me and we found lodgings in Grimsby in the home of a docks' crane driver.

Wives and relatives soon came to stay near the new base, Mrs Ravenscroft the wife of the first lieytenant with Mrs Argles, wife of the flotilla torpedo staff officer, shared accommodation. Chief ERA Hathaway's wife was another of several ladies who found digs within easy reach of these desolate docks.

From Immingham Captain D7 directed the operations of his destroyers, providing two during the dark hours for each FS or FN convoy moving along the swept channel inside the mine barrier. The destroyers were there to give protection against enemy destroyers, E-boats or U-boats which had penetrated the mine barrier. The anti-aircraft cruisers took over from dawn to dusk to counter air attacks which were growing in frequency. Because of the constraints of the swept and buoyed channel the convoys could steam only in two columns of ships which stretched 15 or more miles making protection a difficult and often hopeless task. On dark, gale tormented and snow showered nights, even without enemy interference, navigating the channel filled with lumbering merchant ships of all types and conditions made the night patrols a dangerous occupation.

Captain Mack spent many nights out on the east coast convoy route in different destroyers of his flotilla, while, in November, *Jervis* sailed just three times to take her part in the escort of northbound convoys FN34, 36 and 39. By the night of 18th/19th November new German magnetic mines plus the conventional type were everywhere in the Humber and life for shipping along the east coast was difficult and potentially lethal.

The main star in *Jervis*'s immediate future was the promise of a refit and some leave, but the ship was having problems. The long periods of November spent in Immingham resulted in many of her ship's company being seduced by the fleshpots and good beer of Grimsby. Access to this east coast Shangri-la was via a tramline that ran exposed to the full blast of easterly gales; single decked cars, blacked out, stifling with tobacco smoke and packed with beer-laden bodies, heaved, bucked and plunged back to Immingham reducing all but the super-human, into vomiting wretches. After one return trip of libertymen, a leading stoker had to be forcibly restrained from diving from the ship into the ice-floed Humber, and it became commonplace for stretchers and bearers having to meet the arriving tramload of helpless libertymen. Sadly seven punishment warrants were read in November, which was not a good month for the flotilla leader. Three warrants were read on Thursday the 22nd, a black day.

It was with some sense of relief that *Jervis* left Immingham next morning for Hull where she berthed on Alexander quay later that same morning to become refit Job Number 101; the starboard watch were sent on seven days leave.

The refit and leave for both watches was soon over and on 7th December all hands were turned-to, re-storing ship and preparing for sea. During the morning grim news became known – damage and casualties sustained by *Jersey*. She had been in company with *Juno* patrolling the convoy swept channel route during the night 6th/7th when both J's were surprised by a sub-division of German destroyers laying mines off the Haisborough light vessel. The enemy ships, *Erich Giesse* and *Hans Lody*, attacked with torpedoes and hit *Jersey* which almost broke in half, killing ten and wounding thirteen of her men. While the German destroyers sped away unseen or challenged, *Juno* succeeded in taking her stricken flotilla ship in tow and made for Immingham. While this was going on two merchant ships struck and sank on the new German minefield.

Jervis returned to Immingham on the 9th berthing on the East Arm at 1600. Captain Mack gave his ship and flotilla little time to ponder on the 7th DF's first casualties; after releasing *Jackal* to proceed to Hull for her refit he took the remainder of the flotilla, *Jervis*, *Juno*, *Janus*, *Jaguar* and *Jupiter* across the North Sea to seek U-boats off Terschelling, returning at mid-day of the 11th without success or opposition from the enemy.

A few days later *Jervis*'s sister 5th Flotilla Leader *Kelly* ran into the second of what was to become a series of disasters. *Kelly* had been back in the builders yard, Hawthorn Leslie, since 16th November for repairs to damage acquired in a high speed dash in heavy weather and had been out of action for a month. *Kelly* left the yard on 14th December and, a few hours later, struck a mine aft so within 36 hours she was back in the yard where she would remain until 28th February 1940. Her ship's company, who had expended their free travel privileges in two weeks' leave, were to be funded for their next unexpected round of leave by Captain D5's wife, Lady Edwina Mountbatten. This leave which included Christmas and the New Year would, to the chagrin of the remainder of the 5th Flotilla and the ribald envy of the 7th Flotilla's Js, shelter the *Kelly*'s crew from the rigours of that first dreadful winter weather of the war.

Meanwhile *Jervis* and her destroyers operating out of Sullom Voe had successfully completed an important convoy operation. They had collected a group of ore ships from off the Lofoten Islands and brought them safely to Rosyth in the teeth of a succession of vicious snow-laden gales. The destroyers arrived back in the bleak and comfortless port of Immingham at dawn Christmas Day where the 7th Flotilla base staff, led by Ralph Engledue greeted Captain (D) and his ships with their Christmas mail. *Jervis*'s share was 50 bags. This, the first Christmas Day of the war, was a low key and sombre affair full of uncertainties over the future, but the ships were at least in harbour for a few hours and the mess-decks which had been awash and noisome were soon cleansed, decorated and a meal of sorts put up to the galley.

The Admiralty sent Philip Mack their congratulations for the safe arrival of the convoy from Narvik. The iron ore ships had been urgently needed as the east coast blast furnaces were in danger of having to close down for the lack of ore. On the afternoon of Thursday 28th December, Captain Mack departed for a conference at the Admiralty and left the first lieutenant in temporary command of *Jervis*. Cadet David Dykes pondered in his diary on the reasons for his captain's summons to London:

> Captain left in the afternoon, having had a signal asking for his presence in the morning. What is it for? I hope for some great operation in the offing, is he to be decorated, re-appointed, plans for the Immingham base, or merely a visit to explain our activities since the war was declared? All very mysterious. All sorts of rumours prevail.

On Friday afternoon with Captain Mack still in London, *Jervis* sailed with Ravenscroft in command and joined *Janus* off Humber Light to commence a routine convoy route patrol. It was a strange experience for the flotilla leader to be steaming in line astern of and under the orders of what was normally a junior flotilla unit. *Jervis* remained on patrol longer than expected and until Sunday 31st December because mines had been sighted being dropped by parachute into the Humber. *Janus* refused to allow her charge (his Captain (D)'s ship) to return to harbour until confirmation had been received that a check sweep had been carried out in the Immingham approach channel. The First Lieutenant at 1345 berthed *Jervis* on the Killingholme oiling jetty, 'where we secured alongside beautifully'.

The fact that the first lieutenant had assumed command in the captain's absence, the normal procedure in a private ship, had caused some disquiet and not a little jealousy in the case of at least one of the more senior flotilla staff officers. Philip Mack was nevertheless firm in his decision that his first lieutenant and executive officer was the second in command even though this was by no means the general rule in all destroyer flotilla leaders where some flotilla staff officers were senior to the ship's first lieutenant. After refuelling *Jervis* berthed on the east arm where Captain Mack was waiting after his return from London. That evening his officers led by Lieutenant King Church tried to pump him for hints on the scope of the forthcoming operation. Philip Mack gave little information except to say that the bows would have to be strengthened for steaming in ice covered seas and that if the operation was successful it could shorten the war. After further departures of Captain (D) to London and several 'false dawns' the projected operation was called off.

While Captain Mack was away a small stir occurred at Immingham. *Javelin* had completed her collision repairs and arrived at the base with *Jupiter* in company and for the first time, in this first week of January 1940, all eight J class ships of the 7th Flotilla were in port and in company.

On Saturday, Captain (D) returned to his bleak and frozen base a disappointed man. The politicians had called off the operation into northern waters because of the deteriorating situation in Europe and of fears that Holland was about to be attacked.

There followed days of patrolling off the enemy coast seeking shipping in wild seas and freezing conditions. After the 1st Flotilla Leader *Grenville* was mined and sunk and only one small enemy freighter intercepted, the operation was called off. Then came searches off the Norwegian coastline looking for German ore ships and while still at sea on 29th January Captain Mack tackled the task of forming 29 merchant ships – only three British – into some semblance of a convoy. For the next three days in bad visibility caused by recurring snowstorms the *Jervis* and two other J's shepherded their charges south-west towards Scotland. The flotilla gunnery officer, H.H. Mulleneux wrote, '. . . conditions were so bad that at dawn 31st January only 15 convoy ships could be seen and then dawn next day another night of gale and snow only 7 ships were in sight.'

Despite these difficulties all 29 ships were brought safely across to the Firth of Forth. When Captain Mack led his trio of exhausted destroyers up to Rosyth to fuel he was less than pleased to find that *Jackal* and *Javelin* – which had been ordered to the Forth to hunt U-boats – had been in port and unemployed for several days. This was 2nd February and on the 6th *Jervis* arrived at Hull for a boiler clean and degaussing.

Jervis completed her boiler clean which had allowed each watch three days leave. On the 14th she returned to Immingham leaving *Juno* and *Jersey* in Hull to carry out a refit and boiler cleaning. The remainder of the flotilla had been recalled from convoy escort duties and ordered to join Captain D7 at Immingham in readiness to sail at 1600/14th for a raid on enemy shipping reported to be concentrated in an anchorage three miles from Borkum island. Captain Mack was in the act of proceeding to carry out the operation when it was cancelled, reconnaissance from the air had failed to find any of the shipping in the anchorage which was now blocked with ice floes.

The flotilla returned to the routine of protecting and shepherding north- and southbound east coast convoys. A demanding task in good weather with clear visibility, it became a nightmare in darkness and freezing gale conditions of February 1940. The times of greatest tension came when convoys, north and southbound, passed each other within the confines of the swept channels, with their numerous bends to avoid many of the dozens of mined and bombed wrecks. Some convoys were of great length; *Jervis* sailed from the Tyne at 0400/24th to escort a FS convoy of 73 ships that stretched in two columns for 16 miles along the tortuous swept channel. At 1700 one of the convoyed ships struck a mine and sank in mid-channel; it took all the skill of the escorts to guide the following ships round the stricken vessel and the ever active minesweeping flotillas, then to restore cohesion in the great ship formation. *Jervis* berthed at Immingham at 2230 after relief escorts had taken over.

These perilous escort routines went on with collisions – especially at night – a constant peril; on 27th February *Jackal* collided with and sank a small Swedish steamship *Storfors*. The crew was fortunately picked up without loss or serious injury by *Jackal*. The flotilla gunnery officer Hugh Mulleneux was doing a short spell in the destroyer and was duty staff officer on watch on the bridge when the collision occurred and later wrote in his diary: 'I was on watch and am feeling a Jonah.'

Jackal with her bent stem returned to the Tyne and was to be out of action for three weeks.

Captain Mack had a couple of 'dress' idiosyncrasies which were typical of his many expressions of individuality permissible within the constraints of a disciplined and uniformed Service. At sea, at night, he always wore white trousers stuffed into black sea-boots, it was thus possible on the blackest night for those on watch always to spot if and where the captain was on the bridge. Another unusual item of dress – possibly an inheritance from his Victorian or Edwardian naval predecessors – was that when in No 5 uniform, he always wore a stiff fronted 'boiled' shirt and very frequently with a winged collar.

Kelly, with her mine damage repairs completed, sailed from the Tyne on the 28th to join her flotilla destroyers at Rosyth. *Jervis* left the Humber with *Juno* and *Jupiter* to escort a FN convoy to the Tyne on 1st March, then proceeded to Rosyth to take charge of a Norway-bound convoy. During the night of 2nd/3rd March after leaving the FN convoy and leading her two destroyers towards the Firth of Forth, lookouts in *Jervis* sighted the dark shape of a southbound ship. When challenged the ship revealed itself to be the *Kelly* bound for a dockyard in the Thames. The astonishing news was that the unfortunate and damage prone flotilla leader had been in collision with the Tribal class destroyer *Gurkha* which had, with its propeller, torn a hole in the *Kelly*'s bow. The 5th Flotilla leader was not to emerge from the Thames shipyard for eight weeks. In this period of five months since November 14th 1939 while his ship, except for a few days, had been continuously out of action, Captain D5, Lord Louis Mountbatten, had been frequently at sea directing his flotilla from other K class destroyers. His flotilla staff officers were also carrying out their specialist flotilla duties afloat.

Jervis departed from Rosyth with Convoy ON17A, on Monday, 4th March bound for Bergen, Norway. Passage of the convoy apart for one day of gale force winds and a high sea that reduced speed to 3 knots, was uneventful. On the return journey, in position 61 degrees north and 01 degree 20 minutes east *Jervis* and her two consorts were in firm asdic contact with a submarine. The depth charge attacks, however, produced no concrete result so, after a short search, Captain Mack broke off the hunt and arrived back at Rosyth on Saturday evening. There followed eight days of escorting MT and FN convoys until Monday, the 18th, when *Jervis*, *Janus* and *Javelin* set out from Immingham, bound to Rosyth and a new convoy to Norway. In the early hours of the 19th, steaming at 22 knots, *Jervis* was involved in a devastating collision with a neutral ship. Midshipman C.B. Featherstone Dilke, Cadet David Dykes' relief, was on the bridge for the middle watch, and a day later he wrote up his journal:

> At 0145 we passed a MT convoy, an hour later I sighted a single white light at green 02 degrees – bearing remained steady so the OOW ordered the helmsman to alter course 5 degrees to starboard, I was ordered to call the captain and navigating officer. Captain Mack was on the bridge within 30 seconds and when he saw the light ordered the OOW to steer a further 5 degrees to starboard and to switch on dimmed navigating lights. Just before 3 oclock the light became extremely bright – probably a steaming light – and 3 minutes later in the inky darkness almost dead ahead I spotted her bows heading straight for our port anchor, a fraction of a second later the OOW spotted her also and at once gave the order, full astern and hard astarboard.
>
> But she was too close and, the next moment struck us just abaft the port anchor; our degaussing gear was severed and fused in a shower of sparks. The Swedish ship, as she turned out to be, bumped down our port bow tearing into the ship as she did so. She finally came to a stop

abreast 'B' gun and then her engine going astern took effect and she drew clear to drift away on our port beam.

We signalled to *Janus* and *Javelin* to standby us and I left the bridge to report on the situation below. I went down a ladder inside the bridge structure to find men pouring from the forward mess-deck in various stages of undress. One badly injured man was being carried by three of his messmates. Just then I heard a cry for help that seemed to come from the water abreast the motor cutter. I ran aft to the port torpedo davit and there I saw Signalman Todd RNVR who had been washed out through the hole in the side with a mess table, he was hanging on to this table and floating around on it. Yeoman Evans who was on the bridge shone an aldis lamp on the water and with two ratings we managed to get Todd inboard. We had a 15 degree list to port, 3 to 4 feet down by the bow at the time which helped considerably to get him out – ship going astern at ½ knot. When we had picked up all the men in the water the captain ordered 80 revolutions astern on both engines, the ship appeared to stand it quite well; he shortly afterwards increased to 100 revs. About ¾ hours later Able Seaman Connery died of severe injuries in the head in spite of all the doctor's efforts. 0500, *Hasty* and *Vivian* escorted us as far as the Tyne where two tugs joined us at the South Shields breakwater and a launch with two doctors. The tug *Malta* secured aft and the *Washington* secured to what remained of our starboard bow. The banks of the Tyne were black with people and ambulances awaited our berthing.

Telegraphist D.W. Hague was on watch in the w/t office:

I had the middle watch with my mate for that watch, 'Fanny' Fanthorpe. We were about fifty miles due east from Newcastle and I was decoding a signal that Fanny had just received concerning a new German minefield laid by U-boats in the approaches to the Tyne when 'BANG', I was lifted out of my chair, as was Fanny, and we both finished up hard against the control panels of our main transmitter. Power went, so we switched to emergency and collected ourselves together. Naturally we thought that we had struck one of those mines. The ship started to list quite sharply to port, so after switching off and collecting our confidential books, Fanny and I made for the upper-deck. We stopped near the 'cut-away' waiting for instructions from a higher authority but none came and as the ship seemed to settle but still with a pronounced list, we went back to the W/T office. Soon mostly naked and soaking wet people came in, our mates from the messdeck, both W/T and V/S personnel. I checked out our emergency transmitter and on my Petty Officer Telegraphist's instruction transmitted a signal to the Admiralty. We could hear banging going on and it turned out to be the repair party shoring up the forward bulkhead in the boiler room . . . My mess-deck and forward magazine was flooded. My mates could not remember how they ever got out as the ladder from our mess to the seamen's mess above was twisted like a corkscrew. We had a count and two were missing, Ordinary Telegraphist Lambert and Leading Signalman Short. The worst was Leading Signalman Sampson whose head had been hit by two mess-deck stanchions.

Stoker 2nd class George Morel had a narrow escape from death. He should have been in his hammock, but had been detailed by the chief stoker to substitute for another stoker on the sick list:

> I was in the gear-room when there was a crash and I was tossed into the bilges. I was then sent to examine the stern glands, I didn't know if the ship which was listing, was about to sink. I later found that the port side of the ship was ripped back to No 1 boiler-room. Arthur Mann who I relieved was gone and so was my hammock and kit. My brother was told that the *Jervis* had been lost.

A Swedish merchant ship, ss *Tor* (Master, Captain A. Herman Pettersson) had rolled back the entire portside plating of *Jervis* like a sardine tin, from the stem to the forward bulkhead of No 1 boiler-room, exposing to the elements the whole of the lower messdecks and the seamen's messdeck above. The miscellaneous and stokers' messes were flooded to the deckhead.

Signalman Bill Snape was in his hammock:

> I awoke with a start, something was wrong, but what was it? I heard no explosion, no snores from my mess-mates, no lights visible, not even the pilot light but I could hear water swirling louder than normal. The ship seemed to have a most unusual motion . . . she was wallowing. I remember shouting at the top of my voice something like, 'What the bloody hell is going on?' No reply, I shouted again my oppo's name, 'Bob'. No reply, there was an awful stench of paint and oily water, so I fell out of my hammock onto the mess table underneath and found myself up to my neck in icy water. It was pitch black and instinct and knowledge of my whereabouts in the mess enabled me to somehow reach the ladder leading to the upper messdeck . . . made my way direct out onto the upper-deck. There in a state of controlled confusion men were turning out the boats and apparently preparing to abandon ship. Then a cry went up, 'Has anyone seen the following ratings?' When I answered I was told to make my way to the W/T office where a muster had taken place. I hurried to the office and found the Chief was not amused and told me so. However I told him what I had been through and pointed out that what he thought was blood was in fact red lead paint that covered me from head to foot.

Stoker Alec Shirley also escaped from his hammock:

> I awoke with the screams of men in my ears. From the advantage point
> my hammock afforded, I put out my hand and touched the sea that
> gushed through the gaping hole the tanker had cut into our ship. At first I
> thought that I was in the midst of a nightmare and that the bloodied
> bodies I saw on the portside lockers were figments of this dream but, as
> realization dawned, I joined the press of shouting, fear-driven men at the
> bottom of the hatch. At last I stood naked on the seamen's
> mess-deck. . . . A quick muster told us that five stokers were missing and
> we probed the dark waters that were rising in our messdeck for signs of
> life. The waters were three-quarters of the way up the bulkhead when we
> heard Micky shout for help. His Irish voice entreated us from the dark
> depths and drove us frantic at our inability to succour him. The water
> was only one foot from the hatch when he began to scream; it was then
> they closed the hatch to keep the sea at bay. I could still hear him when
> the officer ordered us aft.

The collision casualties were grievous, 2 dead and 15 missing in
Jervis, the Swedish ship had no one hurt. Three more bodies were
found as soon as the dock at Swan Hunters yard began to pump out;
then later when it was possible to probe the underwater wreckage
four more bodies were found in No 2 magazine, a leading signalman,
a stoker and two seamen.

This collision was a major, though only a temporary setback – as
events were to prove – to what was to be a remarkable and successful
war record of a fighting flotilla leader which was to triumph in every
function for which the ship was designed.

Captain Mack, once he was cleared in the ensuing Court of
Enquiry, moved with his staff to his base at Immingham, named
HMS *Beaver* II, and from there put to sea regularly in the remaining
active ships of the flotilla; he did, however normally use the *Janus* as
his temporary flotilla leader. The staff specialist officers dispersed
themselves into the private ships. At the base Ralph Engledue had
been relieved by a term-mate, Paymaster Lieutenant Richard
Carter.

On the Tyne all the *Jervis* ship's company had been housed ashore
with the exception of the duty watch sentries and fire party.
Lieutenant Ravenscroft remained in charge. He took the opportunity to send away to their home manning-port all ratings due for extra
courses or promotion examinations. There were also the next-of-kin
to console; Captain Mack and the divisional officers had written to
them all and had visited the widows who had moved into the vicinity

of Immingham. In this, the captain was assisted by the ship's company, the flotilla chaplain and by Chief ERA and Mrs Hathaway in particular.

CHAPTER TWO

Mediterranean and the 14th Flotilla

While *Jervis* remained in dry dock having her shattered port side forward rebuilt, the German blitzkrieg on Denmark and Norway commenced on 9th April. Units of the J's in the 7th Flotilla immediately became involved in the abortive efforts to contain and stop the German fleet landing and then reinforcing its army in Norway. The British destroyers were soon employed on the transport of troops to support the Norwegians on operations within the long narrow fiords and sea leads, then later the rescue of the expeditionary force, all in the face of overwhelming air attacks.

Three of the J's, *Javelin*, *Jackal* and *Janus* shared with the other fleet units the strain of continuous air bombardment from screaming dive bombers coming out of clear, cloudless skies in round the clock daylight attacks within the confines of the fiords.

The 7th Flotilla ships shared the agony of the Norwegian campaign as it continued towards an inevitable and humiliating collapse.

Kelly had completed her third long repair period in dockyard hands on 27th April and arrived in Scapa Flow. On 2nd May she was off Namsos, as part of a mixed British and French force under the command of Vice Admiral J.H.D. Cunningham, to extricate 5,400 troops in an operation codenamed Maurice. The task was successfully accomplished from under the noses of the enemy by the destroyers commanded by Captain Philip Vian in *Afridi* but with the loss of two ships, a French destroyer *Bison* and the *Afridi*. The remainder of the force with the troops in French transports arrived back at Scapa Flow on 5th May.

Janus was with *Kelly*, *Kandahar*, *Bulldog* and the cruiser *Birmingham* when the force sailed from Scapa Flow on 7th May to intercept an enemy mine-laying group of destroyers, minelayers and E-boats reported to be on passage towards the UK east coast. In a bank of mist, at a position east of the Dogger Bank, *Kelly* led her destroyers at speed into an E-boat ambush and was torpedoed with 27 killed or missing. *Janus* remained with the stricken flotilla leader as part of a protective escort for what turned out to be an epic 91 hour tow in bad weather and subject to several air attacks.

Kelly was eventually towed into the Tyne and drydocked at her builders yard at Hebburn just two weeks after completing her last repair period on the Thames.

The sister flotilla leaders, *Jervis* and *Kelly*, lay in nearby shipyards on the river Tyne. *Jervis*'s ship's company watched the 5th DF leader with only a skeleton crew left in the ship, dock down and virtually crumble onto the blocks. The *Kelly*'s crew was sent straight away on leave while men from *Jervis* looked for their missing shipmates. Telegraphist D.W. Hague recalls:

> She was put into drydock close by and literally fell to pieces. Her survivors were sent on leave and we of *Jervis* went aboard *Kelly* to help salvage bodies. I found a young 'sparker' in what was left of the W/T office – dead of course.

Janus was saved from any further traumatic experiences in the North Sea: on her return to Immingham she embarked Captain Mack and most of the flotilla staff and sailed for Plymouth with orders for Captain (D) to sail to the Mediterranean and to assume command of the 14th Flotilla. He left Plymouth in *Janus* on 18th May at 0035 hours, taking with him *Juno*, two Tribal class destroyers, *Nubian* and *Mohawk* and four destroyers of the K class (ex-5th Flotilla) *Khartoum*, *Kimberley*, *Kandahar* and *Kingston*. The flotilla of eight destroyers sped south at 22 knots, in calm brilliant sunshine, away from the rigours of the North Sea, the disasters of Norway and the gut-worrying news of a German panzer breakthrough via Belgium into France. The flotilla in a long line astern entered Gibraltar harbour in the evening of 19th May.

The destroyermen were given no time ashore to sample the unblacked-out night life offerings of Gibraltar. Captain Mack sailed next morning eastward into lovely Mediterranean sunshine tempered by only the lightest of westerly breezes. The sailors emerged from their blue serge and jersey chrysalises and exposed white limbs and torsos to the warm sunshine. The destroyers were required urgently to reinforce the Mediterranean Fleet and the naval forces based on Aden and the Red Sea, as tensions mounted with the likelihood of Italy entering the war on the side of Germany. With a short call to refuel at Malta on the 22nd they arrived at Alexandria, the fleet's main base on the 25th where Captain Mack assumed command of the 14th Flotilla and awaited the arrival of his destroyer leader *Jervis* following completion of her repairs on the Tyne.

In home waters *Javelin* and *Jaguar* were committed to the evacuation of the British Expeditionary Force out of the European mainland from 25th to 29th May before they were suddenly withdrawn, because of the heavy losses of fleet destroyers, to join a reserve group of destroyers made up from H, I and J's to act as an anti-invasion flotilla. The withdrawal of the J's did not save *Jaguar* from receiving bomb damage aft as she raced for Dover filled with troops. She was towed into port and then taken to Sheerness for urgent repairs.

Javelin retired to Hull for a short refit, so with *Jaguar* at Sheerness and *Jupiter* completing repairs to her fractious engines, only *Jackal* remained as the one fully operational J class in Home waters on 1st June. She was at Harwich with *Kelvin*.

The K's had taken no part in the Dunkirk evacuation, Operation Dynamo. *Jackal* was already under the administrative control of the 5th Flotilla and of Captain D5, Captain Lord Louis Mountbatten; the other three, Home waters, J's followed rapidly and became part of his flotilla.

Captain D5 had taken over the destroyer base, HMS *Beaver* II set up by Captain Mack at Immingham, but instead of using the offices for himself and his staff in the old dock building and the accommodation in the hulk *Dunluce Castle*, it was perhaps characteristic of Captain Lord Louis to install himself and staff in the local county hotel.

As *Kelly* was again out of action for an even longer period than previously, the private ships had, from time to time, again to act as flotilla leader with Captain (D), his staff officers and extra communication ratings embarked. Even for the J's when Captain Mack was the Captain (D) involved, it was never a comfortable period when carrying the flotilla captain and his staff. There was the dislocation and discomfort of having to provide accommodation, which entailed the captain of the ship having to vacate his quarters. Then there was the embarrassment of having two senior officers functioning from the same small bridge area. Captain (D) was in command of the flotilla, but in these circumstances the ship was not commanded by him. There was also the other factor that one of Captain (D)'s staff officers stood a watch alongside the ship's officer of the watch, with the staff officer responsible only for the reports which he made to Captain (D) – not to the ship's captain.

It was with considerable misgiving that the commanding officers of the J's contemplated the arrival of Captain D5, Lord Louis Mountbatten, and his staff in their ships to conduct a flotilla operation. From his charismatic charm there were few dissenters, and he was universally recognised as a highly inventive and professional naval officer with a flair for publicity and an infinite range of influence and connections. He had nevertheless a reputation of being a Jonah in any ship in which he went to sea, a superstition backed by more than circumstantial evidence and the fact that his claims of U-boat sinkings and other successes against the enemy had not been confirmed. *Kelly* had a continuous succession of misfortunes under his command, not all of them through enemy action.

Commander Pugsley in *Javelin* observed with some charity:

> There was no great enthusiasm to be selected as Lord Louis' temporary ship. In due course, I was to suffer through sharing his bad luck.

In the eastern Mediterranean for the moment there was an uneasy calm, while the fleet exercised, patrolled and prepared for war. Yet there was still time to play. Ships' companies bathed in the waters of the harbour or, on 'make-and-mend' afternoons, groups hired feluccas whose crews arrived alongside for their passengers, well stocked with bottles of Stella beer buried deep in ice-filled old gasoline cans. The feluccas sailed to locations outside the harbour where bathing could take place from golden beaches fringing a desert still safe and free from defilement by mines and warlike obstructions. The vast palmtree-dotted beer-garden of the Fleet Club was the venue for Tombola sessions and beer under clear, star-packed Egyptian night skies. Alexandria – free from blackout restrictions – offered every indulgence of the flesh and vice, subject only to the controls imposed by the Provost Marshal.

The four K's, *Kimberley*, *Kandahar*, *Kingston* and *Khartoum* had departed from Alexandria and sailed on through the Suez Canal to their Red Sea station and for a while the 14th DF consisted of only four destroyers. With two other groups, the 2nd Flotilla and the 19th Division of Australian destroyers, the ships exercised hard with the battleships and cruisers of the fleet. This consisted of 48 hour spells at sea, then 24 and 36 hours in harbour to refuel, store and ammunition, with appraisal sessions of the exercise lessons.

This continued until 10th June, a black day for the Allies. Narvik had finally been evacuated, Norway and its army abandoned when the British force sailed from Harstad; on the western front the

German army drove on irresistibly toward Paris and it seemed that the French would seek an armistice. News came through to the Mediterranean Fleet that Italy would declare war and hostilities would commence at 0001/11th June.

The expected did occur; Italy was at war with the Allies, and the fleet left Alexandria harbour at 0230. With his flag in *Warspite*, Admiral Sir Andrew Cunningham sailed with *Malaya*, aircraft carrier *Eagle* and cruiser *Caledon* screened by the destroyers (Captain D14), *Juno*, *Nubian* and the Australian 19th Division. The fleet proceeded westward along the North African coastline seeking units of the Italian fleet to be found operating out of their Tripolitanian and Cyrenaican bases, and specifically for submarines assumed to be moving from Tobruk towards Alexandria. In the afternoon of the 11th, the cruiser *Calypso* and *Mohawk* and *Dainty* of the 2nd Flotilla joined the fleet. At midnight on the 12th, the fleet reversed its course eastward.

During the night the Italian fleet drew first blood – the submarine *Bagnolini* passed through the asdic screen and torpedoed *Calypso* which sank at 0330 with the loss of one officer and 38 ratings. The fleet returned to Alexandria, making a very cautious entry because during its absence several minefields had been laid by enemy submarines. Malta was being bombed day and night and the situation at Alexandria was full of uncertainties. The French squadron based on the port had also sailed on the 11th. Its Admiral Godfroy in his flagship *Lorraine*, having made an offensive sweep into the Aegean without contact with the Italians, returned again to Alexandria, troubled by divided loyalties, while his government parleyed with the Germans. Units of the French squadron sailed once more with their British allies and bombarded the Italian coastal Tripolitanian township of Bardia on Friday the 21st, then returned to harbour and to years of inactivity. The squadron's officers and men became confused with dissension between those who wished to carry on the fight and those that wanted to return to ports in unoccupied France. Moreover all were restless because they had not been paid for some time.

The British Commander-in-Chief could not sail with his Mediterranean fleet in case the squadron sailed for France or alternatively scuttled their ships to blockade the fleet base. Although he trusted the intentions of Vice Admiral Godfroy he knew that the French Admiral was not in firm control of his men. Tension reached dangerous levels when men of the 14th DF were put on standby to board and overpower the crews of the French ships under the guns of battleships and cruisers during the night of 3rd July and the following day made more acute, when at 0800/4th five Italian planes bombed the harbour. The tension subsided after officers from the fleet (including some of Captain D14's staff officers) visited the French ships. On the 5th a French transport arrived to take away French seamen who had opted to return to France; and then, on the 6th, the demobilisation of the French squadron was begun by taking fuel out of the ships and the removal of breech-blocks from the main armament. While the main units of the Mediterranean fleet remained in harbour little could be done to seek action with the Italian fleet, although some destroyers had entered the Aegean and escorted two convoys from the Dardanelles to Port Said and then maintained patrols outside Alexandria to deter further minelaying by Italian submarines.

Sir Andrew Cunningham and Captain Philip Mack were close personal friends, and so at this very difficult time of dealing with the French squadron, the C-in-C had a senior captain whom he could trust implicitly and whose advice he valued.

Back home in the UK, on 9th June, *Jervis* completed repairs at Hebburn and sailed for trials and a short work-up period. The flotilla leader was under the temporary command of Lieutenant-Commander A.F. Burnell Nugent DSC. The following day the ship received a signal that she was to sail from Plymouth later in the month for the Mediterranean. Before she received her sailing orders, Ravenscroft was relieved by a new first lieutenant, Lieutenant R.W. Scott, a very different type to Ravenscroft who was a rather subdued and introverted man. Scott, robust, forceful, dogmatic, was much dedicated to training, particularly the junior rates and boy seamen; it was a dedication that became very nearly an obsession and was to cause some friction in the wardroom. The ship carried 16 boy seamen in its war complement, as did other destroyers and major war vessels of the fleet.

Jervis sailed from Plymouth carrying a considerable load of stores, a number of specialist officers and senior ratings for the Mediterranean fleet and bases. The most senior passenger was the new Governor-designate for Gibraltar, General Sir Mason McFarlane. The ship sailed on 27th June and berthed at Gibraltar on the 29th. She remained at the fortress base for two days with the ship's company changing into tropical rig, and leave was given in turn to the two watches. The men relished the warm Mediterranean scents in their nostrils, the sights and pubs in the short streets of the town crouching at the base of the great towering rock, a seemingly invincible fortress.

The few days in Gibraltar lifted spirits depressed by the situation existing in the home country, where colleagues in destroyers, ships of the fleet and merchant ships continued with the process of extracting defeated armies from Norway, France and from the clutches of a victorious German war machine. They had also left a country expecting an invasion and an overwhelming air assault.

In the late evening of 2nd July, *Jervis* entered Malta Grand Harbour where her unfortunate 'stand in' commanding officer had some difficulty in berthing the ship. One highly critical member of the bridge staff rather uncharitably wrote: 'He made two clumsy attempts to berth alongside, on the third he damaged our stem – we shall be glad to see our temporary skipper go.'

The realities of the Mediterranean situation came home with a vengeance to a ship's company mildly seduced by the warmth and sunshine. In the 29 days since Italy had declared war, Malta had had 72 air raids, all on the harbour. As work went on feverishly to repair the damage to her stem, *Jervis* experienced her first air attacks trapped within the confines of Malta harbour on Wednesday the 3rd by a squadron of Italian bombers flying at above 12,000 ft, and again on Thursday when three seaplanes made a direct attack on the ship. Considerable damage was done to buildings and dockside equipment, but *Jervis* escaped casualties or damage.

While his flotilla leader was held up at Malta, Captain Philip Mack in *Janus* was with a force engaged in bombarding Italian army installations at Bardia on the 6th and he sailed again with the fleet from Alexandria on the 7th. The fleet began to leave harbour in three groups at 2200 with Admiral Cunningham leading, his flag in *Warspite*, then the *Royal Sovereign* followed and *Malaya*, the 7th Cruiser Squadron comprising *Orion, Neptune, Sydney, Gloucester* and *Liverpool*, and 17 destroyers with Captain Mack the senior Captain (D). Admiral Cunningham had sailed for a twofold purpose: the first and original reason was to give cover to a fast troop and evacuee convoy from Malta to Alexandria. Then on the Sunday morning, as the fleet prepared to sail, news came from Malta that the Italian fleet in strength had been sighted 200 miles east of the island sailing south, probably covering a convoy bound for Benghazi. The British fleet was now on course to contest for the supremacy of the central Mediterranean Sea. The unopposed ventures of the Mediterranean fleet for the first few weeks after Italy entered the war were not to be repeated. Air attacks from the squadrons of the Regia Aeronautica began shortly after the fleet set off westward following the fending-off, of attacks by two enemy submarines at the seaward end of the approach channel into Alexandria.

Admiral Cunningham reported in later years that Italian air squadrons were of high quality in 1940 and 1941. Their high level formation attacks on ships of the fleet gave great concern. Their reconnaissance was highly efficient and seldom failed to find and report a ship at sea. The bombers invariably arrived in an hour or two.

The flagship *Warspite*, over the next five days' excursion which culminated with an encounter with Italian fleet off the Calabrian coast, was attacked 34 times and missed by more than 400 bombs. The two fleets made contact and opened fire on each other between 1500 and 1615 hours on 9th July when the Italian flagship *Cesare* (Admiral Riccardi) was hit by a shell from *Warspite* at 26,000 yards. The enemy fleet turned away under the cover of smoke while skirmishes took place between the opposing destroyers. By the time Admiral Cunningham had skirted the great Italian smoke barrier the enemy had escaped through the straits of Messina albeit under air attack from their own aircraft.

For the next two days while the Mediterranean fleet steered south towards Malta and then eastward they attracted dozens of air attacks which enabled a fast and vulnerable convoy to slip unobserved out of Malta eastbound escorted by four destroyers including *Jervis*. In one of the heaviest raids on the 12th, *Warspite* was straddled by 24 heavy bombs down the port side and 12 off the starboard bow. In the same attack the cruiser *Gloucester* was hit, a fact noticed by Captain Mack in the *Janus*. The following signals were exchanged;

To	From:
Gloucester	D14

    Have just noticed damage, have you any casualties.
    = 1226

D 14	*Gloucester*

    Your 1226. Regret 17 killed including Captain and Commander and 9 wounded.
    = 1230

Gloucester	D14

    Your 1230. I am very sorry.
    = 1232.

After Captain F.R. Garside's death and that of his second-in-command, *Gloucester* continued at her station within the cruiser squadron and fleet, the ship being steered and fought from the after control position. Italian fleet casualties within the *Cesare* were higher: the flagship suffered 29 killed and 79 wounded.

The convoy with its escort arrived at Alexandria on the 14th and shortly afterwards Captain Mack resumed command of his flotilla leader and of the 14th Flotilla which now consisted of *Jervis, Janus, Juno* and the two larger Tribal destroyers *Nubian* and *Mohawk*. One of the convoy ships, ss *El Nil*, which was filled by evacuees from Marseilles to Egypt, included in its passenger list the Commander-in-Chief's wife and two daughters moving from the C-in-C's residence in Malta to Alexandria.

Lieutenant-Commander Burnell Nugent, having completed his ferrying task, departed from *Jervis* to take up his designated appointment, the command of the destroyer *Hostile*.

During the second night in the fleet base, *Jervis* experienced an air raid in the strange situation of there being no blackout in the city of Alexandria; only the ships in harbour and the dockyard were in darkness and had been blacked out since the June day when Italy had declared war. This first raid started at 2230 hours Tuesday, 16th July, the Italian airmen were meticulous in their accuracy, avoiding the Egyptian city and bombing only the harbour installations and ships, inflicting some minor damage. The crash of bombs and uproar of anti-aircraft fire from the fleet and army batteries ashore caused considerable alarm and panic in the very crowded and cosmopolitan city.

When the raiders returned the following night much of the city was blacked out and continued to be so, as successive raids were made on the port area. Indiscriminate bombing of the city would follow upon the arrival of the Luftwaffe in the Mediterranean.

These early raids did little to disturb the routine of the newly arrived *Jervis*. Leave was given to each non-duty watch which in turn departed with confidence in the duty watch to engage the raiders with the pom-pom and close range weapons. The watch ashore enjoyed the experience of sitting out on the pavement seats and tables of Avenida cafes, restaurants and the Fleet Club beer garden watching the extraordinary spectacle of a night display of searchlights which coned onto high flying silver moth-like aircraft and the eruption of pyrotechnics from tracer anti-aircraft artillery fire, being showered from time to time by falling shrapnel. Later, when they returned to the ship they found evidence of the night encounters, as the duty watch topping up depleted ammunition ready-use lockers, and they listened to embroidered tales from their shipmates of nearer than near misses from falling bombs and to their claims of probable hits on the raiders.

There was limited sea-time for *Jervis* in the latter half of July. The 2nd Flotilla which had sailed with the Australian cruiser *Sydney* encountered two Italian cruisers. They helped to sink one of them, the 6″ gun cruiser *Bartolomeo Colleoni*. The 14th DF sailed when heavy units of the fleet set off at noon of the 16th to intercept the suspected route of retreat of the second enemy cruiser, *Bande Nere*, toward Tobruk. Without encountering the escaping ship the flotilla returned to Alexandria next day, after making a vain search for a missing Walrus seaplane flown off from the flagship *Warspite*.

Six clear days followed in harbour which the new First Lieutenant Scott and his henchman the Buffer (chief bosun) used to achieve what was nearest to their seamen hearts, the overall repainting of the ship.

Very few escaped their 'press-gang' recruitment for hands to wash-down and paint ship. Junior wardroom officers were sent aloft to reinforce the telegraphist and visual signal ratings detailed off to paint the topmast, signal yards and tripod. Others reported to the chief yeoman to paint inside the bridge and flagdeck. Stokers scraped and repainted the funnel and the casings which housed the main boiler and engine room air intakes and exhaust while the bulk of the seamen ratings painted the superstructure or dangled on stages over the ship's side and manned borrowed dockyard catamarans used to paint in the black bottom colour. The remainder of the seamen gunners and torpedomen painted the gun shields, guns and torpedo tubes.

The Buffer and his small party of assistants dressed in overalls and sweating in the Egyptian sun, on a portion of the iron deck protected by canvas paint cloths, mixed and blended, with carley float paddles, the colours in old steel petroleum drums, light Mediterranean grey, dark grey, black for the bottom colour and funnel top plus red for the flotilla identification bands. They filled the paint fannies, tended the staging lanyards and kept the sun-kissed painters on the move. The first lieutenant and sometimes the Buffer embarked in the skimmer or motor cutter to observe progress, watch for paint holidays and to see that the bottom colour line was straight and to spot any painters who dozed on their stagings under the forecastle flare and out of sight from their part of ship petty officer. It was a popular task in the Mediterranean sunshine, the paint-ship hands worked semi-naked and after the mid-day tot issue and lunch continued in high good humour with many deliberate falls into the clear warm harbour water until 1600, after which the non-duty watch scampered off ashore.

Jervis, immaculate in her repainted livery, sailed at 0200/27th with her flotilla in the lead of the great ships of the fleet to cover the progress of a large convoy from the Dardanelles bound for Port Said and Alexandria. That evening an Italian air squadron based on Scarpento bombed the fleet at intervals between 1800 and 2000. *Jervis*, in her station at the centre and head of the destroyer screen surrounding the battleships and cruisers, was selected as the target in one of the attacks, as recalled in the flotilla gunnery officer's diary:

> Four bombers actually attacked *Jervis*, who was in the central position of the screen and dropped eight bombs which fell very close. I had popped my head up through one of the holes on the top of the DCT.* I looked up and saw four aircraft and their bombs descending upon us, I thought, hoped that they would miss aft, although they actually fell about ten yards ahead. I popped back into the DCT very quickly. Quite a lot of splinters came inboard.

The only hurt was to the Buffer's pride; he was incensed that 'Wop bomb' splinters had spoiled some of his pristine paintwork.

The high level attacks on the fleet patrolling SW of Crete were highly disturbing to the Commander-in-Chief as he strove to protect the convoys operating between the Egyptian ports, Athens and the Dardanelles especially after the failure of an attack by the very few available fighter aircraft carried in the aircraft carrier *Eagle*. The Gladiator fighters encountered thick weather while seeking the Scarpento air base which delayed their attack, and so ran into fully alert defences. Half the small formation with their highly skilled fighter pilots were lost.

July ended with a flurry of fleet activity. After returning from sea to refuel and embark ammunition the fleet again departed next day at mid-day so as to attract maximum attention of the enemy agents in Alexandria. Operation MA9, was a demonstration to distract the Italian air force and fleet away from an operation in the Western Mediterranean where Force H based on Gibraltar was bringing the

---

* Director Control Tower.

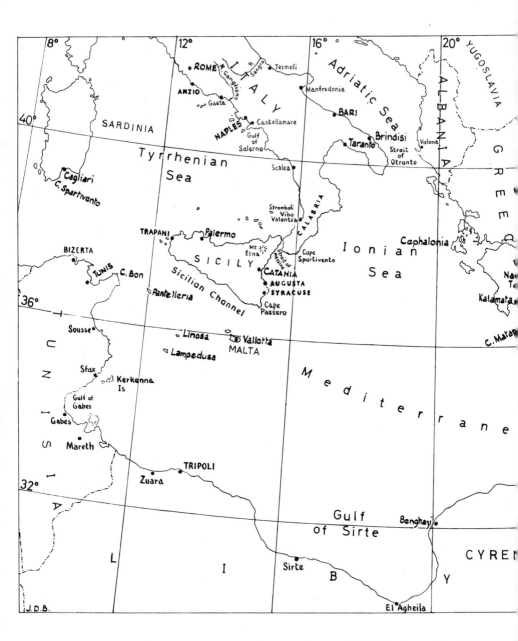

Central and East Mediterranean seas. Operational areas of HMS Jervis and the 14th Destroyer Flotilla, 1940 to 1946.

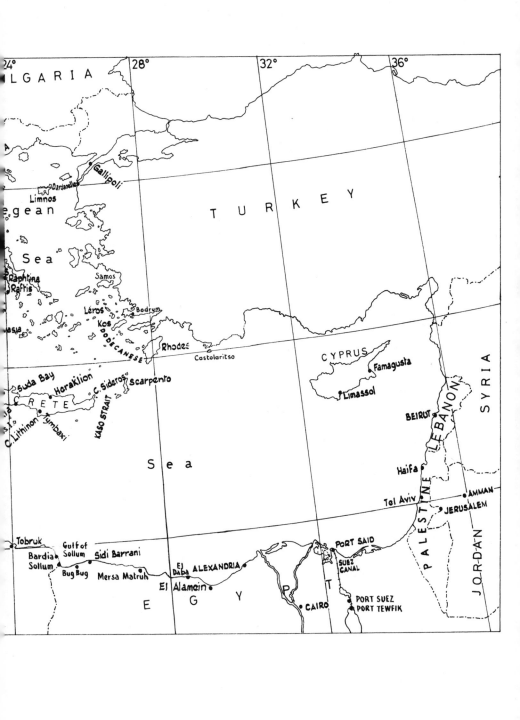

ageing aircraft carrier *Argus* to a position 8 degrees east and from there, was to fly off Hurricane fighter reinforcements for the defence of Malta. The joint operations were concluded successfully, but after *Jervis* had returned to Alexandria, escorting *Malaya* which was having serious boiler problems. They entered harbour on 1st August to learn that *Liverpool* had been hit by a bomb on the bridge and also informed of secret intelligence reports advising the Mediterranean fleet that invasion of England was imminent.

Problems multiplied when, on the 2nd, Captain Mack became aware that the French squadron, despite its cosmetic demilitarisation carried out in July, was making preparations to move its ships. Boilers had been flashed up and steam was on several capstans. The squadron consisted of the old battleship *Lorraine*, two modern cruisers and some destroyers. Captain Mack sent some of his staff officers to visit the cruiser *Suffren* where they found that the previously friendly, co-operative officers as well as their commanding officer had changed in their attitude and that the majority view was '*La France est vaincu*.'

The 14th DF staff, their flotilla colleagues and the staff of the Commander-in-Chief (as the fleet had again re-entered Alexandria) exerted their sympathetic understanding and Admiral Cunningham's personal friendship with Vice Admiral Godfroy and other senior French staff officers. This had the desired effect and defused a tense situation. The French warships unshipped and landed the main armament obdurating pads into the safe keeping of the French Embassy, and completed the disembarkation of the main armament ammunition.

Following seven days at sea with the 7th Cruiser Squadron, the 14th Flotilla passed through the Kaso channel into the Sea of Crete and into the Gulf of Athens to within sight of the Parthenon, giving many in the destroyers with a feeling for Greek history and legends an opportunity to ponder on Socrates and the flowering of Greek genius. After these few days patrolling unopposed among the magical and scented Aegean islands, the force returned to Alexandria on 11th and *Jervis* proceeded to an alongside berth and commenced a boiler clean.

That boiler clean and self-refit was to last until Thursday, 20th August. Opportunity was taken to give all night leave to men over 20 years of age or rated at least as able seamen. Accommodation was available ashore organised by the Fleet Club and a few religious bodies. For men less than 20 years or rated no higher than ordinary seamen, leave expired at 2300 hours. The boy seamen's leave was very restricted; regulations allowed from 1300 to 1800 hours on Saturdays and Sundays and – because their ship was on an overseas station – they could also have Wednesday afternoon out of their ship. Thus the 16 boys in *Jervis* were exposed to all the dangers of violent death or terrible wounds possible in a ship at her war station and confined to their ship every night and most days even though it was undergoing repairs in a harbour subject to attack.

On the 14th two of the flotilla staff officers, Lieutenant Mulleneux and Lieutenant (N) J. Cochrane had a day in Cairo bearing despatches to the Desert Army's headquarters; they flew to the Egyptian capital and returned by train.

Next evening the harbour was again under air assault. This time the Regia Aeronautica dropped mines and torpedoes into the harbour. No damage was done to major fleet units and the fact that she lay alongside saved *Jervis* from some of the tension of being at her normal buoy in mid-harbour. It was this raid that probably motivated First Lieutenant Scott to give the ship's company members under the age of 20, and especially the boy seamen, a break away from the ship with an opportunity of sleeping ashore, free for a few hours, of the dangers of shipborne life. With the support of the flotilla Chaplain Reverend Booth he formed 'The Under 20 Club' which gave the junior seamen more recreational opportunities; conducted parties in the charge of volunteer officers, senior ratings and the Chaplain, visited places of interest. Funds were made available for these young men to have meals ashore and whenever possible a chance to sleep in a bed in safe accommodation.

Following completion of the boiler clean, *Jervis* sailed on the morning of Tuesday the 20th with five other destroyers, *Janus*, *Nubian*, *Mohawk*, *Hero*, *Hostile* screening the cruiser *Liverpool* on a sweep into the Aegean to clear the way for a convoy sailing from Athens, Operation MD7. The convoy was sighted on the 22nd south of Gavdo island, where the covering force and convoy received attention from Italian bombers from Scarpento. *Jervis* and her destroyers brought the Athens convoy safely into Port Said, then turned west and the flotilla returned to Alexandria. Captain D14 remained in harbour until sailing on 29th August on a major fleet operation in co-operation with Force H based at Gibraltar.

After the encounter in July with the Italian fleet off Calabria, Admiral Cunningham had made it clear to the Admiralty that his fleet required another battleship which, with the *Warspite*, could match the Italian capital ships in speed and range of their guns. The enemy airfields dominating the central Mediterranean made it imperative that he should have another and more modern aircraft carrier and some anti-aircraft cruisers. This major operation Hats was to bring through to the Eastern Mediterranean some of the reinforcements requested by the Commander-in-Chief. These were the refitted and modernised battleship *Valiant*, the aircraft carrier *Illustrious* (built with an armoured flight-deck) and two anti-aircraft cruisers *Coventry* and *Calcutta*. The joint operation started with the East Mediterranean fleet sailing in strength on the 29th making a demonstration to distract the attention of the Italians away from the west. At the same time *Jervis*, with *Juno*, *Dainty* and *Diamond*, sailed as close escort to the first convoy of ships from the east to Malta since the Italians entered the war.

From the west the reinforcements, formed as Force F, sailed from Gibraltar with Force H as a covering and protection operation with Vice Admiral Sir James Somerville in his flagship the battle-cruiser *Renown*, the aircraft carrier *Ark Royal*, cruiser *Sheffield* and 12 destroyers. Aircraft from the *Ark Royal* attacked Italian air bases in Sardinia on the 31st before Force H turned back to Gibraltar, leaving the Force F reinforcements to link up with Admiral Sir Andrew Cunningham's fleet south of Sicily.

Jervis with its convoy, ss *Cornwall* carrying troop reinforcements to the island, the RFA tanker *Plumleaf* and storeship *Volo*, continued at 12 knots westward but did not escape the attention of Italian air squadrons. One bomb hit the *Cornwall* aft, killing one man and wrecking the steering, but the ship after a short stop regained station and maintained the convoy speed. The convoy with its escort entered Grand Harbour on 2nd September where it was joined by units from Force F including the battleship *Valiant* to refuel, to disembark passengers and off-load eight 3.7" army anti-aircraft guns and ten Bofers; and the two anti-aircraft cruisers entering harbour to take in fuel and to add to the anti-aircraft gun-power while the battleship was in harbour. *Illustrious* remained to the west with the main fleet. It was a wise precaution as heavy air raids developed, with German Ju87's for the first time sharing in the attacks on the harbours of Malta and the fleet lying off.

Shortly after *Valiant*, the two AA cruisers and *Jervis* with her destroyers emerged from Malta harbours, Admiral Cunningham detached the 3rd Cruiser Squadron, *Gloucester*, *Kent* and *Liverpool* with the destroyers *Nubian* and *Mohawk* from the main fleet to enter

February 1941. *Jervis* alongside an oiler in Suda Bay – Crete.

22nd February 1941. Malta convoy MC 6. *Jaguar* G34, sweeps across the front of the convoy to attack a submarine contact.

March 1941. Crete – interlude in the mountains, overlooking Suda Bay. George Jago, Doc Hamilton, Richard Wells with café owner; taken by Hugh Mulleneux.

28th/29th March 1941. Battle of Matapan. *Jervis* leading change of destroyer screen prior to the battle squadron's alteration of course – *Warspite, Formidable, Valiant* and *Barham*.

(*Below left*) Matapan. Italian crew of cruiser *Pola* line the rails to embark in *Jervis*. (*Below right*) 29th March 1941. *Pola*'s POW crew crowd *Jervis*'s iron deck. (*Bottom left*) March 1941. After Matapan Leading Telegraphists R. Maxted, D. W. Hague and R. Richardson pose with captured headgear.

the Gulf of Nauplia to collect a convoy of five steamships and to protect them on their passage to Port Said. The remainder of the fleet he divided into two groups: Force E, consisting of *Malaya, Eagle, Coventry* and five destroyers led by *Jervis*, took under their wing Convoy AS3 from Athens to Port Said; the second group, Force I, the C-in-C in his flagship *Warspite, Valiant, Illustrious, Calcutta* and seven destroyers proceeded north of Crete until late on the 4th when *Eagle* from Force E joined *Illustrious*. The two aircraft carriers flew off Swordfish to attack enemy airfields at Kalatho and Maritza on the island of Rhodes, but four of the Swordfish were shot down by Italian CR42 fighters.

Jervis with her flotilla returned to Alexandria on the 5th. All day the fleet in squadrons and flotillas entered, and it became a very crowded base with three battleships, two aircraft carriers, seven cruisers, 17 destroyers, the French demilitarised squadron, several fleet tankers and supply ships. The fleet remained concentrated in the base for the next few days while great activity went on between the staff of the Commander-in-Chief and the British Army of the Nile headquarters. There were clear indications that the large Italian desert army which greatly outnumbered the British was, after weeks of minor skirmishing and inactivity, about to advance into Egypt.

At dawn on the 11th with *Jervis, Janus* and *Nubian* giving close anti-submarine protection, the monitor *Terror* and two gunboats *Aphis* and *Ladybird* opened fire on the main enemy army camp and the coastal road on the west side of Sollum bay. The bombardment went on all day causing an immense amount of damage; by midnight *Terror* had expended her entire outfit of 220 rounds of 15" high explosive (HE) ammunition, each shell weighing 9/10ths of a ton, and the gunboats their individual outfits of 6" shells. Retaliatory fire from ashore was intermittent and rarely accurate and the air attacks very light; in the afternoon *Jervis, Janus* and *Nubian* closed the shore and, from close range, joined in the destruction of the army encampments, stores and vehicle laagers.

Less than 24 hours back in harbour had passed when in the morning of 13th September came the information that Marshal Graziani's army had started a cautious move down the pass toward the Sollum railhead of the line to Alexandria and on along the coast road a few miles to Buq Buq.

In the early hours of the 13th the 3rd Cruiser Squadron with *Jervis, Hero, Hasty* and *Hereward* on the screen sailed on a contraband patrol and offensive sweep into the northern reaches of the Aegean Sea steaming as far as the Thermia channel and the Stino pass close to the Dardanelles, a fact that excited the special interest of Captain Philip Mack who regaled the bridge watchkeepers with his memories, humorous and macabre, of the times he served as a young and junior officer in these waters. The cruisers and their attendant destroyers steamed unmolested in this area of stunning beauty, blue purple islands set in a sea that reflected the azure unclouded sky; war seemed to be an even greater obscenity in this setting. Gun crews, always alert, sunbathed round their guns and men off watch crowded the upper-decks. These were the days before the horrors of flash burns experienced in ships bombed and torpedoed in Home waters had been fully analysed. Fleet orders would shortly transmit the lessons to the fleet, men would soon be issued with face and arm flash covering and be forced to keep their bodies covered at all times when at sea.

Flag Officer 3rd Cruiser Squadron led his force out of the Aegean via the Kithera channel and joined a powerful section of the main fleet, *Valiant*, *Illustrious*, *Orion* and seven destroyers. The Italian army had pushed forward a few more miles to Sidi Barrani where *Janus* and *Juno* with the gunboat *Ladybird* were ordered in to bombard an enemy transport park. *Valiant* and three destroyers returned to Alexandria while Captain Mack commanding the screening destroyers remained with the two anti-aircraft cruisers *Coventry* and *Calcutta* giving support to *Illustrious*. This force steamed south to a position 100 miles north of Benghazi where at midnight *Illustrious* flew off 15 Swordfish to lay mines and then attack the ships in the Italian supply port with torpedoes. The result was most satisfactory, the enemy destroyer *Aquilone* was lost on a mine, a second destroyer *Borea* was torpedoed (later salvaged) and two freighters, *Gloria* and *Maria Eugenia*, were also sunk by torpedoes.

On passage back to Alexandria the cruiser *Kent* with two destroyers detached herself from the 3rd Cruiser Squadron and closed the coastal town of Bardia to bombard enemy troop concentrations. The action ceased abruptly when the ships came under heavy air attack and *Kent* was hit aft by an aerial torpedo, which killed 32 of her men and caused much damage. The cruiser was with considerable difficulty towed east with *Jervis*, *Juno* and *Janus* assisting the operation, and they succeeded in getting the badly damaged ship into Alexandria late on the 19th.

The following morning (20th September) with a correspondent from the *Daily Telegraph* embarked, Captain Mack in *Jervis* with

Janus, Juno and *Mohawk* sailed for Mersa Matruh which was just to the east of the Italian army's furthest point of advance into Egypt. The ships arrived at 1030 hours, 'a sunbaked spot but attractive in its way with a little blue lagoon'. *Jervis* entered the lagoon leaving the other destroyers outside on anti-submarine patrol. The ship was boarded by the Naval Liaison Officer (NLO) and the Army Liaison Officer (ALO) for discussions with Captain (D) and his staff, to plan the bombardment of the enemy-occupied airfield and the troop and transport concentrations at Sidi Barrani. While this was going on, other army officers came out to the ship for 'Baths and Gin'. In late afternoon *Jervis* sailed and steamed eastward with her flotilla until after dark, then doubled back at speed to a position off Sidi Barrani where the destroyers closed to within 4500 yards of the coast. At 0400/22nd the ships opened fire together, 'making two runs past the target area from 0400 firing 553 shells in all'. 'Returned to Mersa Matruh and dropped the ALO, whilst the Colonel had a bath'. The destroyers arrived back at Alexandria at 1600. When Captain Mack called upon the fleet flagship, the assembled army commanders expressed themselves satisfied with the bombardment results, fires were still burning and the material damage had been very great.

For the remainder of September and into October, *Jervis* and the 14th DF were engaged with two runs to Malta: the first was with the cruisers *Liverpool* and *Gloucester*, carrying 1200 troop reinforcements to the island fortress. On the second, the operation commenced with a full fleet exercise carrying out day and night encounters – it was a massive and impressive vista with the sea occupied by four battleships, two aircraft carriers, six cruisers and 22 destroyers joined later, at the conclusion of the fleet evolutions, by a convoy of six merchant ships from Port Said with their own escort of two anti-aircraft cruisers and four destroyers. On its passage to Malta the armada ran into very bad storm conditions. The high seas and strength of wind surprised many who were newcomers to the Mediterranean, but the storm helped the fleet to avoid detection, for enemy reconnaissance aircraft had been grounded.

Jervis entered Malta with her destroyers to refuel, and Lieutenant Mulleneux wrote in his diary:

All the destroyers, *Coventry, Calcutta, Ramillies, Plumleaf* (fleet tanker) *Janus* and *Jervis* all secured in a heap in the middle of the harbour for about four hours – a wonderful target for the bombers – but nothing happened, this may have been due to the weather, showery and thundery . . . We left again with *Ramillies* at 1830; on the way in, *Imperial* had sat on a mine and will be about four months in Malta refitting.

The fleet's passage back to Alexandria was full of incident: on 12th October, *Ajax* ran into what was intended to be a trap set by the Italian 1st Torpedo Boat flotilla but, with the use of her radar, *Ajax* outwitted the enemy ships, and sank the *Airone* and *Ariel*. The cruiser was hit several times by gunfire but avoided the many torpedoes launched at her. She was then attacked by five ships of the 11th Destroyer Flotilla and again succeeded in fending off the attack, at the same time badly damaging two of the Italian ships. One, the *Artigliere* was found and finished off by the cruiser *York*.

Ajax was then joined by *Jervis* and *Janus* in the following afternoon and ordered to collect a convoy out of Piraeus and to shepherd it eastward under the general protection of the main fleet. From *Jervis* observers noted; '*Ajax* has a few holes, the damage cannot be bad but she is burying bodies in the afternoon.'

After collecting the six convoy ships at 1400/13th the AA cruiser *Coventry* arrived and the convoy sailed south through the Kithera channel to link up with a convoy from Malta to Alexandria. The formation was attacked twice, each time by five bombers dropping 20 bombs and described by those present as a 'poor attack'. However that evening, attacks developed by Italian torpedo carrying aircraft and at 1900 *Liverpool* was hit. The ship's bows were destroyed as far back as the A turret and bad fires raged. When *Jervis* with her convoy passed the scene at midnight the fires had been overcome and *Liverpool* was in tow by *Orion*. *Jervis* re-entered Alexandria at 1630/16th, and from 1900 with other ships in harbour endured a prolonged air-raid which was the first of many raids which occurred over the next six days while the fleet remained in port. Much damage was done to shore installations but there was only minor damage to shipping.

In this six day period *Jervis* sailed twice to carry out flotilla exercises taking with her an officer of the still neutral navy of the United States of America as an observer, a Lieutenant-Commander Opie, who remained in the ship for several days. On the 25th, *Jervis* and *Janus* in company with the cruisers *Orion*, *Sydney* and *Calcutta* departed on another contraband control sweep in the straits of Doro and Kaso and along the coastlines of Crete. Several small steamers and caiques were stopped and boarded without incident before the next major shock news arrived by signal. In the early hours of the

28th the ships were informed that Italy and Greece were at war and that the Italians were invading Greece via Albania. The optimists in *Jervis* thought that it would simplify matters as the Mediterranean fleet would now have access to the Greek mainland .nd Crete ports and anchorages.

On 6th November, *Jervis* sailed. Captain Mack was the senior Captain D of the destroyer flotillas accompanying the fleet on a combined operation, MB8, with the objective to support a supply convoy to Malta from the east and to link up with Admiral Somerville's Force H bringing from the west further reinforcements to join the Mediterranean fleet. These were comprised of the battleship *Barham*, cruisers *Berwick* and *Glasgow* and three destroyers, *Greyhound*, *Gallant* and *Griffin*. The Mediterranean Fleet met its reinforcements just to the west of the Sicilian narrows, passing them through safely to the east and on to Alexandria.

While this operation proceeded smoothly without being sighted by Italian reconnaissance aircraft and also unobserved by patrolling submarines, Admiral Cunningham took his fleet northward into the Ionian sea where under the cover of darkness *Illustrious* flew off 21 Swordfish aircraft armed with torpedoes. In the early hours of 12th November the Italian battlefleet was attacked in Taranto harbour. The new battleship *Littorio* and two older capital ships of the *Guilio Cesare* class were sunk at their moorings in the face of intense anti-aircraft fire which shot down two of the Swordfish. While the attack on the Italian fleet base was under way, British cruisers intercepted an enemy convoy in the Strait of Otranto, bound from Valona in Albania to Brindisi. In a short engagement the four convoyed merchantships were sunk and two escorts badly damaged. Thus the British Maritime supremacy in the central basin of the Mediterranean was for a while reasserted.

While all this excitement was going on, *Jervis* continued on the screen of the fleet battleships and remained with the flagship until they returned to Alexandria on the 14th. During the day Captain Mack's staff officers made contact with the three newly arrived Greyhound (G class) destroyers, *Greyhound*, *Gallant* and *Griffin* who now joined the 14th DF. Two days later *Jervis* sailed again with six other destroyers, the battleships *Valiant* and *Barham* and *Eagle*, covering troopship convoys sailing out of Alexandria and Port Said bound for Piraeus.

On the morning of the 17th, *Jervis* and her destroyers entered Suda Bay for the first time and Lieutenant Mulleneux describes his first impressions of what was to be an important base:

An excellent harbour and quite a picturesque spot. The harbour was full of shipping and most of the Greek destroyer navy. Several transports were embarking Greek Cretan troops for passage to Salonika.

Flags (Lieutenant (S) Richard Wells) and I landed to spy out the land, it was really most interesting and refreshing. The town itself is a tumbledown affair but picturesque in its way with little white houses with red roofs, dusty roads and the hills behind. The soldiers seemed to be coming down from the hills – some walking and some on mule or horseback. They varied from magnificent moustached mountain chieftains well equipped and mounted, to rather miserable-looking specimens who appeared to have only half their equipment and wits about them. A fusillade of musketry went on all the time as the local army, through sheer joie-de-vivre, let off their guns in the air and anywhere.

The naval offices have been taken over from the Imperial Airways and is apparently the only building to boast of a WC – within the strict meaning of the act! . . .

After our visit to the office we were given a car to take us out to the PWSS (Port War Signal Station) which is also the site of the main gun battery. It was a pleasant quarter hour drive along the coast. Flags and RA Flags (Flag Lieutenant to the Rear Admiral 3rd Cruiser Squadron) had a look at the PWSS whilst Hicks showed me the battery and then gave us all a glass of vino at the local Ritz. The sailors live in the local prison and up to a few days ago had the prisoners as their messmates – a delightful crowd apparently ranging from generals, convicted of political crimes, to local brigands.

Needless to say the domestic arrangements are a little rustic but they seem to have worked marvels in the 3 weeks they have been there as besides mounting the battery of 4 x 4" and 2 pom-poms they have succeeded in building themselves little 'houses' near the gun positions as well.

After a glass of wine at the office we returned to the ship. *Jervis* sailed at 1500, relieving *Vendetta* who had been doing an anti-submarine sweep with the other destroyers outside.

The cruiser squadron with the 14th DF arrived back at Alexandria at noon on 19th November.

Jervis with her flotilla remained in harbour until the 25th and survived a particularly heavy air raid on the night of the 23rd/24th. It was the worst raid to date on the base and, while ships in harbour escaped serious damage considerable damage was done to shore and repair installations, upsetting the morale of Maltese and Egyptian workers in the port.

The fleet capital ships had been divided into two divisions, referred to by those who served under Admiral Sir Andrew

Cunningham as the first and second elevens, *Jervis* sailed as part of the 1st XI on 25th November. She departed from Alexandria at 0300 with the fleet flagship *Warspite*, *Valiant*, *Gloucester*, *Glasgow*, *Orion*, *Illustrious* and 12 destroyers; the 2nd XI followed an hour later. This was Operation MB9, which included the main operation, *Collar*, whose objective was to bring through from the west two cruisers, *Manchester* and *Southampton*, carrying 1400 troops and war *matériel*. On passage westward aircraft from *Illustrious* 'beat up' the enemy airfields in the Dodecanese and, later *Eagle*'s airmen raided Tripoli. The fleet entered Suda Bay in succession to refuel and then continued westward. Part of the operation was to send the battleship *Ramillies* through to the west and then on home for a refit. Admiral Sir James Somerville in *Renown* with Force K was also at sea bringing the two troop-laden cruisers to meet the Mediterranean fleet. This time an Italian fleet set out from Naples to oppose the eastward passage of British ships. The Italian Admiral Campioni, with a fleet of two battleships, seven cruisers and sixteen destroyers, was constrained by orders not to engage superior forces. He was badly served by reconnaissance reports from the Regia Aeronautica which misled the admiral into believing that he was outnumbered when, in fact, his forces were superior.

The Italian fleet south of Sardinia had a short skirmish at long range with Force H and elements of the Mediterranean fleet, a skirmish later to be glorified by the name Battle of Spartivento. The British cruisers *Manchester*, *Newcastle* and *Berwick* were for a time near missed by successive salvoes from the Italian battleships and cruisers, but only *Berwick* was hit in the running fight before the Italian admiral turned back. *Berwick* was able to continue on westward with *Ramillies* while *Manchester*, *Southampton* and three merchantships proceeded east without further opposition and were met by the fleet including *Jervis*. Captain Mack arrived back at Alexandria 'after a singularly uneventful operation as far as our end of the Mediterranean was concerned'. Lieutenant Opie USN, the neutral observer, left the ship. Bad news about the *Javelin* was awaiting Captain D who was expecting her and possibly the remaining J's at home to join him in the near future. He now learned that *Javelin*, with Captain D5 embarked, had been seriously damaged in enemy action, suffered many dead and was reduced to C & M (Care and Maintenance).

Javelin, *Jackal*, *Jupiter* and *Jersey* had been deployed to operate out of Plymouth as part of the 5th Flotilla. For many nights four German destroyers had been raiding and sinking merchant shipping moving along the swept routes in the English Channel's south-west coastal waters. Captain Lord Louis Mountbatten with his staff, embarked in *Javelin*, left Plymouth Sound in the evening of 24th November on another search for the elusive marauders; Captain (D) for over a month had sailed nightly seeking the enemy destroyers and this was the first time that *Javelin* had been involved since returning from a refit at Immingham where the ship had been fitted with radar.

Commander Pugsley's worst fears of Lord Louis' reputation for being a Jonah afloat were about to be realised. On that night the five destroyers *Javelin, Jackal, Kashmir, Jupiter* and *Jersey* steaming in line ahead found the German destroyers *Karl Galster, Erich Steinbrink* and *Hans Lody* crossing ahead of their track, from right to left, and then disaster struck the 5th Flotilla. Against the advice of Commander Pugsley, Captain D5 ordered an 80° alteration to port together to bring the flotilla on to a parallel course with the enemy ships. The change of course at speed and full helm threw the gun instruments momentarily out of synchronisation and caused the director crews to lose their dimly seen target as the ships careened wildly over. It also presented the flotilla as a prime torpedo target. The result was a catastrophe for Commander Pugsley's *Javelin*. She was hit simultaneously by two torpedoes, one forward and the other aft which caused the after magazine to explode. Three officers and 43 ratings were killed. The ship was left with only 155 of her original 353 foot length.

The Germans escaped unscathed leaving the British destroyers with the melancholy task of protecting their stricken leader from air and submarine attack and to get what was left of a proud destroyer back into Plymouth, in both of which tasks they succeeded. Commander Pugsley's steward, who had had a miraculous escape when the ship had been in collision with the *Jersey*, was among the missing:

> Amongst the ratings lost was my faithful Leading Steward Little who had joined a small party to make sure that the depth charges were set at safe and had been on the quarterdeck when the stern broke off and sank. He was not seen again.

Captain Lord Louis Mountbatten's handling of his flotilla in this engagement was, at the best, highly controversial in the opinion of many of his professional contemporaries and a negation of the traditional old naval signal so often flown in battle, namely to

'Engage the enemy more closely'. It was to be many months before *Javelin* would be able to join the 14th Flotilla and Commander Pugsley, after two further destroyer commands, would return to the J's as Captain D14.

For the first seven days of December *Jervis* remained in harbour or exercised with her flotilla in the approaches to the base with every night in port and able to give leave. At the same time Captain Mack and his staff prepared for the navy's inshore support to the desert offensive which began on the 7th. From the 8th *Jervis*, *Janus* and *Nubian* gave close anti-submarine and anti-aircraft escort to the bombarding squadron, the monitor *Terror* and her small 'widger' consorts, the river gunboats *Ladybird* and *Aphis*, who commenced bombarding enemy positions.

The Western Desert Force started its assault on the Italian front line with the intention of cutting off the Italian desert expert, General Malete, at Sidi Barrani. The bombarding ships and destroyers shelled enemy installations and troops and vehicles retiring along the escarpment road out of Sollum Bay.

Jervis was back in Alexandria on the 12th with *Terror* who had to replenish her empty magazines. The gunboats remained at Mersa Matruh, sheltering from rough seas which threatened those small river craft. In the early hours of the 14th, *Jervis* and *Janus* at an hour's notice were ordered to sea to escort the old AA cruiser *Coventry* which had been torpedoed in the bow the previous evening by the Italian submarine *Naiade* off Bardia. *Coventry* had been giving cover to the *Barham* and *Malaya* during their bombardment of enemy rear positions and line of retirement. The cruiser under her own power was successfully shepherded into port, where she entered Gabarri drydock for repairs to her bow, which had lost 22 feet below the waterline.

After one more day and night in to top up fuel and re-provision, *Jervis* sailed on the 16th with the fleet for the twin operations MC2 protecting the Convoy MW5 to Malta, and MC3 an attack within the Strait of Otranto. Captain Mack sailed leaving behind, adrift, four of his officers. Hugh Mulleneux, Richard Wells, Christopher Argles and Peter Aylwin, the flotilla staff officer's gunnery, communications, torpedo and the ship's sub-lieutenant respectively. This quartet had been ashore at the home of Richard Wells' uncle, Vice Admiral Sir Gerald Wells, who was the Admiral of the Egyptian Ports and Lights. Admiral Wells, his wife and two daughters kept an open house for the officers of their nephew's wardroom and for other officers of the 14th DF. On this evening it had been arranged for the ship's motor cutter to pick them up in good time before *Jervis* sailed but Scott (the first lieutenant) who had been entertaining his brother in the ship ordered the cutter to return the brother to his destroyer and – because a strong gale was creating a nasty seaway in the port – then to return to *Jervis* and be hoisted inboard in preparation for sailing.

The stranded officers, with some difficulty, managed to embark in *Nubian* as she sailed with Convoy MW5 which departed after the main fleet units had gone. They eventually rejoined *Jervis* in Malta at 1400/20th somewhat crestfallen, but were forgiven by Captain Mack because the first lieutenant accepted responsibility for having ordered the boat to return to the ship. It was an action that for a while caused some tension in some wardroom relationships.

In the interim period of the operations, following refuelling at Suda Bay, the 7th Cruiser Squadron, commanded by Vice Admiral Pridham Wippell, *Ajax*, *Orion* and *Sydney* together with *Jervis*, *Janus* and *Juno* made an unsuccessful sortie into the Strait of Otranto while *Warspite* and *Valiant* bombarded the Albanian port of Valona, main Italian Army supply base for the Greek front. *Illustrious* had rather more success, for her aircraft found a convoy escorted by enemy destroyers *Clio* and *Vega* and sank the two merchant ships in the convoy. Then on the night of the 21st/22nd *Jervis* was senior ship of the destroyer escort in the Sicilian narrows conducting the battleship *Malaya* on her way to the Home Fleet with two fast but empty merchant ships, westward into the care of Force H waiting south of Sardinia. That task completed, *Jervis* turned back eastward with her destroyers, but, off Cape Bon, *Hyperion* struck a mine aft. The Italians later claimed that their submarine *Serpente* had torpedoed her. *Ilex* attempted to tow the damaged ship, but twice the tow parted with *Hyperion* settling aft, with cabins and wardroom flooded. Captain Mack decided that it would be impossible to clear the danger area off Pantellaria island before dawn or to get within range of Malta-based fighter aircraft, so he closed the stricken *Hyperion* and with *Ilex*, took off the ship's company – two men had been killed and twelve wounded. *Janus* was then ordered to sink the ship by torpedo.

Jervis returned with the 1st XI of the Mediterranean fleet and berthed in Alexandria at 1600 on Christmas Eve.

Meanwhile at home on the Tyne, Wednesday 18th December, Captain D5 had sailed on trials in his reconstructed flotilla leader *Kelly*. That unfortunate destroyer since her first return to the

Hebburn shipyard on 14th November 1939 had been able to contribute only two weeks and four days to the war at sea.

Far away in a stormy but warmer Mediterranean winter her sister leader *Jervis* was enjoying the remarkable good fortune to be in harbour on Christmas Day. The messdecks had been decorated with bunting and signal flags borrowed from Chief Yeoman Harris and his signal department and, some individual messes, with considerable imagination and ingenuity, had been converted into colourful grottoes. The mess caterers and cooks had succeeded in converting the 'pusser's' issue of pork and rather stringy chickens (obtained from the canteen manager) into palatable seasonal dishes, and some messes found ingredients which – liberally laced with illegally hoarded rum issues – became lethal Christmas pudding substitutes. Aft, the wardroom staff had excelled themselves: 'The Maltese staff competed wonderfully and turned the wardroom into a cross between an early Victorian conservatory, the harvest thanksgiving and the village on a carnival night.'

Philip Mack gave further indications of his stamina – he toured the messdecks at 1000 immediately after an earlier than usual 'tot' issue; he exchanged good humoured and affectionate banter at every junior mess, and accepted innumerable 'sippers'. At 1030 he entertained the chief and petty officers in the wardroom with his staff and ship's officers, then at 1130 he hosted a reception for the flotilla captains and their officers, finally sitting down at the head of the wardroom table at 1445 to commence Christmas lunch with his own officers. Throughout this social marathon Captain Mack's reputation as a raconteur and host became even more firmly established.

Four days later on the 29th, *Jervis* and the 14th DF made their last offensive sweep in 1940; with the cruiser *Perth* the ships swept along the tawny desert coastline as far as Tobruk, which still lay in enemy hands although the Army of the Nile was approaching. The patrol proved uneventful and the ships returned to port that same evening.

Throughout December the Greek army had stemmed the Italian invasion into their homeland and, in some places, had thrown the invaders back into Albania. In the western desert, General Wavell's army had entered Bardia and had taken 60,000 prisoners. Malta was being battered from the air by day and night but the island fortress continued to function as a staging and refuelling port and repairs were still possible for damaged ships.

Jervis remained in Alexandria from 1st to 6th January 1941 carrying out a boiler clean. Leave was given each day from 1600 to

2300 and all night to those who were entitled. It was noticeable that the incidents of drink-based indiscipline and leave-breaking which had been a feature of Immingham were not being repeated in the Eastern Mediterranean. Although there was the occasional, and at times spectacular, deviation from the dictates of naval regulations and discipline by some individualists, there was nothing on the scale of the East Coast misdemeanours. The ship's company had changed little since *Jervis* commissioned; it consisted almost entirely of long service engagement regulars, with just a few ex-regular reservists and peacetime-trained RNVR's.

The ship was the senior flotilla leader in the fleet and Captain Mack was frequently the senior officer of the cruisers being escorted and therefore in command for the many offensive operations which were now a feature of the ship's existence, fleet operations predominated, a total change from the endless convoy escort duties on the East Coast of England. A tremendous pride in their captain and the status that their ship enjoyed within the Mediterranean fleet had developed in the ship's company. They became jealous of their ship's good name and of their captain's reputation.

Much of this development of a happy, close knit and efficient ship was due to the coxswain and his influence on the petty officers and junior ratings. Chief Petty Officer Mortimer was not just the professional who took over the wheel when the ship was called to action stations or when she entered or left harbour, he was responsible for much of the ship's discipline and administration, and he set the example of good behaviour and immaculate seamanship.

Like most coxswains, Mortimer was quite a character and a man of weight and influence, he knew of everything that went on in the ship, he was a friend of everyone who deserved it but could also be a formidable enemy of anyone whom he considered had tarnished the reputation of his captain and ship.

While *Jervis* boiler-cleaned, the remainder of the flotilla was at sea along the desert sea flank of the Western Desert Force as it pushed closer to Tobruk. The flotilla escorted units of the inshore bombarding squadron harassing the rear areas of the retiring Italian army. Flotilla staff officers were embarked in *Nubian* and *Janus*.

This stay in harbour was marred by a second suicide tragedy – this time the victim of his own hand was a chief petty officer, the torpedo gunner's mate. He shot himself with a service revolver in the fire control transmitting station. He was at the time under open arrest facing charges concerning his relationship with a junior rating.

A few days later a replacement joined, Chief Petty Officer, TGM, J.R.C. Edmonds who would remain in the ship for the next three years.

Jervis completed her routine boiler clean in time to join a complex multi-operation MC 4 which included the entire fleets at both ends of the Mediterranean to fight through troop and war supply convoys to Malta and Piraeus. The convoy starting ports were Gibraltar, Alexandria and Suda Bay and at the same time convoys were to be brought out of Malta and Piraeus bound for Gibraltar, Alexandria and Port Said. The core of the operation was to bring Convoy Excess through intact from Gibraltar with ships for Malta and Piraeus. As usual, the convoy from the west would be protected as far as the Sicilian Channel by Force H. Convoy Excess consisted of the fast freighter mv *Essex* (11,063 tons) carrying 4000 tons of ammunition, 3000 tons of seed potatoes and 12 Hurricane fighters, all for Malta, and three other fast merchant ships, ss *Clan Cummings*, ss *Clan MacDonald*, and ss *Empire Song*, loaded with war *matériel* for Piraeus and the Greek front. They were to be escorted by new reinforcements to the East Mediterranean, four destroyers *Jaguar*, *Hereward*, *Hasty* and *Hero* supported by the very new cruiser *Bonaventure* armed by dual purpose anti-aircraft and surface action 5.25″ guns in four twin turrets.

The main objectives of the operation were achieved: the convoy ships reached their destinations after Force H had made contact with the Mediterranean fleet units west of the Sicilian Channel. *Jervis*, beset by condenser troubles, missed most of the bloody sea and air battle. She had sailed with the 1st XI section of the fleet, which included the cruisers *Gloucester* and *Southampton* with 500 troops embarked for Malta and covered Convoy MW5½, *Breconshire* (9776 tons) and *Clan MacAulay* filled with supplies for the island. *Jervis* with her destroyers entered Suda Bay to fuel on the 8th and then departed to rendezvous with Convoy Excess. However she had to enter Malta on the 9th with her condenser problems, leaving the flotilla to proceed without her into the narrows separating Sicily and Tunisia. On the same day Italian reconnaissance located the Excess convoy 100 miles SW of Cape Spartivento, Sardinia, and not long afterwards ten enemy S79's attacked, though without causing any damage.

Then at dusk when the convoy and Force F made contact with the

14th Flotilla destroyers, at a position south of Pantellaria island two Italian torpedo boats, *Circe* and *Vega*, made an abortive torpedo attack. They were both badly damaged by *Bonaventure*'s formidable broadsides and *Vega* was sunk by a torpedo from *Hereward*. The convoy and escort avoided a salvo of torpedoes fired by the submarine *Settimo* but the *Gallant* struck a mine which destroyed her fore-end back to the bridge, killing 60 officers and men. She was taken in tow by *Mohawk* and brought into Malta where she was beached. The convoy, as it approached Malta, came under a murderous air attack by high level Italian squadrons and German Ju87 and Ju88 aircraft which were held off by *Bonaventure*'s rapid and accurate AA defence with her 5.25″ main armament. Meanwhile the fleet, its 1st XI, standing off east of Malta came under intense and skilful dive bomb attacks for the first time. Supported by Italian high level and wave-hopping torpedo-carrying aircraft, two German Ju87 squadrons, (1/StG and 11/StG) formed a circuit above *Illustrious* whose fighters had been lured away by the Italian torpedo bomber threat. The Ju87's in turn peeled off from their circuit and plunged down onto the aircraft carrier which was hit seven times and near missed by many more. She was badly damaged with 60 dead and 70 wounded and had to limp into Malta for emergency repairs.

At midnight *Jervis* rejoined the fleet manoeuvring to the east of the approaches to the island. Here it was difficult to discover with certainty what was happening. The Excess convoy ship *Essex* had berthed without damage in Malta and the other three ships of the convoy were passing through the Strait of Kithira on course for Piraeus. Other convoys, ME5½ and ME6 had slipped out of Malta's harbours and were making their way towards Egypt and yet another convoy was passing north of Crete, bound for Port Said. In the central basin the 1st XI of the battle fleet was breaking away from the remainder and setting course to arrive off Tobruk for a further bombardment of the port and defences, but other events intervened. Mid-afternoon signals were received that the cruisers *Gloucester* and *Southampton* were being dive-bombed and that both ships had been hit. *Jervis*, *Janus*, *Perth* and *Orion* were detached at 1700 and ordered to proceed at speed to the cruisers' assistance, 'while the fleet also turned back and plodded along behind'.

We arrived, about 200 miles east of Malta, at 2130 and found *Southampton* blazing and abandoned with *Gloucester* and *Diamond* in attendance. When we arrived *Diamond* had taken off all the survivors and transferred them to the *Gloucester*. We circled round while *Orion* finished *Southampton* off with a torpedo. The fire had got such a hold that any hope of saving the ship had to be abandoned. She blew up with a simply gigantic explosion which, if it hadn't been so tragic, must have been the best display of fireworks on record, a truly Wagnerian funeral.

So wrote Hugh Mulleneux in his diary.

Southampton had been hit aft where one bomb had exploded outside the wardroom, killing most of the officers.

The fleet returned to Alexandria on the 13th accompanied by an unexpected replacement for *Gloucester*. *Bonaventure* which should have returned to the west had expended all her 5.25″ ammunition outfit and had to proceed to Alexandria, under the protection of the fleet's guns, to re-stock, after which she remained with Admiral Cunningham's fleet.

Jaguar joined the 14th Flotilla and her three sister J class destroyers. Four days later Captain Mack in *Jervis*, and with *Nubian* and *Hero*, departed from Alexandria with the cruisers *Orion* and *Bonaventure* to carry out a further softening-up of the Tobruk defences. The army had timed their assault on the port for 20th January, but the ships ran into high winds, mountainous seas and visibility cut down to nil by blinding sandstorms. *Nubian* had to be detached to close the coast and stand by the gunboat *Aphis* which was in trouble in the high seas. The weather continued unsuitable for bombarding so the force made for Suda Bay where they arrived on the 20th in the evening, where Captain Mack found *Juno*, *Janus*, *Ilex* and *Greyhound* of the 14th DF waiting for him.

After refuelling and spending a night in harbour Captain D14 sailed at 0600/21st with *Jervis*, *Juno*, *Janus* and *Greyhound* for Malta, Captain Mack's task was either to bring out *Illustrious* if this was at all possible, or to escort convoy ME7 of empty supply ships back to Port Said. The flotilla learned that German Ju87 squadrons had been systematically bombing the island, selecting gun sites, grounded fighter aircraft, the dockyard and the berthed *Illustrious*. On arrival in the Grand Harbour 24 hours after leaving Suda Bay and steaming fast through seas that were going down, the men in *Jervis* found after their nine days' absence from the island, that the bombing by the German dive bombers and Italian high level formations had changed the situation. New damage to property and dockyard installations was very obvious and work in the dockyard over the last few days had been badly disrupted: Maltese dockyard workers' and civilian morale was shaken and houses near the dockyard were being abandoned.

Jervis berthed on Boathouse Wharf just astern from *Illustrious* – which had been hit again – and opposite the mv *Essex*. The supply ship had been hit by a bomb which, fortunately, had missed her huge cargo of ammunition. Stevedores were refusing to unload the military stores and ammunition from the ship, and this was now being done by soldiers and sailors. The best news for the beleaguered islanders was that Tobruk had fallen and that the Western Desert Force was pressing on westward.

That afternoon Hugh Mulleneux and Doc Hamilton managed to get a couple of hours out of the ship and away from the dockyard, and went for a walk in the Maltese countryside as far as Notabife and visited the local church. In *Illustrious* the engine-room staff, ship's company and dockyard experts slaved without stop to get the ship fit enough for a dash to Alexandria. All day long on 23rd January those in the aircraft carrier and her waiting destroyer escort held their collective breaths. For some inexplicable reason the day passed without a repetition of air raids – just the solitary snooper aircraft high up circling the island but no attacks. BBC radio broadcasts had announced that *Illustrious* lay grievously damaged in Malta's Grand Harbour, and this may have led the enemy to believe that the ship was unable to steam for some time to come.

That evening, not long after 1800, Captain Mack put to sea with his destroyers, followed by the great shape of *Illustrious* being towed and nudged by tugs out through the harbour entrance. To the surprise of the escort, *Illustrious* 'cracked off' to the south-east at 25 knots. At dawn the 24th the cruisers *Orion*, *York*, *Ajax* and *Bonaventure* were nowhere in sight; they had miscalculated the damaged carrier's speed and were astern doing only 17 knots. Because of this the 50 high and low level bombers sent out to find *Illustrious*, once the dawn snooper had found that her berth was empty, came upon and pounded the jinking cruisers, while the prime target and her 14th DF escort escaped. *Illustrious* entered Alexandria on the morning of 25th January to be greeted by the flagship *Warspite*'s ship's company, cleared from the lower deck to cheer her in with the C-in-C's Royal Marine band playing on the quarterdeck.

The Western Desert Force captured Derna on the 30th but on the Greek front ominous events were beginning to happen; the Germans, impatient with their Axis partner's failures, had begun to move Panzer regiments into the Balkans and there were indications that they would soon confront the Greeks.

Within the 14th Flotilla there had been a staff change. On 17th

(*Left*) Jack Caswell, Boy Seaman 1st Class. (*Right*) Ronald Bone, Boy Seaman 1st Class.

(*Left*) Stokers 1st Class George Morel and Bernard Smith. (*Right*) Chief Stoker Gabey and company.

(*Above*) *Jervis* — ship's company — Alexandria.

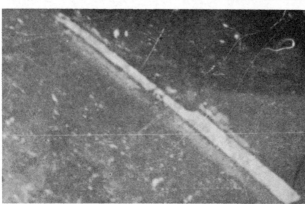

(*Left*) 16th April 1941. Enemy convoy destroyed by *Jervis* and the 14th DF. Three escorts and five supply ships with one 14th DF ship lie in the shallows off Sfax. From top:

    Mohawk
    Tarigo
    Supply ship.

January the navigator Lieutenant (N) J. Cochrane had been relieved by Lieutenant (N) J.B. Laing DSC. Cochrane had always been less than satisfied with the situation in that he, who was senior staff officer and senior to any of the ship's officers, had not been nominated by Captain Mack as second-in-command of *Jervis*. He had found this difficult enough to accept when Ravenscroft had been the first lieutenant, but now with the new man Scott, forceful, robust and not especially popular, and again junior to him in seniority, Cochrane was most unhappy with his status in the ship. There were of course, sound operational reasons for Captain Mack's decision; the first lieutenant's action station was aft in the ship where he would be able to take over command should the bridge be knocked out, whereas the flotilla navigator's action station had to be on the bridge by the captain's side or close by in the plot and was therefore especially vulnerable should the bridge be hit in action. So Cochrane, a great friend of Hugh Mulleneux, departed from the ship in Alexandria.

On 7th February *Jervis*, *Janus*, *Jaguar* and *Mohawk* left Alexandria in extremely rough seas and a thick sandstorm, and many of *Jervis*'s ship's company – including their captain – were sea-sick. The flotilla was on passage to Suda Bay where it was to be based, a move which promised to bring a break from the pressures and responsibilities of escorting the 1st XI of the battle fleet. On passage the destroyers watched over the safe progress of two AS convoys from Greece. News came through, while the ships were still at sea, that the Western Desert Force had entered Benghazi and *Jervis* received a signal asking for particulars of Lieutenant Cochrane's next of kin. The signal depressed and worried his friend Hugh Mulleneux who knew that Cochrane had been sent to join the staff of the Naval Officer in Charge (NOIC) at Tobruk. A few days later Mulleneux's fears were realised; Cochrane had been killed at Tobruk in an explosion.

The Western Desert Force captured Benghazi on 6th February; the British forces (which at no time exceeded two divisions) had routed an Italian army of ten divisions and was pressing on beyond Benghazi in the direction of El Agheila deep in the Gulf of Sirte. Less good was the news that it was estimated that a million German troops had occupied Romania or were passing through Bulgaria towards Greece. The Greek government had asked for British front line troops – and these were being earmarked from the small victorious Desert Army, a fact which would contribute to halting the British advance westward to Tripoli and prevent the elimination of the Axis forces from Tripolitania and Tunisia.

From Suda Bay the flotilla patrolled the Kithira and Kaso straits at opposite ends of Crete, as well as the Stampalia channel and joined the 3rd Cruiser Squadron covering the passage of a convoy to Malta plus several Aegean convoys. The flotilla sailed with troops embarked at Suda Bay to invade the island of Kaso, but the operation became abortive when the advance landing party could not find a way to scale high cliffs that barred the way into the island.

The British Army advance came to a halt at El Agheila and the fleet prepared to transport a division of troops with its support artillery, tanks ammunition and stores to Greece. The Germans had commenced dropping magnetic mines into the Suez canal bringing the flow of traffic to a stop. *Illustrious* could not be got away for repairs, and by the beginning of February 93 ships including the aircraft carrier *Formidable* (to take the place of *Illustrious*) were held up at the southern end of the canal.

Jervis and her flotilla were back in Alexandria for the first four days of March, then proceeded to sea for two days, exercising with the fleet and trying out a new anti-aircraft barrage fired by the destroyers on the screen to form an umbrella over the capital ships to deter dive bombers and another as a protection against wave-skimming torpedo-carrying aircraft. This second barrage was created by the battleships and cruisers firing low over the sea with ammunition fused to explode at 2500 yards, inside the destroyer screen stationed at 3000 yards from the outside columns of the big ships. At the same time the destroyers fired a barrage 'away' from the fleet and close range-weapons of the attacking planes broke through and over the destroyer screen. The barrage over the fleet increased the downpour of shell splinters and shrapnel that rained down on the ships and foamed the sea in heavy attacks, while the low level barrage became an effective and terrifying deterrent for many enemy torpedo bomber pilots, but to the long-suffering hard-worked destroyers a special peril – many men on the screening ships would be killed or injured by faulty ammunition or badly fused shells.

The fleet sailed on the 6th to cover the first convoy of Operation Lustre, whose objective was the fast transfer of British troops and *matériel* to Greece from Egypt and the captured desert ports. Before they sailed, *Jervis* learned that their old bombarding partner, *Terror*, had been mined while withdrawing from Benghazi in the face of intense dive-bombing and then was sunk under further massive attacks as she struggled to reach Tobruk. At the same time the destroyer *Dainty* was sunk by a bomb as she left Tobruk.

Jervis returned to Suda Bay and, from the 8th, sailed frequently to cover Lustre convoys moving along the north coast of Crete, or northbound through the Kithira straits; air attacks were frequent and often heavy.

When *Jervis* had had her collision damage repaired on the Tyne in 1940, the after set of five torpedo tubes was lifted out and replaced with an elderly 4″ high angle gun for extra anti-aircraft defence. Lacking sophisticated control equipment, this gun became a priceless morale booster as well as a crude weapon to fire barrages against diving aircraft. Yet it was their captain's calm skill that gave his sailors their greatest confidence. *Jervis* was not fitted with RDF (Radar) but Philip Mack had an uncanny ability to sight aircraft before his lookouts and bridge staff and when under attack he watched every diving aircraft until he saw (or sensed) the bomb release and then, only then, with an adroitness which constantly amazed his ship's company would he give helm and telegraph orders that eluded the falling bombs. Their captain's skills were backed by the pom-pom crew whose joint outpouring heavenward of prayer to the Almighty formed an impregnable umbrella over their ship!

The ship spent a day and a half in Suda Bay and part of a watch was allowed ashore to stretch their legs and to sample the sparse offerings of the local township, Canea. Four officers also went ashore to walk and explore; George Jago, Doc Hamilton, Richard Wells and Hugh Mulleneux who later wrote:

> . . . the first part was up rocks and scrub which was rather like the Scottish moor. We came to a little wood of firs and olives where goats with little bells were grazing tended by a shepherdess and an old shepherd – altogether a most idyllic scene. A stone path wound up through the wood to a small cluster of little white houses over the ridge near the top. Over this ridge we got a most lovely view of the mountains – in foreground the firs and the little white village, in the background these lovely snow-covered mountains. We stopped at a small estaminet on the ridge, admired the view and drank Cretan wine, we got a fine view of the mountains, the harbour, green fields and woods, Canea and other villages in the distance. We filled our lungs with the magnificent mountain air and had our lunch at the top.
>
> We climbed down a different way, a pretty steep slope. The flowers were just beginning to come out, lovely little anemones, poppies, daisies, a few pheasant's eyes and a species of a small lily. A grand day.

The flotilla returned to sea screening *Valiant* and *Barham*, the great ships contributing their bulk and menace to the security of the 'Lustre' convoys passing through the Kithira straits into the Gulf of Nauplia and the Greek ports and of empty ships returning to reload at Port Said and Alexandria. A gale started to blow during the night of the 13th; by dawn next day it had reached storm force and the seas were mountainous. It was 'just like old times in the North Sea without the cold.' Transit fore and aft along the destroyer's iron decks became a perilous venture and in *Jervis* all upper-deck movement was restricted, and between decks became a sodden hell of swirling water and debris.

The wind began to moderate on the 15th and an otherwise dull patrol continued as the covering group moved south-east following a convoy returning to the Egyptian ports. *Jervis* and her flotilla followed the battleships into Alexandria on the 18th where, to everyone's surprise *Illustrious* had gone and in her old berth lay her replacement, the new carrier *Formidable*. It was obvious that the Suez Canal had been re-opened as the port was full of freighters discharging war *matériel* or preparing to sail on, in convoy, to Greece.

The first convoy sailed at 0630/20th for Operation MC6, the passage of ships from Haifa and Alexandria to Malta. *Jervis* and her destroyers screened the three battleships *Warspite*, *Valiant* and *Barham*, and the aircraft carrier *Formidable*. In extremely rough weather, which no doubt grounded enemy aircraft, the convoy arrived at Malta without being sighted or attacked. This was to prove to be the last occasion, for the next two years, that a convoy to the island from the east or west would escape being attacked. The fleet was back in Alexandria where *Jervis* prepared to enter dry dock to carry out a self boiler clean and at the same time, have her rudder repaired. Plates had peeled off leaving most of the rudder with little more than a bare steel framework.

The Germans had entered Italy in force. Convoys of German and Italian transports were at intervals passing round the western end of Sicily and south of the island of Pantellaria to Tripoli where heavy armoured units of the German army and Italian reinforcements were being landed. The German High Command was putting increasing pressure on their Axis partner to adopt a more aggressive policy in the Eastern Mediterranean with their fleet, to disrupt the flow of Lustre convoys to Greece. Additional fuel was made available from Romania for the Italian ships, and firm undertakings were made that the Luftwaffe and Regia Aeronautica, operating together, would provide extra and constant reconnaissance to support the fleet and squadrons to attack the British fleet should it sail to challenge the Italian fleet. German intelligence had erroneously reported that the British had only one battleship, *Valiant*, ready for sea and action.

The Mediterranean Fleet had returned to Alexandria after exercising with *Formidable*, an excursion to test the effectiveness of the new AA barrage over the fleet. Some Ju88's tried to intrude on the fleet's business and one came out of the vortex of fire and smoke over the ships, to crash to its death in a final, gigantic splash.

Then came a report, long awaited with impatience and eagerness by the Commander-in-Chief: at 1220/27th a British Sunderland flying boat had sighted three enemy cruisers and a destroyer 80 miles east of the south-eastern tip of Sicily steaming a course roughly in the direction of the south coast of Crete. This was just what Admiral Cunningham had hoped for; he was convinced that this was an advance squadron of the main Italian fleet seeking to intercept convoys to and from Greece and Egypt. These lightly escorted convoys were being covered by Vice Admiral H.D. Pridham-Wippell, Vice Admiral Light Forces (VALF) with his squadron of four cruisers, *Orion*, *Ajax*, *Perth* and *Gloucester* and the four destroyers *Ilex*, *Hasty*, *Hereward* and *Vendetta* operating out of Suda Bay. The VALF was currently patrolling south of Crete and the situation was a tempting bait for the Italian fleet.

At 1400/27th an Italian snooper plane from Rhodes flying high over Alexandria reported that an aircraft carrier and three battleships lay at their moorings with awnings spread. Later that afternoon to deceive enemy agents in the city Admiral Cunningham landed with light hand luggage as if he were about to spend the night ashore. Guests who had been invited to dine in the flagship were at dusk collected by boat and taken out to the *Warspite*. As soon as it was dark the guests were landed and the battleships struck their awnings and raised steam. The convoys on passage north and south from Piraeus and the Egyptian ports were ordered to reverse course and to clear from the central sea. *Jervis* – about to enter dry-dock – had her boiler clean and rudder repair postponed and was ordered to immediate notice for steam.

The fleet sailed at 1900 steaming at 20 knots towards a position 20 miles south of Gavdo island where VALF had been ordered to rendezvous with his Commander-in-Chief. The fleet consisted of *Warspite*, *Barham*, *Valiant* and *Formidable* screened by *Jervis* (D14), *Janus*, *Nubian*, *Mohawk*, *Stuart*, *Griffin*, *Hotspur* and *Havock*. Only *Valiant* and *Formidable* were fitted with radar, type 279 sets. None of the destroyers had sets of any kind and in VALF's cruisers, the flagship *Orion* had an early primitive set, but *Ajax* had a type 279.

Admiral Cunningham's intelligence information was about to mature. At 0800/28th VALF reported that he was in contact with two groups of Italian cruisers. By 1100 the British squadron had been lured into an uncomfortable and potentially dangerous position planned by the Italian Commander-in-Chief, Admiral Iachino, with his flag in the *Littorio* class battleship *Vittorio Veneto*. VALF had the powerful 8″ Italian cruisers closing in on his starboard quarter and the Italian battleship coming in on his port beam. The faster enemy ships were overtaking the British squadron which was being out-ranged and straddled by accurate fire.

This action was taking place about 50 miles north-west of the British Commander-in-Chief's position who rescued his cruisers by launching an attack of torpedo-carrying Albacores and Swordfish from *Formidable*. The attacks indicated to Admiral Iachino that the British fleet with an aircraft carrier was approaching and was probably very close but he had received no reports or warnings from Axis reconnaissance sources. The Italian battleship and cruisers broke off their attack on VALF's cruisers, and retired westwards. The Italian flagship continued under attack throughout the afternoon from Fleet Air Arm planes and RAF Blenheims from Crete. Between 1500 and 1530 one torpedo hit was obtained aft on the *Vittorio Veneto*, the aircraft and its crew of three were shot down and lost. The flagship's speed was reduced.

The Battle of Matapan which followed has been researched and documented in great detail in many naval historical works, and so only the movements and activities of Captain Mack, *Jervis* and the 14th Flotilla will be discussed here.

The 14th DF was sent off in pursuit by the following signal;

To: General   *From : C-in-C*
Following are my intentions. If cruisers gain touch with damaged '
battleship, 2nd and 14th DF's will be sent to attack. If she is not then
destroyed, Battlefleet will follow in. If not located by cruisers, intend to
work round the north and then west and regain touch in the morning.
Mohawk and *Nubian* join the 14th DF at dusk and destroyers form, 2nd
DF and 14th DF, 45 degrees, one mile on either bow. 10th DF ahead.
1810 28/3/41.

At this point Admiral Cunningham estimated that the *Vittorio Veneto* was making slow progress westward; the enemy battleship was actually doing 19 knots.

To: 2nd and 14th DF   *From: C-in-C*
Destroyer flotillas addressed attack enemy battlefleet with torpedoes estimated bearing of enemy battlefleet 286 – 33.
2238 28/3/41.

Captain Mack had in fact an impossible task, the enemy forces were too far ahead and making sufficient speed to avoid being attacked under the cover of darkness. The British battleships following behind had been alerted by the radar in *Valiant* that a large vessel was lying stopped not far from the battlefleet's line of advance. It turned out later to be the Zara class cruiser *Pola*. Unknown to the C-in-C she had been torpedoed in the last FAA attack at 1930 on the Italian fleet. The cruiser had been hit amidships between the boiler and engine rooms and had lost all electrical as well as propelling power; her armament could not be trained or elevated. Admiral Iachino had sent back two cruisers and three destroyers from the stricken ships squadron to see if they could assist. These ships were also detected in *Valiant's* and *Formidable's* radar.

The Italian ships had no radar and their gunnery optics were not suitable for night vision nor was flashless ammunition carried; their fleet policy was that no major vessels should fight at night, only the escorting destroyers would defend with torpedo attacks. In complete contrast the British Navy had constantly exercised night action with the gun between the wars and with superior night optics, and some ships were now fitted with the priceless aid of radar.

Admiral Cunningham, handling his battleships as if they were destroyers, manoeuvred so that the three ships at point blank range, 3000 yards, poured successive 15″ broadsides from the turrets and 6″ from the secondary armament into the *Zara* (Admiral Cattaneo) and the *Fiume*. The Italian cruisers were at the same time held in the unblinking merciless and blinding beams of searchlights in the battleships and escorting destroyers. After the terrible holocaust that overwhelmed the helpless enemy ships, the C-in-C turned the battle squadron ships together and retired north-west away from the torpedoes launched by Admiral Cattaneo's destroyers. One, the *Alfieri*, was sunk a quarter of an hour later, at 2315, by a torpedo from *Stuart*. Another Italian destroyer, *Carducci*, was sunk by a torpedo from *Havock*.

Away to the west Captain Mack, steaming at 28 knots to work

ahead of the Italian flagship, had actually crossed the track astern of the enemy battleship who was still retiring with her remaining cruisers and destroyers. At 0030 *Jervis* received a signal addressed to the C-in-C and D14 reporting that *Havock* was in touch with the stopped Italian battleship; *Havock* had in fact mistaken the *Pola* for the *Vittorio Veneto*. Before *Havock* corrected her signal Captain Mack's flotilla had turned back towards the gun flashes and star shells sighted far astern, which indicated that the battlefleet was engaged in some spectacular action. The flotilla was steering ESE and working up to full speed toward the position given by *Havock*. An hour later, when *Havock*'s corrected sighting report was received, Admiral Iachino was 85 miles away to the west – and uncatchable.

With *Nubian*, *Mohawk*, *Janus*, *Ilex*, *Hasty*, *Hereward* and *Hotspur* in line astern of *Jervis*. Captain Mack arrived at the scene of the night action at 0200. The sea was filled with boats, rafts and swimming men; Hugh Mulleneux recalled:

> At about 0200 we passed through a whole party of Italian survivors from some ship or other and it was awful hearing their pitiful and despairing cries for help. It rubbed into one the evil of war . . .

The cruiser *Fiume* had sunk: *Zara* was still afloat but abandoned and with a small number of fires burning. Captain Mack ordered his rear destroyers to start picking up survivors and – so as not to imperil his own ships – restricted the firing of torpedoes to *Jervis* which fired a salvo of three torpedoes. The cruiser erupted into a huge fire ball. The unfortunate Italian cruiser flagship and her consort *Fiume* had been paralysed with surprise and terror when fired upon out of the night darkness by the British battlefleet; *Zara* had been hit by four 15″ broadsides from *Warspite* and five each from *Valiant* and *Barham*, *Fiume* had received two from the *Warspite* and one from *Valiant* and had sunk within 45 minutes.

In the light of the explosion caused by *Jervis*'s torpedoes which lit a desolate sea scene of wreckage, boats and swimming men, *Zara* rolled over and sank. Two miles away witnessing the death throes of her squadron ships that had come to her assistance lay *Pola* which had been torpedoed seven hours earlier. She had not been touched in the point blank massacre of the rescue ships. Captain D14 made the following signal;

To: C in C (R) VALF   *From: D14*
Have sunk *Zara* and am about to sink the *Pola*.
0311 29/3/41.

There were two options open to Captain Mack, namely to sink *Pola* or to board and capture. Philip Mack quickly made up his mind; to try to tow the cruiser back to Alexandria could expose the fleet to overwhelming air attack so he decided to take off the survivors, then sink the cruiser. He ordered the first lieutenant to fall out the 4.7" gun crews keeping only the pom-pom closed up and to prepare wires and fenders starboard side. When No 1 at his action station aft received this order he sent for the Buffer from his action station in the director and told the incredulous chief bosun's mate to prepare to berth on *Pola*. The No 1 mounting guns crew, in high excitement armed themselves with cutlasses and stood by to board ship.

Jervis, under the firm controlling hand of Philip Mack, made a perfect approach and lay alongside at 0325/29th. There was no hesitation by the men in the cruiser when Petty Officer 'Duggy' Garret, captain of the foc's'le, sent over a heaving line shouting 'Catch hold of this, you buggers!' Wires fore and aft were quickly secured by the Italians and No 1 gun's crew, waving cutlasses, rushed onto the cruiser's forecastle rendering blood-curdling cries. There was no resistance from the wretched survivors. Only 257 remained, all who could swim out of the complement of 1000 had abandoned ship earlier. Many of those who cowered on the cruiser's deck were inebriated; the ship's wine store had been broached.

A brow was quickly rigged between the ships and all 257 filed, in an orderly manner, into *Jervis*. The destroyer's gunners' party made a quick round of the cruiser and removed several Breda machine guns badly needed to augment the ship's anti-aircraft defence. Fifteen minutes after securing alongside *Jervis* cast off, stood off and fired one torpedo into *Pola*. It hit her but the cruiser was reluctant to sink. *Nubian* was ordered to fire a second torpedo. This had the desired effect; the cruiser blew up and disappeared. 2400 Italian officers and men died that night; the British lost three of its Fleet Air Arm airmen. The British destroyers at dawn began picking up enemy survivors, a potentially hazardous task, for the ships were within easy range of German and Italian shore-based bombers. In little over an hour 900 men were picked up, then the C-in-C withdrew the destroyers and ordered them to rejoin the fleet, which was retiring towards Alexandria. A signal had been sent from Malta to the Italian Chief of Naval Staff so that, two days later, the Italian hospital ship *Gradisca* picked up 13 officers and 147 men. Earlier during the night of the 29th, Greek destroyers had picked up 110 survivors.

Some of the *Jervis*'s ship's company remembered different aspects of the part played by their ship. George Kean was one of the signalmen on the bridge;

> I was on the bridge . . . when we were leading the destroyers in search for the damaged battleship. I stood on a stool in front of the signalman's table on which I had a trigger lamp and a box lamp – both fitted with coloured shade and a Very light pistol. Round my waist I had tied a 'tack line' and tucked into my left side I had red cartridges and on my right green cartridges, into my stomach white ones. My instructions were to immediately copy any challenge from an enemy ship. As I had been reared on stories of destroyers being wiped out making torpedo attacks, I was not too disappointed that we failed to catch the battleship.

Telegraphist Hague came off watch shortly after the surviving ship's company of the *Pola* had been embarked;

> We took off over 200 of them; they were everywhere and for the want of something better to do, Bob Richardson and I went over to one who was standing alone and we tried to open up some sort of communication. Imagine our surprise when he suddenly blurted out in broad American, 'I'm f. . k. . g fed up with this war!' Afterwards we found out that he was on a visit to the land of his birth and became conscripted into the navy. We fed the prisoners on their own grub – tinned items taken from a captured Italian freighter.

Among the 257 men taken off by *Jervis*, 22 were officers, including the commanding officer Capitano di Vascello Manlio Piba and 26 petty officers. Captain Piba had been in command of *Pola* for 2½ years and was highly regarded by his men for whom he showed great concern while he remained in *Jervis*. His distress over the loss of so many of his men and his command was aggravated by the fact that he was suffering from an acute attack of piles.

Congested with prisoners, *Jervis* was sent on ahead of the fleet and arrived back in Alexandria at 1700/30th; after disembarking the Italians the destroyer entered drydock that same evening for repair to her long outstanding rudder defect.

CHAPTER THREE

Leader of the J's and K's

While in drydock, those in *Jervis* learned of the sinking and abrupt end to the short career of the new cruiser *Bonaventure*. She had been torpedoed by the Italian submarine *Ambra* on 31st March at a position not far from where four nights earlier the *Zara, Fiume, Pola* and two destroyers had been obliterated. It was an act of partial revenge by the Italian navy.

Benghazi was abandoned by a weakened Western Desert Force on 3rd April and General Rommel's heavy tank units were pressing on eastward. On the 6th, the day that *Jervis* undocked, came the news that German divisions that had passed through Yugoslavia had launched attacks on the Greek positions in northern Greece, an altogether gloomy situation, for the Allies.

Enemy convoys of troop and supply ships, escorted by Italian destroyers were flowing on a regular basis from Italy and Sicily to Sousse, Sfax, Tripoli and – now that it had been recaptured – to Benghazi. The only serious opposition to these convoys came from the submarines based still on Malta, and the occasional attack by RAF and FAA aircraft from Malta and Crete. The losses in these convoys had been light, about 2% of the cargoes carried, and the Commander-in-Chief was under considerable pressure from the Chiefs of Staff in London to stem the flow of enemy troops and armour into North Africa. The movement of British forces to succour the Greek nation, which had commenced on 4th March, had been a predictable disaster. The hitherto victorious Western Desert Force had been forced to give up its initiative by an action that was to prolong the desert war for two years and it was now in full retreat. The troops that had been syphoned out of the desert and taken at such cost in terms of lives, effort and material to Greece were on the brink of an overwhelming defeat. The fleet was left with the task of salvaging what was possible in the face of appalling odds.

The arrival of the battle-experienced Fliegerkorps X, with its Ju87 and Ju88 squadrons who had learned their anti-ship skills in the narrow fiords of Norway, had already made its presence felt. The RAF in the face of increasing fury of the raids on Malta had withdrawn its Sunderland and Wellington aircraft.

Nine ships sailed in Convoy AN25 on 8th April from Alexandria escorted by the *Coventry*, *Jervis* and *Janus*, bound for Piraeus. On passage Captain Mack received a signal from the Commander-in-Chief informing him that he was creating a small destroyer strike force to operate from Malta against enemy convoys. This was all the C-in-C could spare out of his limited resources, at the same time taking into account the deteriorating situation at Malta in the face of enemy air attacks. Captain Mack was to command the strike force of four destroyers: *Jervis*, *Janus*, *Nubian* and *Mohawk*. *Nubian* had sailed from Alexandria with *Hero* and *Defender*; her two consorts relieved *Jervis* and *Janus* as escorts to AN25 as the convoy approached the Gulf of Nauplia, while *Nubian* made for Suda Bay to await the arrival of Captain D14. *Mohawk* which was part of the escort to Convoy AG11 left the convoy and proceeded to join D14 at Suda Bay, where the cruiser *York*, which on the night of 26th March had been badly damaged by two of six Italian explosive motor boats after they had penetrated the harbour defences, still remained beached.

After fuelling in the evening of the 8th, the designated Malta Strike Force destroyers remained in Suda Bay for the following daylight hours while their commanding officers conferred with Captain Mack. The force sailed on the evening of the 9th, its passage through the Kithira channel and across the Ionian sea being given protection by the cruisers *Perth* and *Ajax*. The destroyers arrived off Malta at 0600/11th without being subject to air attacks but, because of severity of raids on the island they dispersed to widely separated berths, *Nubian* and *Mohawk* up by Mersa, *Janus* at Sliema and *Jervis* in Dockyard Creek.

Throughout the day small air raids disturbed the destroyer's stay in harbour, but the enemy aircraft directed their attention to targets away from the dockyard. On the previous days many magnetic mines had been dropped, both inside and outside the harbour, which kept nerves at full stretch as they exploded from time to time without any warning.

Hugh Mulleneux noted in his diary after arrival:

Our job is to nip out and attack the Tripoli convoys by night – during the day presumably we remain in harbour and provide a target for the bombers. One of us (D's staff) has to go to the operations room at 1600 daily to get the latest reconnaissance reports. If anything good comes through we sail out to attack at about 1900. I was the duty officer today and duly sat about the operations room from 1600 until 1830.

A report came through of a convoy of four large 8000–10,000 ton ships escorted by four destroyers steaming at 15 knots for Tripoli. The Strike Force sailed at 1900 but Captain Mack's destroyers were spotted leaving and the convoy escort warned. After several hours' search along the estimated track of the convoy nothing was found and a rather disconsolate force returned to harbour 0800/11th.

Another convoy was sighted during the day and tracked by shadowing aircraft and the submarine *Upholder* was ordered toward the area. The enemy consisted of five merchant ships and an escort of three destroyers. Captain (D) sailed at 1733 with his four ships, but again the convoy escort commander was warned that the destroyers were out, and took avoiding action. As the force returned to Malta after several hours of fruitless searching off the Kerkenah islands it was dive-bombed as the ships steamed in line ahead through the Coino channel. No damage was suffered but one large bomb fell into *Jervis*'s wake and exploded just ahead of *Janus*, the next astern. The ships entered harbour at 0630 in the midst of an air raid. Raids on a small scale went on all day – Easter Sunday, 13th April.

No new reports came through of enemy convoys within the range of the Strike Force, but there was intelligence that a convoy had been loaded with German troops and transport at Naples and was ready to sail. As the force did not sail, leave was given after dark for men to stretch their legs and to seek out the dwindling stocks of Maltese beer in Valletta. After these first two unsuccessful sorties, signals had begun to flow between Vice Admiral Malta, the Commander-in-Chief and the Admiralty for explanations as to why the Strike Force had failed to make contact. Admiral Cunningham reminded the Admiralty that as the RAF was unable to retain suitable reconnaissance and shadowing aircraft on the island, and that the Fleet Air Arm Swordfish were not suitable to replace them during daylight hours, when the convoys were given protection of fighter aircraft.

The convoy reported as being ready at Naples and which departed at 2300/13th was sighted at 1600/15th off Cape Bon on the Tunisian coast steaming at 9 knots on a southerly course.

The convoy and escort was made up of the following ships:

Convoy		Cargo
German ships:		
Adana	4205 tons.	3000 German personnel embarked
Arta	2452 tons.	3500 tons of military stores
Aegina	2447 tons	300 vehicles
Iserlohn	3704 tons.	
Italian ship:		
Sabaudia	1590 tons.	Fully loaded with ammunition
Escorts		
Luca Tarigo	Capitano di Fregata de Cristofaro (Senior Officer) (1628 tons. armed by 6 x 4.7″ guns and 4 x 21″ torpedoes and 12 anti-aircraft weapons. Speed 38 knots.)	
Lampo *Baleno*	Capitano di Corvetta Marano	
	Capitano di Corvetta Arnaud (1220 tons, armed by 4 x 4.7″ guns and 6 x 21″ torpedoes and 8 anti-aircraft weapons. Speed 38 knots.)	

The Strike Force sailed into bad weather but most of the crews were hopeful that this third sortie would prove successful. The expectations and some of the preparations made in the destroyers are recalled by ex-CPO E. Wheeler, who was at that time serving as an able seaman in *Mohawk*;

> We slipped out of Sliema creek that evening, we knew that something was definitely on that night, you could sense and smell it. At the first turn of the screws the older hands rolled their paper money carefully into thin rolls and placed them into condoms which had been drawn from the sickbay on the last run ashore – and then stowed the packets in our belts ... Night action – ship to ship was a hell of a lot different from the constant air attacks which were the normal daily routine at sea. This was the Navy against Navy and we were confident. We were battle-wise – we were good and we knew it.

Weather improved as Captain Mack led his destroyers at 26 knots on a direct course towards No 4 buoy which marked a route around the Kerkenah bank; he was under considerable pressure to bring this enemy convoy and its escort to action. His intention was to arrive ahead of the convoy's route to Tripoli, then to steam north and to intercept the oncoming ships.

The convoy had been sighted by an RAF patrol aircraft at 1700 as it crossed the Gulf of Hammamet at an estimated speed of 8 knots. This information was passed by signal from Vice Admiral Malta to D14. It seemed certain that the convoy escort commander knew that he had been sighted for he was heard to ask for air support and for reinforcements to sail from Tripoli. Some S79's took off from Syracuse but had to turn back because of bad weather conditions and so Capitano de Cristofaro stood on for Tripoli unaware that British destroyers were at sea looking for the convoy, but he was alert to the possibility of an attack.

Arriving off the Kerkenah Bank No 4 buoy, Captain Mack considered his intelligence information. It was very dark; there was the possibility that the convoy had passed, or it could have turned back towards Pantellaria. If it had taken the second option it would not be possible to catch the ships before dawn. Mack decided on a third possibility; the convoy speed was actually slower than the reconnaissance aircraft's estimate, so he steamed north on a reciprocal course to the one he believed the convoy to be following. His hunch proved to be correct, and he received confirmation from the w/t office. Telegraphist Hague was on watch:

I had been on watch for Italian W/T traffic and taking bearings, they could not leave their transmitting keys alone. I picked up some traffic and reported bearings to the bridge and shortly afterwards our force contacted the convoy and its escorts.

At 0130 Captain Mack estimated that he had reached the 'farthest on' position of the enemy convoy proceeding at 7 knots. There was still no sign of the convoy so D14 altered course to close the shore and return inside the possible route of the convoy. At 0200 the enemy ships were sighted, D14 had manoeuvred into a perfect position, the convoy was silhouetted against the moonlight – five merchantships, one small destroyer astern on the starboard quarter of the convoy, and ahead a large destroyer with a smaller ship.

Undetected by the convoy or its escort, Captain Mack, with his destroyers in close company and in line ahead, approached the enemy destroyer *Baleno* on the starboard quarter of the formation. *Jervis* opened fire at point-blank range. Her first two salvos passed over the *Baleno* but *Janus*, the next in line, opened fire on her radar range and hit the destroyer's bridge killing the captain and all the ship's officers. *Jervis*'s three twin-gun mountings went into captain-of-the-quarters firing, each mounting selecting its own target and opening with rapid fire into the stopped *Baleno* and the merchant ships, starting fires. *Nubian* and *Mohawk* were firing into every ship in sight. Smoke, fires and explosions shattered the Mediterranean night. Captain de Cristofaro turned his ship *Tarigo* and, with *Lampo* working up to full speed, turned back immediately from their station at the head of the convoy and charged into the mêlée of ships. He steered his destroyer between the convoy and Captain Mack's line of destroyers – the surviving crew members of the *Baleno* had managed to beach their ship and were fighting their fires. As *Tarigo* steamed down the line the gunnery control officer in *Jervis* was struggling to regain control of his guns, which were reluctant to give up their independent actions. He succeeded in time to deliver a full broadside into the *Lampo* as the small destroyer tore past, working up to full speed. *Lampo* fired her outfit of torpedoes and as other salvoes from *Janus* and the Tribals astern poured into her frail hull, she came to a stop and drifted onto a sand bank, full of dead and dying men.

Tarigo, as she passed between the British ships and her convoy, was hit full on the bridge by a broadside from *Mohawk* which destroyed her main steering position and mortally wounded her captain who lost a leg. Captain de Cristofaro continued to command his ship; hand steering had been connected and he manoeuvred to attack with torpedo, with one of his few surviving officers, a young ensign, directing the firing of the ship's torpedoes. One torpedo fired at *Jervis* was seen from Captain (D)'s bridge to pass underneath, but the second hit *Mohawk* aft destroying 'Y' gun, the after magazine and shell room and killing all the crews. *Mohawk*'s remaining guns continued to engage the convoy under director control. The merchant ships although armed failed to bring their guns into action, no doubt because of the suddenness of the Strike Force attack, but two masters tried to ram their tormentors.

Jervis had an extremely narrow escape; she was almost struck amidships by the towering stem of one ship, a danger which Captain Mack avoided by emergency full ahead and violent helm action. The *Nubian* had a similar narrow escape with only a few feet to spare.

In *Mohawk*, her engineer officer had reported that while the entire quarter-deck had gone, the propellers and shafts seemed to be intact and that he would see if he could get the ship moving. Then, five minutes after the first torpedo, the disabled *Tarigo* fired another,

(*Top left*) Cruiser *Fiji* 22nd May 1941. *Fiji* bombed and sinking off Crete. (*Top right*) 23rd May 1941. *Kelly* capsized and sinking after being dive-bombed south of Crete.

26th May 1941. *Formidable* being bombed and hit on the flight deck.

May 1941. *Jervis* – near misses.

(*Top left*) May 1941. *Jervis* pom-pom crew. (*Top right*) May 1941. Italian escort destroyer *Lupo* and flotilla transport German troops to Crete.

May 1941. Malta and Gozo islands with Sicily on far horizon.

April/May 1941. Malta's bomb damage – destruction of Opera House.

hitting *Mohawk* in the boiler rooms. *Tarigo* then sank, close to No 3 buoy, Kerkenah Bank.

In the middle of the action with *Tarigo* and *Lampo* the aerials in *Jervis* carried away and telegraphists, Richardson and Hague had to go aloft:

> Once the action started I closed down on D/F and had a good view of the scrap from my position outside the D/F office. None of us are sure why it happened, possibly gunfire or the excessive whipping and twisting of *Jervis* but the main aerials carried away. Bob Richardson and I were the 'jury' aerial party so after collecting the temporary aerials we went aloft, Bob sitting at one end of the yard and me at the other end unshackling and disconnecting the damaged parts and fitting the replacements. We had just finished when one Italian destroyer passed down our port side. *Jervis* illuminated her with the searchlight and she likewise did us. Bob and me wore blue pants but white shirts, we must have stood out like two penguins. We were targets for all kinds of small arms; red, white and green tracer came uncomfortably close. I shouted to Bob, 'Are you a bloody hero' and to this day neither of us can remember coming down the masthead ladder, we must have done for we picked up the loose ends of the aerial and scampered aft to attach it.

Nubian closed the position where *Mohawk*'s hull floated bottom up and began to pick up survivors; the enemy destroyers had all been silenced and every ship of the convoy was on fire, beached or sinking, *Jervis* was preparing to torpedo the Italian ammunition ship *Sabaudia* when the ship blew up. Hugh Mulleneux recalled the moment:

> We were much too close for it to be at all pleasant. There was a gigantic explosion, conflagration and blast effect, the latter knocking everyone on the bridge down except for the pilot and myself and it blew our tin hats off. Then for what seemed like an eternity it was like living in an inferno and one got also a good idea of how the unfortunate inhabitants of Sodom and Gomorrah must have met their end. We were entirely surrounded by fire, and directly above our heads ammunition was blowing up like so many Chinese crackers. The sea boiled and sizzled as all the bits started to come down – some white hot – and at the same time reflected a fiery glow. Great lumps came pattering down from the sky and harmed no one.

E. Wheeler of *Mohawk* remembers his ship sinking;

> We started to sink by the stern and also listing heavily to port. The captain ordered abandon ship; my abandon ship station was the starboard whaler but it was so much matchwood now. So it was over the

side and swim for it. I had a lifebelt on and uninjured too, I wasn't too badly off, at that moment after a few minutes in the water I spotted a Carley raft ahead of me and made for it. There were about eight of the crew onboard it, mostly to my surprise stokers; how in the hell did they get out of that flaming inferno? One stoker petty officer was badly injured but managed a grin and said, 'You damned near missed the last boat, young Wheeler.' I remember chaps calling for their oppos hoping to find them safe and well . . . About two hours later the fight was over and *Jervis*, *Janus* and *Nubian* turned to pick us up. The Carley raft I was on bumped alongside *Nubian* and we were soon scrambling up the nets to the safety of *Nubian*'s deck. The hospitality of *Nubian*'s ship's company was overwhelming, we survivors were treated like long lost brothers.

There were a dozen of us *Mohawks* washing each other down in *Nubian*'s ship's company bathroom. Suddenly in steps my oppo H.G. Fleming covered in blood and oil fuel but with his cheeky smile on his face. 'Anyone want to buy a battleship?' he asks. His smile was short-lived however for when he started to strip he took off his service belt and undid the pocket to take his money out. Then with a look of horror and disbelief he held up the oily soggy mess. The pocket had been slashed by a piece of shrapnel during his escape from 'X' gun and the waterproofing condom had been torn to shreds. 'I was keeping this for Carmelita,' he said as we all howled with laughter, for his Carmelita worked in the 'Lucky Wheel' down the 'Gut' and she was fifty if a day.

Jervis moved slowly and cautiously in the dark through groups of *Mohawk's* men in the water, her bridge signal lamp beams picking out the oil-drenched survivors and two in particular clinging to the keel of the upturned destroyer. Captain Mack's voice came out of the darkness encouraging the men to slide into the sea and swim across, but they seemed incapable of doing this so he edged his ship closer until lines could be thrown across and the two men hauled inboard.

Stoker George Morel was a member of the after ammunition supply party and had heard and felt rather than seen any of the action. He came on deck to see in the wavering lights of the bridge signal-lamps, groups of *Mohawk's* men struggling to make the ship's side. He went down one of the scrambling nets to help survivors out:

> Some of them were so bemused and shocked that I swam out a few yards to help get them inboard quickly. I remember thinking that if the ship had to shove off quickly I would be left behind.

Nubian and *Jervis* picked up 169 of *Mohawk*'s men including the commanding officer Commander Eaton. Captain Mack ordered *Janus* to sink the hulk by gunfire, then collecting the remaining three ships of the Strike Force, left the area at 0400 leaving eight enemy ships either sunk or run aground.

The next morning the Italians set in motion a massive rescue operation, nine destroyers and escort vessels plus two hospital ships picked up 1271 men out of the 3000 personnel embarked, but the vehicles, stores and ammunition carried were a total loss. A few weeks later the destroyer *Lampo* was patched up and salvaged, and later she was re-commissioned.

Flying their battle ensigns Captain Mack's destroyers made a triumphant return to Malta, entering harbour at 1000/16th. No doubt in retaliation for the annihilation of the convoy Malta was subjected to a virtually continuous day and night air bombardment interspersed with mines dropped by parachute. On the night of the 18th/19th for the first time Ju87's dive-bombed the ships in harbour by moonlight. *Jervis* at her berth experienced a bomb ahead and another astern but suffered nothing more than splinter damage.

There was considerable satisfaction in London, Admiralty and Government circles with this first total destruction of a supply convoy, but supplies continued to flow into North Africa escorted by units of the Italian fleet, and the growing strength of the Axis forces in the Western desert confirmed this. The Prime Minister issued directives that the task for the Mediterranean fleet was to halt the flow of supplies into North Africa and that the battle fleet could be sacrificed to achieve this objective. He suggested that *Barham* should be used as a blockship to end the use of Tripoli as a supply base. This directive was strongly resisted by the Commander-in-Chief on the grounds that chances of getting the blockship in its correct position against the opposition of the coastal defences were remote, casualties to the men manning *Barham* would probably be in the region of 1000, the sinking of one of the fleet's three battleships would be an enormous boost to Italian Naval morale and, finally, the C-in-C could not countenance the reduction of his battle squadron. Admiral Cunningham informed Admiralty that it was his intention to conduct a full fleet bombardment on the port of Tripoli. The operation was to coincide with bringing through the *Breconshire* to Malta carrying aviation fuel supplies and the passing of a convoy of empty store ships from Malta to Alexandria. This operational plan received the support of the Chiefs of Staff.

The bombardment was to take place on 21st April and so, as part of a complex multi-operation, *Jervis*, *Janus*, *Nubian* and *Diamond* sailed as escorts to Convoy ME7, which was comprised of the steamships

Clan Ferguson, City of Lincoln, City of Manchester and *Perthshire.* The convoy sailed on the evening of the 19th after a long day of frequent air attacks on Malta island and the dockyard, men manning the ships were 'looking forward for a "quiet" night at sea! although we all expect to have to return to Malta'.

At dawn on the 20th the convoy was joined by the anti-aircraft cruiser *Calcutta* and the new 8 x 5.25″ gun cruiser *Phoebe.* At noon the entire fleet appeared over the eastern horizon. The convoy with the two cruisers and *Nubian* with *Diamond* continued eastbound for Alexandria. *Nubian* was carrying the *Mohawk*'s survivors as passengers. *Jervis* and *Janus* joined the screen of the fleet.

The fleet remained on its westerly course organised in two forces, the bombarding force consisting of the three battleships and the cruiser *Gloucester* with *Jervis, Janus, Juno* and *Jaguar* as anti-submarine screen and the carrier force, *Formidable* and three cruisers, *Orion, Ajax* and *Perth* with four destroyers. At 2120 the C-in-C in *Warspite* brought the bombarding force round to a course of 235 degrees for Tripoli and detached the carrier force. Four H class destroyers *Hotsput, Hero, Havock* and *Hasty* with minesweeping gear streamed proceeded ahead of the battle squadron formed in line ahead with *Gloucester* astern. *Jervis* and *Janus* were stationed on the port bow of the flagship and *Juno* and *Jaguar* to starboard, the entire force went to action stations at 0300. The bombardment was to be carried out at 0500 with the aid of flares dropped from FAA and RAF aircraft. The RAF would commence a bombing air raid on the city and port area half an hour before.

At 0445 the force rounded the submarine *Truant,* which had been stationed as a datum mark in the port approaches; at the same time *Jervis* and *Janus* dropped back and took station on the quarter of the battleships, to clear the line of fire. The force steadied onto the firing course and at 0502 opened fire at a range of seven miles, Hugh Mulleneux later wrote:

> The party was started by the RAF and FAA who bombed the place. This was highly spectacular with guns firing, bombs dropping, flares and best of all the bright red and green tracers from the 'Wop' close range AA guns. A real Brocks benefit, which however was improved upon when we started our performance at 0500. More flares were dropped and more guns went off including the 15 inch from the battleships which are always a fine sight at night. We could see few ships in harbour and we fired blind all over them – the director's crew claimed three hits! After the battleships had been going for about 20 minutes the coastal defence

batteries eventually opened fire. We could hear the shells whizzing and whistling over our heads which was quite alarming at first. Luckily they didn't correct the range much and as most of the shells continued to fall miles over we shortly recovered our poise. I think that the size of the guns must be about 6 inch. At about 0545 we all withdrew, having given Tripoli a tremendous plastering which I should think would have an adverse effect on the enemy war effort in Africa. *Formidable* and Co joined us at 0730 and we proceeded eastwards at 21 knots expecting to be bombed at any moment. Strange to relate, we weren't!

The bombardment had lasted 40 minutes and 530 tons of shells had been poured into the port area, namely 478 x 15″, 562 x 6″, 334 x 4.7″ and 602 x 4.5″ shells. The buildings on the wharves and the city suffered badly but not permanently and only one cargo ship loaded with fuel and bombs was sunk and the torpedo boat *Partenop* was damaged. The attack had, however, taken the Italians completely by surprise and no air attack was mounted on the fleet.

At 2000 Captain Mack was detached from the fleet and ordered to return to Malta with a re-organised flotilla, *Jervis* and *Janus* accompanied by *Juno* (Commander St J.R.J. Tyrwhitt) and *Jaguar* (Lieutenant-Commander J.F.W. Hine). Captain Mack and his ships arrived without incident on the morning of the 22nd, and the fleet returned to Alexandria also without problems the following morning.

At Malta, increased air attacks greeted the return of the Strike Force. *Jervis* berthed in Sliema creek. Stoker J. Clifton was taking some air:

> It was during the evening I was strolling on the iron deck with another stoker when something made me look up. Out of the sky came a parachute with what looked to be a forty gallon drum hanging below. Slowly it came down until I felt that it could only get caught in the top of the mast. At the last moment it swayed clear and zoomed down out of sight the other side of the jetty where there was a tremendous explosion.

As there had been no sightings of enemy convoys during the day, Captain D followed his policy of giving shore leave to his destroyers at every opportunity. A party of telegraphists from *Jervis* were among the libertymen:

> That evening Bob, Tubby Maxted and myself [D.W. Hague] were ashore when the sirens went again for what turned out to be a heavy raid, in fact in the following morning there was only a smell left where the fish

market used to be. The three of us went into a shelter to get out of the way but after a while got fed up with it and decided to go outside into Strada Reale, a bomb had dropped nearby and Tubby thought that he heard cries for help. The street was as light as day because of parchute flares and the three of us in white uniform looked very conspicuous. An aircraft dived down at us we could see bullets and cannon shells bursting along the Strada towards us. Most shops and buildings had blast walls and sand bags behind them. I dived for one hoping the others would do the same, Tubby chose my doorway and all umpteen stone of him crashed on top of me, I left a large imprint on the bags. It was the nearest that I got to getting hurt in Malta.

The Strike Force sailed in the evening of the 23rd; a convoy of four ships, three German and one Italian, escorted by four destroyers had been sighted passing Palermo and later rounding the eastern end of Sicily. A covering force of two enemy cruisers and two destroyers had been located patrolling off Cape Bon. Captain D14 had a task that was not to be easy, cutting out the convoy without being attacked by the covering force. In a position south of Lampedusa Island at midnight *Janus* reported that she had intercepted a signal from an aircraft which had located a surface contact four miles to port. Captain Mack reduced speed to 25 knots and turned towards the target position. Fifteen minutes later *Jervis* sighted a single-funnelled vessel ahead which appeared to be an enemy cruiser; Captain (D) ordered the flotilla to train torpedoes to port, then as he ordered a turn in succession to starboard to fire torpedoes the ship was seen to be an armed auxiliary. Captain Mack countermanded his signal to attack with torpedoes, but before she could act on the new order *Juno* fired a salvo of four and one torpedo hit the Italian ship in the bow. *Jervis*'s first salvo of 4.7" fired at a range of 1000 yards, hit the ship on the bridge; the other three destroyers also opened fire with their gun armament scoring hits, *Jaguar* firing star shell by mistake.

There was no return fire and the auxiliary was soon on fire in three places and stopped. At 0048 Captain Mack ordered *Juno* to finish the ship off with a torpedo, which struck as the crew were abandoning ship. *Juno* reported soon afterwards that the ship was awash and sinking. The auxiliary was the *Egeo* (Capitano di Fregatte Ugo Fiorelli) of 3311 tons and armed with medium-sized guns forward and aft; she had left Tripoli the previous evening and was on passage to Palermo. Of the 126 ship's company only 26 were picked up later by an Italian hospital ship.

There was no time to pick up survivors. Captain D14's task was to locate and sink the convoy, and he had been delayed. Now he led his destroyers away at 29 knots to find the main target in the Gulf of Hammamet, but it was to no avail; the convoy and its escort, 30 miles away had witnessed the flares put up by *Jaguar* and had reversed course out of harm's way.

The Strike Force returned to Malta and, when it entered harbour at 0845/24th viewed, with mixed feelings, the large bulk of the cruiser *Gloucester* which had arrived during its absence. The cruiser had been sent as reinforcement to Captain Mack's destroyers because the Italians had commenced to cover their convoy movements with powerful cruiser units. One of Captain (D)'s staff looking at the *Gloucester* remarked, 'I am afraid that she may be as big a liability as an asset.'

The big ship certainly seemed to attract extra enemy bombers. The raids, previously frequent, became incessant and reached blitz proportions for more than an hour from 2100. One 1000 lb bomb near missed and shook up the *Gloucester* and bombs fell all round the destroyer's berths. This continued with only the briefest breaks for two days and nights. The ships were emptied of personnel except for the close range weapon crews and fire parties; non-essential and off duty officers and men slept ashore in the deep shelters. No reports of convoys on passage came through following the sinking of the unfortunate *Egeo* so to get some relief for the crews and to preserve his ships from the aerial bombardment, Captain Mack took his destroyers and *Gloucester* to sea after dark and spent an uneventful night patrolling east of the Malta approaches and watched the distant pyrotechnics of the night air raid on Valletta and the island's air bases.

The same routine was carried out on the following night but soon after the return to harbour at 0600/28th, the 5th Flotilla led by Captain Lord Louis Mountbatten in *Kelly* entered Grand Harbour. In addition to *Kelly* the 5th DF consisted of *Kashmir, Kelvin, Kipling, Jersey* and *Jackal*; they had brought with them the new 5.25″ cruiser *Dido* and the equally new fast minelayer *Abdiel*. *Kelly* had completed her fourth and longest period in dockyard hands on 18th December 1940 and since that date had avoided any further catastrophe while she had operated in the English Channel and the Western Approaches. Comment from Captain D14's staff was: 'The 5th Flotilla has come to relieve us from our job, we don't know quite why.'

The facts were that the Admiralty had sent out the 5th Flotilla to reinforce the Strike Force and to intensify pressure on the Axis North African supply routes but because of the collapse of Allied resistance in Greece, the impending evacuation of British troops and continuing advance of the enemy in the Western Desert, the Commander-in-Chief could not afford to keep the 14th DF in Malta; he required the destroyers with the fleet together with the support and counsel of his friend, the senior Captain (D). It would also be suicidal to keep so many ships exposed to the mounting weight of air attacks on the island fortress. The 14th Flotilla sailed that evening leaving *Janus* who required some essential repairs but taking with them *Dido* and *Abdiel*. As the ships steered eastward into the night, the sky astern was lit by the flashes and flares of the nightly blitz baptising the newly arrived 5th Flotilla.

The group making for Alexandria were dive-bombed in the 'Dog Watches' of the 29th, no one was hurt and the aircraft also escaped unscathed.

Over the 36 hours following their arrival back in Alexandria at 2135/30th the impact of the disasters suffered by the army began to be understood by the 14th DF: Greece had been overrun, soldiers taken at immense cost in terms of blood and *matériel* in the Lustre operation had been evacuated out of small ports and off beaches at Raftis, Raftina, Kalamata and Monimvasia. The men who had been lifted out came from the Greek army, British Home Regiments, Australian and New Zealand Brigades. Armour, artillery and transport had been abandoned; units which were tolerably intact with their personal weapons had been taken by destroyers to Suda Bay for the defence of the island, and the remainder returned to Egypt for re-equipment and re-training. The Greek and Yugoslav Royal families and Governments had also been evacuated. Losses at sea had been heavy, the transports *Pennland*, *Slamat*, *Costa Rica* and HMS *Ulster Prince* had been sunk by dive bombers. In the case of the Dutch ship *Slamat* the circumstances of her loss were particularly horrible; after having been struck by bombs when coming out of Nauplia, her 500 soldier passengers and her crew were taken inboard by her escorts the destroyers *Diamond* and *Wryneck* but shortly afterwards the speeding destroyers were both hit and sunk in an overwhelming attack from Ju87's. Then for several hours in a flat calm, warm, sun-kissed sea the survivors were machine-gunned by successive waves of aircraft. Out of about 1000 men only one officer, fourteen ratings and eight soldiers were picked up.

By night, 50,672 troops had been lifted out of Greece. All but

14,000 came over open beaches and were ferried by small boats to the waiting warships and transports; every destroyer in Alexandria had been committed, and without destroyers the battlefleet could not sail to support the evacuation, but the Italian fleet failed to challenge. Nevertheless every move of the ships was challenged by the German and Italian air forces. It was now a grim situation, Greece overrun, an invasion of Crete appeared to be imminent; in the Western Desert Tobruk had been surrounded and invested, leaving the defenders without fighter aircraft protection against enemy bombers. The Axis forces had pressed on and were at the moment at Sollum just 80 miles short of the Egyptian frontier; all the gains of the magnificent British winter campaign in the desert had gone – squandered for political expedients.

One small glimmer of encouragement occurred for the 14th DF. Waiting for Captain Mack's return to Alexandria were the three K class destroyers, *Kingston, Kandahar* and *Kimberley* which after the defeat of the Italian army in Eritrea had been withdrawn from the Red Sea. They now became part of the 14th Flotilla. On 1st May, *Jervis* and *Kingston* together entered the floating dock for a 36-hour below water-line check of the hull, screws, propeller shafts and rudder.

The mental and physical strain on the engine-room staffs had been very great and would increase. At sea, men on watch in spaces filled with racing turbines and auxiliary machinery were at constant risk of sudden death or injury from mine, bomb, torpedo, shell fire and collision that could turn engine and boiler rooms into a vortex of super-heated steam, fire and explosions. Incarcerated below, every call for engine speed change, or sudden alteration of course and distant underwater thuds caused stomach-churning alarms. When the ship entered harbour there was little opportunity for the engineers to relax. The ERA's worked every minute that the machinery was at rest, to service and repair defects and keep plant functioning long beyond the scheduled dockyard overhaul. Work continued in the engine and boiler rooms up to the moment that telegraphs were rung on for the ship to proceed to sea.

The chief stoker, his petty officers and stokers had an unsung task. Whenever the ship under the cover of darkness slid into an anchorage or advance base the opportunity to take in fuel and fresh water could never be missed. While the remainder of the ship's company off-watch snatched at elusive moments of sleep, the stokers were hauling fuel and water pipes across the decks, dipping tanks, ensuring that the bunkers were topped up.

The engine-room departments of the 14th Flotilla ships enjoyed a tremendous advantage in the shape of the professional skill and personality of the staff engineer, Engineer Commander J.A. Ruddy – he was tireless in his support, advice and visits to the destroyers which made up the flotilla.

While *Jervis* had her short break in the floating dock the unfortunate *Kelly* was having another run of misadventures. The 5th Flotilla after their arrival at Malta endured a succession of air raids by 60 and 70 aircraft at a time attacking the island with bombs and mines. The damage was on a large scale and three naval vessels including the destroyer *Encounter* were badly damaged. *Kelly* with her flotilla and *Gloucester* sailed for their first foray to intercept a heavily escorted enemy convoy on the evening of 1st May. Captain Mountbatten and his ships failed to make contact with the convoy and heavy head seas prevented him from engaging a second convoy reported to the north of his position. The force returned to Malta empty handed.

As the flotilla in line ahead in the morning of 2nd May started to enter the Grand Harbour at 0700 disaster struck. *Kelly*, *Jackal* and *Kelvin* passed safely through the entrance but as the fourth in the line, *Jersey*, was about to enter a tremendous explosion echoed round the harbour's encircling battlements. *Jersey* had been mined, killing two officers and 34 ratings. The ship was a complete loss and her hulk blocked the harbour entrance leaving *Kipling*, *Kashmir* and *Gloucester* outside but Captain D5 and his two K's and *Jackal* bottled up inside.

When the fleet departed from Alexandria on 6th May for a major operation, Tiger, involving both east and west ends of the Mediterranean, Captain Lord Louis Mountbatten was still trapped inside the Grand Harbour and the other three ships of the Strike Force, (*Kipling*, *Kashmir* and *Gloucester*) had been ordered to Gibraltar where they had arrived on 4th May. On passage in the Sicilian Channel, however, shortly after *Gloucester* had set off a moored mine in her paravanes, the cruiser had been bombed – a bomb passed through the ship aft without exploding. This was the third time that *Gloucester* had been hit by a bomb since her arrival in the Mediterranean.

The objective of Operation Tiger was to fight through to Alexandria from the west, five large and fast merchant ships loaded with tanks – replacements for the armour lost by the Western Desert Force – and crated Hurricane fighters. At the same time the

Admiralty was passing through reinforcements for Admiral Cunningham's fleet. The fleet from Alexandria which would meet the west/east convoy and fleet reinforcements brought with it two MW convoys for Malta, one of four supply ships and the second consisting of two tankers carrying 24,000 tons of fuel replenishment critically required in the island.

The fleet sailed from Alexandria in heavy overcast weather and, because of the many mines dropped by Axis aircraft in the previous night, it took many hours to get the ships out of harbour: each heavy ship had to be individually led out by minesweepers and handed over to the 14th Flotilla which was on anti-submarine patrol beyond the outer limits of the harbour approach channel.

The first 20 hours of the fleet's passage was quiet and uneventful. Low dense cloud hid the ships from reconnaissance snoopers until, on the afternoon of the second day out, a formation of five enemy aircraft was located by the radar in *Valiant* and *Formidable*. Four of the incoming bombers were shot down by the carrier's fighters before they came into visual sight of the fleet. While on passage, the Commander-in-Chief received a steady flow of reports on the 'mined-in' situation at Malta. The slow progress in opening up the port was becoming critical as the relief convoys accompanying the fleet had to gain entry to discharge their vital cargoes. Furthermore Captain D5 and half of his Strike Force were still bottled in and emasculated, the 5th Flotilla was required to meet the Tiger Operation ships west of Sicily and to share in the escort through the Sicilian narrows.

The blockade was cleared with only hours to spare; *Jersey*'s stern had been blown off to open up a passage in the harbour entrance and then – following a plan conceived by the fleet staff torpedo officer, Commander W.P. Carne, and signalled by the approaching flagship to Vice Admiral Malta – MTB's and ML's from the dockyard dropped dozens of depth charges at close intervals along the approach channel. These explosions set off or neutralised a great many of the contact and magnetic mines laid by the enemy. A way in had been partially cleared by the 10th allowing the entry of the two MW convoys, which were preceded down the channel by the corvette *Gloxinia* streaming her magnetic sweep setting up a dozen mines in her wake. All six merchant ships of the two convoys entered harbour undamaged and immediately afterwards Mountbatten who had been chafing to get out, sailed – but too late to make his appointment with the Tiger ships west of Sicily. He joined up with the remainder of his flotilla which had returned from Gibraltar and were with the fleet in a position 40 miles south of Malta where a junction had been made with four of the Tiger convoy ships and the fleet reinforcements. One of the convoy (ss *Empire Song*, 9224 tons,) had been mined and sunk in the Sicilian channel.

The clouds were still low and dense: under this natural umbrella an impressive battle-line had taken shape astern of *Jervis*, leading the escort screen of 25 destroyers. First came the fleet flagship *Warspite* followed by *Formidable, Barham, Valiant* and *Queen Elizabeth*. There were also six cruisers of the 5th and 15th Cruisers Squadrons, the Tiger convoy had its own escort of cruisers, the three AA cruisers *Coventry, Calcutta* and *Carlisle* as well as *Fiji* and *Gloucester*. The entire fleet with its convoy had formed up and were steaming eastward on the evening of 9th May. Soon after sunset a number of enemy air formations tried to attack the armada of ships but were prevented from breaking through to the capital ships by a spectacular fire blitz. The fleet moved under a dense umbrella of bursting AA shells linked by hundreds of coloured tracer strands; several bombs dropped near the screening destroyers, but *Jervis* reported, 'We are in greater peril from the battleships' close range barrage; shells, shrapnel and bullets are whistling, bursting and splashing all round us.'

While the fleet had been on its outward passage to meet the Tiger convoy, Admiral Cunningham detached *Ajax* (Captain E.D.B. McCarthy) and three destroyers to bombard Benghazi. This was carried out during the night of the 7th/8th, the only opposition encountered coming from the coastal batteries. The harbour and shipping were thoroughly scourged by naval gunfire before *Ajax* and her destroyers withdrew to rejoin the fleet and as they did so the bombarding force fell upon two unescorted Italian supply ships approaching the port. Both ships were sunk. Now as the fleet returned eastward the Commander-in-Chief detached Captain Lord Louis Mountbatten and the 5th DF to repeat the bombardment of Benghazi before returning to Malta to resume operating as the Strike Force.

Captain D5 led away *Kelly, Kashmir, Kelvin, Kipling* and *Jackal* and arrived off the port at midnight on the 10th opening fire at 0043/11th. In the glare of falling star shells the harbour seemed to be full of wrecks with only one undamaged ship berthed on the mole inside the harbour entrance. 866 rounds of 4.7″ were fired by the five destroyers and several hits were observed to damage the berthed vessel. The flotilla was engaged by the shore batteries which straddled the destroyers several times, then as Captain D5 left the area and made for the Italian Messina to Benghazi convoy route they came under a heavy air attack, and the first night time dive bombing and machine gunning experienced in the Mediterranean. A bomb closely near missed *Kelvin* abreast the bridge and *Kelly* had two bombs in her wake.

The flotilla found no enemy shipping and again returned empty-handed to Malta on the morning of 12th May where it remained for the next nine days hoping for a report of convoy sightings from air reconnaissance. As none came, the 5th Flotilla sailed on 21st May to join the fleet off Crete.

The fleet with its Tiger operation convoy and reinforcements returned to Alexandria without further problems on the 12th. The gamble taken to pass the convoy through the Mediterranean to avoid the long haul round the Cape of Good Hope had succeeded. Forty-three crated Hurricane fighters and 238 tanks were being unloaded from the convoy ships. In the ships joining the fleet came mail and news of German air raids on the homeland – raids on London, Portsmouth and Plymouth. *Jervis*'s ship's company, like everyone else in the fleet, were starved of news from home; mail was infrequent in this period of acute anxiety, and so men from the newly arrived warships were sought out ashore in the Fleet Club and elsewhere for news of what was going on at home.

BBC news bulletins were of course received in the ships, but these were regarded as less than adequate for giving an accurate picture of the war situation in the home country, in view of the broadcasts of events in the Mediterranean theatre which were heard with amazed derision by their participants.

The war in the central Mediterranean basin had reached a critical turning point: the fleet, with minimal air cover or support, was facing up to the imminent invasion of Crete, whilst the enemy possessed overwhelming air superiority operating from airfields that dominated the Aegean and eastern Mediterranean.

An invasion of Crete by German air and seaborne troops was forecast for 15th May and to meet this possibility the fleet had been deployed. A battle squadron, *Queen Elizabeth* (flagship of Vice Admiral Sir H.D. Pridham-Wippell) and *Barham* with *Jervis* (D14) and four other destroyers had been sailed and were on station to the west of Crete to oppose any moves by the Italian fleet. The Commander-in-Chief had formed three groups of light forces, cruisers and destroyers; these were deployed south of Crete during daylight hours and would, after dark, move north through the Kaso straits and the Antikithera channel to patrol north of the island, seeking invasion shipping. Admiral Cunningham remained at Alexandria to maintain close contact with the Middle East Army Command and to be able to co-ordinate the movements of his four forces to support the army. He also held in reserve at Alexandria the battleships *Warspite* and *Valiant*, three cruisers and a few destroyers. The carrier *Formidable* was out of action until 25th May with engine defects and furthermore she had only four serviceable aircraft.

Other aircraft available for the defence of the army in Crete or to give cover to the fleet, hardly existed or only in pitiful numbers. None of the terrible lessons learnt with the lives of hundreds of seamen and their ships in Norway and at Dunkirk had been digested by the Government and the Chiefs of Staff. The only aircraft available to take on an Axis air armada of hundreds of aircraft were three Gladiators and three Fulmars of the Fleet Air Arm, and three Hurricanes, RAF survivors from the Greek débâcle.

The first 24 hours after the expected D-day of 15th May passed quietly for the ships at sea, except for snoopers observing the formations south of Crete, but throughout the day bomb attacks commenced with increasing ferocity on Maleme and Heraklion airfields and on army positions defending the airfields. These attacks continued without let-up in the daylight hours of the next four days. The light forces swept round east and west of the island and along the north coast on the night of the 16th/17th, and again the following night. *Jervis* as part of Vice Admiral Pridham-Wippell's force patrolled the Kithera and Antikithera channels, retiring south into the Ionian sea at daylight. The battleships refuelled the screening destroyers in turn and then, as the invasion continued to be delayed, they themselves had to return to the fleet base for refuelling. This happened on the 19th and they passed their relief battle squadron, *Warspite* (Flag, Rear Admiral A.B. Rawlings) *Valiant* and five destroyers.

Following their return to Alexandria in the middle watch of the 20th, Captain Mack and his staff learned that the army had recaptured Sollum, but this morsel of good news was expunged by the knowledge that the Luftwaffe were using Vichy French airfields in Syria and by the grim incoming signals that told of the dawn invasion of Crete; airborne troops and paratroops had commenced landing from gliders, transport planes and by parachute at Maleme and Heraklion.

The battle for Crete and the evacuation that followed have been the subject of many works by military historians and the autobiographies of senior commanders – and so again this account is confined to the part played by *Jervis* and the ships of the 14th Flotilla.

Jervis sailed after refuelling, at 1400/20th with *Nizam* and *Ilex* in company, with orders to bombard the airfield on the island of Scarpento. At about 0130/21st the dark shapes of land that were the islands of Kaso and Scarpento were in sight. As the destroyers approached the bombarding position in line ahead, there came a heart-stopping alarm signal from *Nizam* – 'Torpedoes to starboard'. Then followed the underwater thumps of explosions as torpedoes reached the end of their runs. The E-boat or submarine which fired the missiles escaped detection. An hour later the destroyers opened fire on the unseen airfield, without observing any fires or explosions caused by their gunfire. The ships then searched Pigada Bay using star-shell but the anchorage was empty of shipping. Some flares landed ashore and started two large fires which could still be seen 20 miles astern as the destroyers retired. Captain D received a signal ordering him to join CS15 who, with the cruisers *Dido* and *Coventry* and the 14th DF ships *Juno*, *Nubian*, *Kandahar* and *Kingston*, had been in action with six Italian MTB's in the Kaso Straits. Before Captain Mack's force made contact with CS15 however, another signal received at 1300 ordered *Jervis* and her destroyers to return with all despatch to Alexandria. As they neared Alexandria news came through that at the time that *Jervis* reversed course *Juno* had been bombed and sunk with heavy loss of life.

The sinking is recalled by Able Seaman E. Wheeler who a month earlier had survived the sinking of *Mohawk*. In the Mediterranean fleet survivor's leave was an unknown luxury;

> On the 15th May I joined *Juno* at Alex: I wasn't happy about this as I was the only ex-*Mohawk* and *Juno* was a Chatham ship but there was nothing I could do about it except to grin and bear it . . . we were patrolling between Kaso and Leros but on receiving information of an airborne landing on Crete the force swept through the Kaso Strait. We were at action stations all this time, my particular station being ammunition number, left gun, B mounting. We fought off six Italian motor gun boats that night and at dawn we were attacked by Ju87 Stuka dive bombers. The attacks were non-stop, a mixture of German dive bombers and Italian high level bombers. At 1249 we were hit by three bombs out of a stick of five; the other two dropped in our wake, from Italian high level bombers. The ship just split in half from the bridge aft to the stern. She sank in 97 seconds (timed by someone in *Kandahar*). It was a case of every

man for himself, everything happened so fast. When I recovered my senses B gun deck was almost awash so over the side once again I went. Looking in front of me I saw *Kandahar* stopping and lowering her whaler and that's where I swam for. Someone yelled out, 'Wheeler, Jock can't swim.' Turning my head to the right there was Jock going through the water like a torpedo. For one who couldn't swim he beat me to *Kandahar*'s whaler . . .

There were very few survivors. *Kingston* also stopped and lowered a whaler which picked up eight men of whom five died before the ship reached Alexandria.

Jervis, *Nizam* and *Ilex* departed soon after midnight on the 21st/22nd to patrol the eastern approaches to the island, moving after dark into the sea area off Heraklion. In the same night and to the north, *Janus* and *Kimberley* of the 14th DF with *Hasty* and *Hereward* forming part of Admiral Glennies' Light Force of cruisers and destroyers that included *Dido* (flagship) and *Orion*, came upon an enemy mixed convoy of small steamers and caiques protected by one escort destroyer. In a 2½ hour action three steamers and a dozen caiques packed with German troops were sunk before the action had to be broken off in face of overwhelming air attacks, 4000 of the enemy troops died. *Janus* sunk several caiques by gunfire and another by ramming, cutting it in half. Low in ammunition the Force retired through the Antikithera channel.

Rear Admiral King's Force, comprising *Naiad*, *Perth* and the 14th DF ships, *Nubian*, *Kandahar* and *Kingston* were off Heraklion with orders from the C-in-C to sweep north-west in daylight to seek further convoys. One caique packed with troops was sighted and sunk. Then the force came under a ferocious air attack as it came within sight of a convoy of over 30 caiques. Squadron followed squadron of Ju87 and Ju88 bombers; one of *Nubian*'s bridge staff later described the scene: 'The sky was black with bombers and the sea bubbled with bombs.'

In face of this onslaught, Rear Admiral King gave the order to retire. The single Italian escort destroyer *Sagittario* succeeded in masking the front of its convoy with a smoke screen and, reversing its course out of harm's way, and at the same time it launched a torpedo attack on the British cruisers.

It turned out to be a terrible day for the fleet. The first to be sunk was the destroyer *Greyhound*, which was dive-bombed after she had found and sunk a caique, then, while *Kandahar* and *Kingston* picked up their flotilla shipmates, they were dive-bombed and machine-

(*Top*) June 1941. Damour river crossing destroyed by *Jervis* and her flotilla. (*Centre left*) *Jervis* closes *Queen Elizabeth* for hand messages. (*Centre right*) French Alexandria Squadron's liberty cutter sets off an Italian mine. (*Bottom right*) *Jervis*. 'Woggles' the ship's cat and others on the bridge watch *Barham* pass.

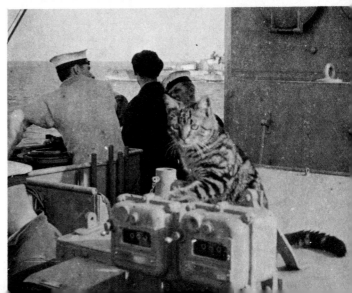

(*Left*) July 1941. Hugh Mulleneux 14th DF — Gunnery Officer, diarist and photographer. (*Right*) Air raid over Alexandria.

(*Centre left*) 11th July 1941. Tobruk run — *Defender* hit by Italian bombs and sinking off Bardia. (*Centre right*) 19th August 1941. Tobruk run — *Jervis* with Polish troops embarked. (*Bottom left*) August 1941. Tobruk harbour. (*Bottom right*) August 1941. Tobruk run — *Jervis* returns with British and Australian wounded.

gunned. The flagship *Naiad* received damage from a near miss and shortly afterwards the AA cruiser *Carlisle* was hit on the bridge, killing her captain. *Warspite*, also in the Kithera channel, was hit by a large bomb which wrecked her starboard 6″ and 4″ gun batteries. *Gloucester*, steaming at high speed was hit by several bombs, set on fire and became a total loss. Italian S79's hit *Valiant* aft with two bombs but caused little damage, then in the late evening *Fiji*, which had survived twenty attacks and was down to using practice ammunition, received a very close near miss from a bomb released by a Me109, which blew in the cruiser's bottom and brought the ship to a stop with a heavy list and her engines crippled. The cruiser was hit by three more bombs and, at 2015, rolled over and sank. *Kandahar* and *Kingston* were again the rescuing destroyers; they lowered their boats and rafts and then withdrew from the area until after dark. The two K's had both been attacked 22 times over the previous five hours. They returned and picked up 523 *Fiji* survivors, and now both being very short of fuel were ordered to return to Alexandria.

In the afternoon the 5th Flotilla (which had been ordered from Malta to the Kithera channel) joined the battlefleet. Captain Mountbatten had with him *Kelly, Kashmir, Kipling, Kelvin* and *Jackal*. The flotilla had first been ordered to see if they could pick up any of *Gloucester*'s or *Fiji*'s men but before they reached the area the order was countermanded and D5 was sent to patrol north of Canea and Maleme. In the night the flotilla destroyed two unarmed caiques full of troops, then bombarded Maleme airfield which was now held by enemy paratroops. *Kelly, Kashmir* and *Kipling* were ordered to leave the area and proceed to Alexandria. Soon after 0800/23rd the three destroyers were under attack from 24 dive bombers. *Kashmir* was hit first and sank within two minutes; shortly afterwards *Kelly* turning under full helm at 30 knots was also hit – still moving through the water the destroyer capsized.

In a flat calm sea under brilliant sunshine the survivors from both ships in the water were repeatedly machine-gunned. *Kipling* (Commander A. St Clair-Ford) remained at the scene for three hours picking up survivors in the face of these repeated air attacks. Forty aircraft dropped more than 80 bombs while *Kipling* picked up 279 men. Later she arrived 70 miles off Alexandria, where her fuel ran out and she had to be towed into harbour. This marked the end of the 5th Flotilla. *Kipling* and *Jackal* joined the 7th Flotilla commanded by Captain S.H.T. Arliss in *Napier. Kelvin* joined the other three K's in the 14th DF.

The battered fleet, over the next three days, continued to prevent the landing of seaborne troops on Crete but, because of the total lack of fighters and the absence of an RAF presence of any kind, the enemy continued the uninterrupted supply and reinforcement of its invasion forces with Ju52 transport aircraft.

The battle ashore was fierce and bloody. For days the outcome rested on a knife-edge. At one stage the paratroop force had been driven into one corner of Maleme and were at the point of surrender, but at dawn on the 26th the British, Australian and New Zealand units had gone and were retiring south over the central mountains.

Jervis, Nizam, Ilex and *Havock* sailed from Alexandria in the middle watch of 23rd May for the Kaso strait and Hugh Mulleneux wrote in his diary:

> The other forces at sea have had an awful time with bombs. *Gloucester*, *Fiji* and *Juno* have been sunk. I'm terribly sorry about *Juno*. *Carlisle* hit, *Ajax* and *Naiad* near-missed. It is really a very historic battle – virtually unopposed air-power v sea-power – may the Almighty help us.

He was still able to record; 'A rainbow this evening.'

After a night spent patrolling off Heraklion, *Jervis* and her destroyers passed south through the Kaso Strait and at 0700 came under air attack. First came three Dornier 17's followed by six Ju87's which split up into pairs and attacked *Ilex*, *Havock* and *Nizam*. One Stuka was shot down by *Ilex* but a near miss on *Havock* killed six men. Further attacks developed during the day as the destroyers retired towards Alexandria; the last came from a single Dornier 17 which near-missed *Jervis*. Hugh Mulleneux continued in his diary:

> This is a sad day, I'm afraid that the navy has been seen off by these damn dive bombers. *Kelly* and *Kashmir* are two further casualties and there is probably a lot of other damage. The lesson being learnt is just the same as was learnt in Norway.

In the morning of Sunday, 25th May, ships of the 14th Flotilla held church services dedicated to those who had died in *Juno* and *Greyhound* and the other fleet casualties. Immediately following these shipboard services *Jervis* slipped and led out of harbour *Nubian*, *Kandahar*, *Hasty*, *Hereward*, *Voyager*, *Vendetta* and *Janus* ahead of *Queen Elizabeth*, *Barham* and *Formidable* for Operation MAQ3 to bomb Scarpento airfield by the FAA. At 0300/26th Albacores took off from *Formidable* to attack the island airfield and Hugh Mulleneux wrote on that day, his birthday:

What a birthday! Bombs all over the place. After a fairly quiet forenoon when a couple of shadowers were shot down, at about 1400 we had a terrific attack by Ju88's. Heaven alone knows how many there were, the whole sky seemed black with them – anything up to 60 at a time.

In the attacks *Formidable* was hit twice on the flight deck causing fires. These were brought under control and by late afternoon the carrier was working her aircraft again. *Nubian* next to *Jervis* on the screen was hit aft; the fire set off an explosion that blew off the whole stern, killing seven men and injuring 12 others. The explosion left the ship's shafts and screws intact and *Nubian* was able to proceed at 20 knots. *Jervis* set off to escort her damaged flotilla ship towards Alexandria, when the two ships were attacked by a formation of Italian S79's. Twenty bombs fell into the sea space between the two destroyers causing no damage but considerable alarm to the ships' companies.

Jackal then took over the escort of *Nubian* and *Jervis* returned to resume command of the battle squadrons' screen. A fresh air attack developed next morning 0830/27th by 12 Ju88's. *Jervis*'s pom-pom and Breda guns completed the destruction of one Ju88 damaged by the gunfire from *Janus*. The battle squadron returned to Alexandria that evening without further air assaults.

The extra depression that hit the exhausted and hard-pressed fleet when the news of sinking of the battle-cruiser *Hood* in the North Atlantic, had been received, lifted a little when it became known that the German battleship *Bismarck* had been sunk.

The inevitable evacuation had to be tackled by a fleet strained to the limits of human and mechanical endurance. It was to be a repeat of the experience endured in the fiords of Norway and off the beaches of France and Greece; again here at Crete the Axis squadrons had mastery of the sky over the fleet and operated from airfields that fringed the eastern Mediterranean. Against this opposition the fleet had to try to lift 22,000 soldiers off tiny beaches that crouched at the foot of Crete's southern mountain range.

Twenty-four hours after returning to harbour, *Jervis* departed again with *Janus* and *Hasty* as part of an evacuation squadron consisting of *Phoebe* (flagship, Rear Admiral King) *Perth*, *Calcutta* and *Coventry* with the infantry landing ship *Glengyle*. *Jervis* had embarked a beach control party that was to be landed at Sphakia to supervise the embarkation of troops from small, steep beaches and the few landing places. As the force steamed north-east through the daylight hours of the 29th, evacuation had commenced at other points of the

Crete coastline: Captain Argliss, D7, in *Napier* with *Nizam*, *Kandahar* and *Kelvin* had taken troops off a beach near Sphakia while a force of destroyers and cruisers, *Orion* (Flagship Admiral Rawlings), *Ajax* and *Dido*, had taken 4000 troops out of Heraklion. As the force retired through the Kaso strait all the cruisers had been hit, and the two destroyers, *Hereward* and *Imperial*, filled with soldiers had been lost. In *Orion* the captain had been killed and the admiral wounded; the ship carrying 1100 troops had 260 killed and 280 wounded. The signals bearing this terrifying information were only known in *Jervis* to Captain D and his staff. One bomb only was aimed at the force and this fell very close to *Jervis*. At 2130 Captain Mack increased speed to 30 knots and went on ahead to locate the embarkation point and to land the beach party.

Jervis closed the land in a darkness made blacker by the great unseen cliffs that enveloped everything. Everyone spoke in whispers as the ship at slow speed, crept eastward, flashing a blue shaded light toward the shore and from time to time making cautious calls over the loud-hailer. Suddenly everything happened at once. A light glowed momentarily ashore, then came shouts warning the ship not to approach any closer. Quickly the motor cutter with the beach party embarked was lowered and sent in towards a pinpoint leading light. After a short interval the boat returned filled with walking wounded: 'The poor soldiers had been through absolute hell, they had been bombed and machine gunned from the air practically continuously for eight days – some men had scrambled 12–15 miles with bad and undressed wounds, dead tired, unshaven and dirty, they were still in great heart.'

Stoker George Morel was at the engine controls of the motor cutter: 'I was so concentrating to catch the cox'ns whispered orders, with one hand on the throttle lever the other on the clutch trying to keep everything as quiet as possible – I forgot that I was armed.'

While the motor cutter continued to ferry evacuees from the unseen beach, Admiral King arrived with *Phoebe*, *Perth*, *Glengyle* and the other destroyers. *Coventry* and *Calcutta* patrolled to seaward. *Glengyle*'s landing craft immediately speeded up the embarkation process. *Jervis* with 260 embarked moved out to join the AA cruisers as the other destroyers closed the shore to be filled up.

Able Seaman John Ellis, who joined *Jervis* in April was at his action station at No 3 (X) gun mounting, and later wrote in his diary:

All the time the evacuation takes place, everyone talks in whispers, no lights in case the Germans hear or see what is taking place, all very sad. We load from stem to stern with Maoris, Marines, Cretan men and women and Australians. E-boats and U-boats are reported to be in the area.

Glengyle embarked 5000 soldiers and her landing craft ferried out 1000 to each of the cruisers. The destroyers each filled up with about 250. Nearby Captain D7, with *Napier* and *Nizam*, using extra whalers which had been loaded onto the ships at Alexandria, was embarking 500 troops and then left the boats behind for a further lift. On the way to the evacuation point, *Kandahar* had to drop out and return, due to engine failure, to be followed by *Kelvin* after damage by a near miss.

Rear Admiral King's force set off at 0300 to return to Alexandria. At 0945 came the first high level attack from two planes. One was shot down by *Calcutta*. As the aircraft fell out of the sky, it jettisoned a bomb which hit *Perth* killing 25 men, wounding many others. At noon the ships steaming in a close tight formation were attacked by six Ju88's, on a smooth, deep blue sea and in brilliant sunshine the weaving ships left long curling white wakes while above them aircraft dived down through the barrage of black smoke and shrapnel created by the squadron's massed guns. The attack passed without further damage to the force which entered harbour at 0200/31st. *Jervis* and her destroyers berthed at 38 quay and disembarked their passengers, then moved to an oiler to refuel, at the same time embarking ammunition from a barge moored on the disengaged side. The task was finished at 0600 and hands were then piped to breakfast. As the destroyermen went to breakfast and clean, they saw their flagship *Phoebe* leaving harbour with the minelayer *Abdiel* and *Hotspur*, *Kimberley* and *Jackal* for one last attempt to evacuate some of the 6500 soldiers still remaining at Sphakia. Although the force was attacked three times it succeeded in taking off 4000 and returned safely to Alexandria; 2000 men including 1000 marines were left behind.

May had been a disastrous month for the fleet: two cruisers and seven destroyers had been sunk; two battleships, one aircraft carrier, three cruisers and two destroyers had been badly damaged and would have to leave the station for lengthy repairs. Another six ships would have to be taken out of service for periods from two weeks to two months and would take up the fleet repair facilities.

Then, on 1st June, to complete the dismal toll, a further sinking of a vital ship occurred. *Coventry* and *Calcutta* had been sailed to meet

Rear Admiral King's force to give them extra anti-aircover on their return from Sphakia. The two cruisers were attacked by a strong force of Ju88's. *Calcutta*, hit by two bombs, sank in a few minutes. *Coventry* picked up 255 survivors of her chummy ship and returned to harbour. Rear Admiral King returned safely with the last lift of men out of Crete.

In spite of its crippling losses the fleet had succeeded in taking 16,500 British and Imperial troops out of Crete and landed many tons of provisions and supplies for those who remained behind. The effective fleet on 2nd June 1941 consisted of the battleships *Queen Elizabeth* and *Valiant*, the cruisers *Ajax* and *Phoebe*, the anti-aircraft cruiser *Coventry*, which had a temporary bow, and 17 destroyers. These ships faced a future where they could only operate in a sea encircled by enemy air bases. There was no point at which the ships would be out of range of hostile aircraft.

CHAPTER FOUR

A Fleet Challenges Defeat

The fleet had been savagely mauled in the May fighting to sustain what was a hopeless cause, and some officers in the fleet considered that the surviving ships should withdraw from the east Mediterranean sea. To them there seemed to be little sense in remaining confined to the south-east corner of the land-locked sea with a base at Alexandria which could soon become untenable because of the RAF's inability to counter the Axis air power. As if to emphasise their disquiet, Alexandria was subjected to its heaviest blitz on the night of 4th/5th June. This air raid caused a massive evacuation of the city's population to the outskirts and into the desert.

The sensation of being bottled in did not deter the resolve of the fleet's Commander-in-Chief, Admiral Sir Andrew Cunningham. He made it clear that the Navy would continue to provide an inshore squadron to supply the beleaguered garrison at Tobruk and to bombard the Axis coastal bases even though every movement of his ships would be monitored and opposed by enemy aircraft. He also accepted a commitment to support the army in Palestine, a mixed force of Imperial troops and the Free French, who were about to attack Vichy French and German positions in Syria, with the intention of occupying Beirut and Damascus.

Within the reduced fleet, the 14th Destroyer Flotilla maintained its numbers and strength. Following the ending of the 5th Flotilla caused by the demise of the unfortunate *Kelly*, surviving 'K's' – with the exception of *Kipling* – became permanent units of the 14th. Captain Philip Mack's flotilla from 1st June consisted of *Jervis, Jaguar, Janus, Griffin, Kandahar, Kimberley, Kingston* and *Kelvin. Kipling* and *Jackal* remained with the 7th DF, *Javelin* was still undergoing a long term reconstruction and *Jupiter* operated with the Home Fleet.

Captain Mack's aggressive resolution matched his C-in-C's determination. His philosophy was that the only place for his destroyers was at sea seeking the enemy and if there was no air support, so be it. *Janus, Jackal* and *Kelvin*, hard on the Crete débâcle, and given no time to rest or recover, were already off the Lebanon coast, operating out of Haifa.

Jervis and the rest of the flotilla stayed on in Alexandria for a few days while Captain D14, one of the fleet's most senior captains, conferred with the Commander-in-Chief and his staff. One of the features of these few days in harbour, when the air raids allowed, was that Captain Mack took the opportunity to dine with his officers in the wardroom. He entertained them with stories related to his long and varied career in the Service – on this occasion following the evacuation of Crete, centred on his experiences in South America and his visits to the Andes. He had developed an intense interest in the higher flights of mystical situations based on Inca legends, power of the mind and levitation.

By this stage of *Jervis*'s career, a number of the staff and ship's officers had acquired nicknames, based on the characters of the children's story and film *Snow White and the Seven Dwarfs*. Philip Mack, unknown to himself, was referred to with affection by his officers, as 'Bashful'!

One officer, Surgeon Lieutenant Hamilton had a nickname outside the *Snow White* ambit. Doc was known as 'Umzizi' after a character in *Punch* magazine. Hamilton was highly regarded by the ship's company, his skill as physician and surgeon had been established by the care he gave to wounded survivors picked up by the ship, friend and enemy alike. *Jervis*'s luck and the skill of her captain had, so far, saved her ship's company from death or injury in action. Doc Hamilton – Umzizi – had won the respect and even the love of *Jervis*'s men because of the time he spent at sea, sharing the special strain and fears of those whose watchkeeping duties and action stations confined them below deck where they could not see (and rarely knew) what was going on. They could not share the excitement and adrenalin stimulating activity of those on the upper-deck fighting the armament. He spent time deep down in the ship, inside the claustrophobic confines of the magazines, the boiler and engine-rooms, with the ammunition supply, fire and repair parties, in the W/T office, T/S and wheel-house. He made constant rounds to all these 'below deck' stations bringing good humour, calm reassurance and companionship. He also knew everyone who manned the guns, torpedo tubes, searchlight, flag-deck, bridge and the upper-deck, only retiring to his sick-bay when the probability of casualties seemed imminent.

The three remaining cruisers in the fleet, *Phoebe* (Rear Admiral King, CS15) *Ajax* and *Coventry* with four 14th DF ships, *Kandahar Kimberley*, *Janus* and *Jackal* were despatched from Alexandria and arrived at Haifa on 7th June. Next day *Kimberley* shelled Vichy French positions near Tigre. Then on the 9th two French destroyers, *Guepard* and *Valmy*, were reported to be shelling Australian troops advancing north along the coast. Help was called for, and *Janus* and *Jackal* set off in pursuit. In the running fight that followed, *Janus* was hit five times (on the bridge and No 1 boiler room), suffering 12 men killed and 17 wounded. *Jackal* was also hit once but with no casualty or serious damage. *Janus* was in danger of being sunk by the Frenchmen until *Isis* and *Hotspur* arrived on the scene and forced them to retire.

Janus was towed to Haifa by *Kimberley* whence a few days later she was towed to Port Said and then on one boiler she passed through the Canal making her way to Durban; later she went on to Simonstown for repair.

It was no surprise to the staff of the 14th DF to discover that the campaign in Syria had been under-rated by the Chiefs of Staff, who had assumed that the Vichy French forces in Lebanon and Syria would submit to the threat of Allied infantry, unsupported by armour. This soon proved a costly miscalculation when the British Imperial Force and its Free French Allies found themselves facing heavy tank detachments and had nothing better than Bren carriers and lorries with which to oppose the Vichy armour.

Jervis departed from Alexandria on 12th June with *Hasty* escorting the recently arrived New Zealand cruiser *Leander* to join CS15 off Sidon on the Lebanon coastline and to allow *Ajax* with *Stuart*, *Hotspur* and *Kandahar* to return to Alexandria for a short rest. On the same day, shortly before they sailed, the men in *Jervis* watched their chummy ship, *Nubian*, leave under tow on the first stage of a slow passage to Bombay for her major repairs, and to give leave.

Jervis was soon in action, bombarding armoured vehicles, troop concentrations and artillery hampering the Australian progress along the coast road.

It was a curious unreal campaign, that involved with French formations fighting on both sides and a multiplicity of aircraft types, British, French, German and Italian, which made aircraft recognition almost an impossibility; 'All sorts of queer types of aircraft flying about, it is hard to know whether they are friend or foe!'

Jervis and her destroyers were called upon by the army to engage a wide variety of targets, including tanks which from time to time fired back at the ships. *Jervis* knocked out a powerful battery of twelve

French 75 mm's and then bombarded El Atigua.

In the early hours of the 15th with *Kimberley* she was in action with the two French destroyers which had badly damaged *Janus. Jervis* was straddled several times by the accurate French fire before the enemy ships returned to Beirut. Air attacks from German Ju88's and high flying French aircraft were frequent and heavy; both *Isis* and *Ilex* received damage and the former had to be towed back to Haifa.

Off Beirut, *Jervis* was on patrol in the night of the 15th/16th to intercept the French destroyer *Cassard* which was bringing troops, embarked in Salonica, to the Lebanon, but the destroyer had been forced to turn back by RAF torpedo carrying aircraft operating out of Cyprus. On this patrol *Jervis* had a narrow escape from a torpedo; a submarine was sighted about a cable-length from the ship at the moment that it fired a torpedo. Under full helm and an emergency call for full speed Captain Mack turned *Jervis* away from both submarine and the torpedo which could be seen a few feet off, running parallel with the ship.

The submarine crash-dived; *Kimberley* attacked a firm contact with depth charges and was dive-bombed by three Ju88's for her pains but escaped damage while *Jervis* fought off six dive-bombers.

The Australians' drive north was held up by strong artillery positions and tanks so calls became more frequent and urgent for supporting fire from the cruisers and destroyers; *Jervis* and *Kingston* moved close inshore in the night of the 18th/19th and bombarded Vichy positions south of Damour.

Jervis had a second close shave with a torpedo. Passing close inshore off the city of Beirut but with a wary eye on the coastal batteries, the ship was attacked by one of two Vichy submarines in the harbour which was moored to the mole inside the harbour entrance with bows out. As *Jervis* passed this submarine fired two torpedoes, one passed under the destroyer's bridge – she escaped destruction only because the torpedo was set to run deep. The incident was remembered by George Hesford:

> That day I really saw a chap's hair stand on end with fright – No kidding – I've always remembered it. Quite likely mine did the same – it would have done so if I hadn't been wearing my cap!

That same night *Jervis* patrolled further out to sea with *Decoy, Hotspur* and *Havock*, while inshore *Naiad* and *Leander* supported by *Jaguar, Nizam* and *Kingston*, tried to winkle out the two destroyers *Guepard* and *Valmy* from under the guns of the coastal battery where they had retired for protection. The action was observed by Hugh Mulleneux:

> We were further out to seaward and watched the battle going on – there
> was also another smaller one to be seen on the land close to Damour
> where I imagine our advance will start again soon. An amazing sight –
> Beirut blazing with light like Blackpool on a Bank Holiday with a naval
> battle going on one side of it and an army battle on the other.

It was a strange, unreal situation; the day had started – Sunday,
22nd June – with *Jervis* in harbour at Haifa where the hands had been
piped to bathe, before breakfast in the clear water and then to clean
into dress of the day prior to divisions and church. At morning
service the chaplain announced to his shipborne congregation that
Germany and its allies had attacked Russia.

The following evening the ship returned to Haifa from its station
off Beirut; leave was piped from 1830 to 2330. Next morning John
Ellis and his shipmates paraded ashore wearing gaiters and
webbing, carrying a full pack and an unfamiliar rifle to sweat out a
long morning under the direction of the chief gunners' mate,
preparing to land as a platoon of seamen in support of the 'pongoes'
at Sidon. To everyone's intense relief the expedition was called off.

On the 25th, the chaplain took a party from the lower deck for a
tour of some of the Holy places. 'Padre gets up a party to visit
Nazareth and the Sea of Gallilee – 4/- per man – we visit the Church
of Annunciation, the wishing well and Jesus Christ's carpenter
shop,' John Ellis noted in his diary.

The morning following the visit to the fount of the Christian faith,
Jervis poured 200 rounds of 4.7" into Vichy positions north of
Damour; later *Jervis* was accused by the Vichy command of having
fired upon an ambulance on the coast road. As *Jervis* in company
with *Naiad*, *Kingston* and *Hotspur* returned to Haifa they enjoyed the
rare sensation of having an escort of friendly fighter aircraft, but it
did not save the force from being bombed by five French bombers.
'The fighters did not seem to see or notice anything,' was the
exasperated comment by men in the ships.

Jervis was out again on the 29th bombarding: on completion a
signal was received from the Commander-in-Chief ordering Captain
Mack to return to Alexandria. After *Jervis* had arrived back at the
base in the early morning of the 30th, Hugh Mulleneux recorded his
impression of the bizarre situation:

> Arrived at Alex; to find a sadly depleted fleet. Practically all the works

except *Formidable* have gone, which leaves the mighty Med fleet represented by *Valiant*, '*QE*'*, *Ajax*, *Phoebe* and one or two destroyers besides the Force B at Haifa. How the mighty have fallen – a month ago we wondered what we were going to do with all the ships at our disposal. That problem has unfortunately been solved by the Luftwaffe.

What a fantastic war it is, as here we are lying practically alongside the French cruisers, etc; and all the troops hob-nobbing ashore, when in Syria we are fighting against them! To a lesser degree the situation is the same at Haifa. A couple of girls at the Haifa Club asked us not to bombard Beirut as they had all their furniture stowed there!

Jervis remained at Alexandria for the first few days of July. Army's push towards Sollum (Operation 'Battleaxe') had collapsed in the last week of June; units who made the advance had been outflanked and, with great difficulty, extricated and were back at their original defensive positions close to the Egyptian frontier.

The Tobruk garrison was being supplied at great cost by merchant ships escorted by Australian destroyers. They were subjected to constant attacks from both German and Italian aircraft, the sloop *Auckland*, destroyer *Waterhen* and several supply ships had been sunk: others had been damaged either on passage or when unloading at Tobruk. It had become clear that the garrison could be supplied only by fast warships, arriving, unloading and departing again under the cover of darkness, thus reducing the daylight hours on the double trip during which the ships were exposed and vulnerable to air attacks.

On 9th July the Vichy French in Syria asked for Armistice terms which were accepted on the 12th by the Vichy High Commissioner, General H. Dentz.

After her arrival in the Mediterranean in 1940, *Jervis* was joined by a small, dirty white, Egyptian mongrel puppy – no one had admitted to having brought the small creature inboard. It soon had foster parents, it was bathed, groomed and fed, a small hammock was made and Snowball joined the ship's company. It even became accepted by the large, very independent and aloof ship's tabby cat that had come out with the ship from England. Snowball had now grown and matured and, like the cat, had learned to tolerate and accept the noise and uproar of a ship in action. Gunfire did not frighten either animal. If Snowball was caught on the upper deck when the guns opened up, he would ask to be popped into the nearest shelter or wash-deck locker, from where he would be released at

* Battleship *Queen Elizabeth*

every lull. If he was on No 2 mounting deck, he sought shelter under the canvas cover of the towing pennant, stowed on the flash flare above No 1 mounting.

Snowball had developed a priceless ability; he could hear approaching aircraft long before they were sighted, an attribute which, to some extent overcame the ship's lack of radar and when matched with Captain Mack's uncanny knack of avoiding falling bombs, made the ship's company feel invincible.

Jervis was back in Haifa on 17th July – she had arrived with *Jaguar*, *Kingston* and *Kandahar* to join the cruisers *Ajax* and *Leander*. The entire force sailed that same afternoon, escorting a convoy of troop reinforcements to Cyprus. The ships were back in Haifa on the 20th where the destroyers embarked specialist army personnel and the RAF. *Jervis* had 112 RAF ground staff who were landed at Famagusta. Many of the ship's company doubted whether the High Command knew what they were doing: 'Having virtually evacuated Cyprus after the Cretan "do", we are now about to fill it up again.'

Jervis sailed at 1400/22nd with the cruisers and destroyers to join the battleships off Alexandria the following day. When Force B made contact with the battle squadron it was noticed that two new arrivals were with the fleet – the cruisers *Hobart* and *Neptune*, which had passed through the Suez Canal 24 hours earlier. The fleet manoeuvred; then steamed westward aggressively to distract Axis air attention away from the west, where attempts were in hand to bring from Gibraltar 4000 troops and supplies for Malta, at the same time to sail *Breconshire* and seven fast empty merchant ships to the west from the island.

Operation Substance was successful, although one supply ship was damaged by an E-boat off Pantellaria. All the troops and stores arrived intact but at a cost to the escorting warships. The cruiser *Manchester* was badly damaged by an Italian aerial torpedo and Italian bombs sank the destroyer *Fearless* and damaged her sister ship *Firedrake*. *Breconshire* and the empty merchant ships succeeded in running the gauntlet of enemy air and submarine opposition and arrived safely at Gibraltar.

Jervis and the 14th DF arrived off Alexandria with the fleet in the evening of the 24th but remained outside and waited for *Formidable* to emerge and then escorted the carrier to Port Said for the start of her passage to the USA for repairs. The re-stocking of Cyprus from Haifa continued for the next few days and ended with *Jervis*'s return to Alexandria at 0900/31st July.

August started with a bang: on the 1st, *Jervis, Jackal, Kingston* and *Nizam* set off at high speed from Alexandria to hunt for a submarine which had been sighted several times on the surface off Tobruk. The speeding destroyers were spotted at 1430 by an enemy reconnaissance aircraft and 'soon bombs started to fall on us out of the blue'. The ships were attacked four times before dark. The hunt for the submarine went on all night without results and then next morning on the way back to Alexandria, Italian planes again tried unsuccessfully to damage the ships. The entire 14th DF was in harbour by 1000 Saturday.

The flotilla was about to join the Tobruk 'Death Riders' or 'Suicide Squad', the group of miscellaneous ships which had been keeping the surrounded garrison supplied, *Defender* had been the most recent destroyer sunk, she had been bombed by the Italians off Bardia. The Commander-in-Chief had to undertake a new task with extra hazards, his hard-pressed ships – in addition to keeping supplies flowing – had to replace the entire garrison of Australians by a mixed force of Polish and United Kingdom troops. This seemingly 'crazy' operation was to be undertaken by the fleet weakened in the Crete débâcle, and stretched to the limits by its many commitments and imposed on a protesting C-in-C. Political considerations had prompted the decision; the deteriorating situation in the Far East had brought demands from the Australian Government for the immediate withdrawal of their brigades from the Middle East. Thus, several thousand troops were to be shuttled in successive moonless periods over a stretch of sea completely dominated by enemy aircraft and patrolled by Axis submarines.

This prodigious operation was code-named – 'Treacle'.

On Sunday the 3rd, Hugh Mulleneux heard that he had been promoted to lieutenant-commander and that he had been appointed to a staff gunnery post at the Royal Naval Barracks, Devonport. His promotion was celebrated modestly with friends and flotilla colleagues in the wardroom, everyone aware of the implications of the new operation which was to start within the next few days. Changes in the flotilla staff and ship's officer complement were beginning to take place. First Lieutenant R.W. Scott had gone after just one year in the ship; he had been relieved by a more junior lieutenant, M. Rose. With Rose's arrival in *Jervis*, Captain Mack had changed his nomination of the first lieutenant as his second-in-command; the flotilla staff navigator, Lieutenant (N) J.B. Laing was now nominated.

Jervis, Kingston, Jaguar and *Nizam* proceeded to sea for gun practice with *Queen Elizabeth* and *Naiad* on the 5th, and remained at sea, after the big ships returned to harbour in the evening, to carry out a sweep for a submarine suspected to be in the area. The sweep continued through the night without making contact. At dawn on the 6th, the ships were still sweeping in line abreast formation when they were surprised by a group of Italian S79's flying at 60 feet above the waves. The Italians attacked the starboard wing where *Nizam* had a miraculous escape from destruction, the S79 formation released its torpedoes inside 1000 yards and escaped without a round being fired at them, torpedoes passed close ahead and astern of the startled *Nizam* and the one heading for amidships at the last moment suddenly ran wild, commenced to circle, then sank.

The destroyers returned to Alexandria to experience that night, 'the biggest and most spectacular blitz since our days in Malta'. Most of the damage and fires were ashore – *Jervis* had a number of near misses but, apart from splinter holes sustained little damage and no casualties.

Operation Treacle commenced on Friday, 8th August. *Jervis* and *Kingston* were to be the first away on a 'Beef and Spud' run – the two ships berthed alongside to load up with stores which seemed to consist of . . . 'dried prunes, ammunition and cigarettes'. At 0730 next morning *Jervis* embarked some army staff, 'Brass-hats', connected with the planning of the garrison change-over, they all seemed to be more familiar with deskwork at GHQ than the rigours of front-line combat. The ships sailed at 0815 and made an uneventful passage, arriving off Tobruk at 2345 and cautiously entered the wreck-strewn harbour in near total darkness, while an air raid was in progress on the outer defences. The destroyers berthed 'in this mortuary of sunken ships' and unloaded the stores and passengers in about 25 minutes; then (with all the gentle care that sailors are capable of) embarked wounded Australians, stretcher and walking cases. The galley staff issued endless mugs of tea and coffee to the men able to take in liquid. Free from enemy air interference the ships were back in Alexandria during the afternoon watch on the 10th, and discharged the wounded into a succession of waiting ambulances.

After this first preliminary run, Operation Treacle really got under way with the start of moonless nights on the 18th. That afternoon *Jervis, Kimberley* and *Hasty* each loaded up with 60 tons of stores, then in the early hours of the 19th, the destroyers each embarked 100 Polish officers and men. D14 and his ships sailed at 0830. On passage, only a single S79 made a torpedo attack which was fended off with ease. During this run *Jervis*'s ship's company made their first contact with the Poles: to a man they were impressed by the formidable and grim determination of these men all of whom seemed to have made incredibly dangerous escapes from either Poland or Russia so that they could fight for the freedom of their homeland. Sadly few had any knowledge of the fate of their families and friends.

At midnight the ships felt their way into the darkness of Tobruk harbour, strewn with 80 plus British and Italian shipwrecks; all was quiet. The stores and passengers were quickly offloaded and the wounded embarked, the start of the main lift of Australian combat troops would commence on the next numbered serial run. This started at 0845/22nd when *Jervis*, *Kimberley*, *Hasty* and the fast minelayer *Abdiel* sailed, loaded with stores and packed with Polish soldiers. *Jervis* had also embarked Rear Admiral (Destroyers) Rear Admiral I.G. Glennie, who wished to see for himself the difficulties experienced by his destroyers. On this occasion the destroyers had a covering force of cruisers, *Phoebe*, *Naiad* and *Galatea* and – to the astonishment of the destroyer-men – 23 RAF fighters patrolled the sky above the speeding ships: such numbers had never before been seen, in the memory of those engaged in the East Mediterranean conflict. One sailor was heard to describe the sight, 'It's like the f--king Hendon air pageant'; other cynics said it had all been laid on because R.A.(D) was at sea. The serial went off without a hitch, men and stores were off loaded in complete silence within half an hour, and 200 fully armed and equipped Australians filed inboard the destroyers to be packed into the messdecks, the minelayer taking 500. The ships cleared Tobruk at 0130 and from 0600, things had returned to normal; the ships were bombed comprehensively without a friendly fighter to be seen, but the destroyers and minelayer got back safely.

Jervis, *Kimberley* and *Hasty*, each with 60 tons of stores all of which had to be manhandled by the ships' companies into and out of the ships, and *Jervis* with 200 Polish soldiers embarked (7 cavalry officers and 193 troopers), arrived back in Tobruk at 2315/26th. The scene is described in the diary kept by AB John Ellis:

> Every member of the crew had a job to do, everything was done in total silence. The Germans swept 'No-Mans' and continuously with a

(*Right*) October 1941 – J. C. Stodart, C. Argles' relief as flotilla torpedo officer. (*Centre left*) October 1941. *Jupiter* G85. (*Centre right*) October 1941. HHMS *Queen Olga*.

25th November 1941. *Barham,* torpedoed by *U-331,* heels over and blows up as *Valiant* takes avoiding action.

1942. *Jervis* in the central Mediterranean with RDF (ex-*Janus*) fitted.

(*Left*) *Jervis* – Away sea-boat. (*Right*) September 1941. Lt Rose with Vice Admiral Sir Gerald Wells (Admiral of Egyptian Ports and Lights) and Captain Mack.

(*Left*) 1942. *Jervis* No 3 Mounting at defence stations. (*Right*) 19th March 1942. Captain Philip Mack departs. Pulled ashore by ship and staff officers.

searchlight, the beam would flash across the ship. All the tables in the mess-deck were dismantled to accommodate stretcher cases, we even stacked them on the upper-deck, the stench of blood was terrible.

The destroyers, with every space and cabins occupied by wounded men, sailed at 0100, Doc Hamilton and his 'sick-bay tiffey' assisted by two Australian army doctors, cared for the men on the 14 hour return to Alexandria. The ships entered harbour at 1530, and no men died in *Jervis*.

That night *Jervis* was duty destroyer and lay at the duty destroyer buoy moored by a slip rope, at half hour notice for steam. All, however, expected a night in their hammocks even though no leave had been piped; they also knew with the approach of the full moon period that next day the ship would start a two week refit period. But it was not to be quite like that: at 0100 *Jervis* passed out through the boom, *Phoebe* had been torpedoed by an Italian S79 and, with *Naiad* and *Galatea* in company, was making for Alexandria at 10 knots. *Jervis* joined the escort at 0800 and helped bring the damaged cruiser to port. This was achieved at 2200, the destroyer went straight to the fleet repair ship *Resource* where she berthed alongside and closed down on her boilers. The first stage of Operation Treacle was complete. The Australian destroyers, the 14th Flotilla and the minelayers *Abdiel* and *Latona* had, during the moonless period of August transported several thousand tons of stores to *Tobruk* with 6000 Polish troops and brought out 5000 Australians. The second stage, a new operation, would commence in the moonless period of September. While the garrison remained at Tobruk it was a 'running sore' for the Axis but, at the same time, it had a similar effect on the Navy.

For the next twelve days *Jervis* lay alongside *Resource* while refitting and certain urgent repairs were carried out. Some of the staff officers however continued at sea in the still operative ships of the flotilla, in particular members of a remarkably professional group of flotilla Warrant Officers, notably Charles Sims, Ordnance, Philip Dobson, Gunner DFI, and George Packman, senior commissioned gunner. E.H. (Nutty) Card, Warrant Engineer, remained with *Jervis* to oversee her engine overhaul.

Vice Admiral Sir Gerard Wells, his wife Mary and two daughters Elizabeth and Sue made sure that officers from *Jervis* could relax in their home in Alexandria; they laid on frequent swimming and picnic parties in their yacht *Betha* moored in a quiet corner of the harbour. For the ship's company – even though large areas of the city were placed out of bounds and relentlessly patrolled by the Provost Marshal's staff – Alexandria offered a limitless range of restaurants, cafés and eating houses all catering for the robust appetites and the uncomplicated palates of sailors. The city pandered to all desires of the flesh and there was also the renowned Fleet Club. Admiral Wells also made *Betha* available for the 'Under 20 Club' and the Boy Seamen.

Two lower deck parties, 25 from each watch, travelled to Cairo by train and were accommodated in a luxurious Nile houseboat and looked after by a large staff of servants. It was rumoured that the expenses had been met by King Farouk. Cairo had not been bombed, there was no blackout and there was much to do and – to the delight of the aficionados – an unlimited supply of Whitbreads beer with which to flush out the taste of Alexandria's onion-based Stella beer.

The men who remained in the ship as duty watch on the night of 5th/6th September endured a massive air raid. The Fleet repair ship and the venerable (circa 1907) hospital ship *Maine* had a number of near misses, which caused damage to *Resource* and considerable alarm to the fire and damage control parties in *Jervis*. The hospital ship had seven killed including two doctors.

The repair period, leave and the opportunity for the ship's company to sleep ashore between sheets was soon over. Following a long day at sea exercising with *Jaguar*, *Kimberley* and *Kingston*, *Jervis* with her destroyers and minelayer *Abdiel* were again alongside the jetty – now called Tobruk jetty – loading for the next series of moonless runs to the desert garrison. This second phase (to store and replace the troops) was code-named 'Supercharge'.

The first run outward commenced at 0730/17th loaded with Polish soldiers; this, and the return run with wounded, passed without interference from the enemy. For the second outward run on 20th, *Jervis* carried no stores but had embarked no fewer that 325 officers and men of a Liverpool Territorial Army anti-tank regiment. The destroyer sailors felt sorry for these amateur soldiers – none had seen active service – who were going into the Tobruk perimeter to take over anti-tank weapons and positions vacated by the outgoing Australians and to face battle-hardened veterans of the German tank regiments. Returning to Alexandria, *Kimberley*, sighted a small rowing boat and picked up three British and seven Greek soldiers who had rowed and drifted 180 miles from Crete; a few days earlier,

Kimberley had encountered a caique crowded with British, Australian and Greek soldiers and had towed them into Alexandria. A steady flow of men escaping from Crete continued.

The next Operation Supercharge run for *Jervis* was, serial 9, on the 23rd; she was accompanied by *Kimberley*, *Hasty* and the minelayer *Latona*. The ships sailed into a nasty head sea with the weather deteriorating. *Jervis* had 320 sick soldiers crammed into her messdecks or clinging, soaked and miserable, to every available projection on the upper deck. The bad weather had an advantage in that it kept reconnaissance aircraft away, and the serial was completed without undue problems except for the minor panic caused to Stoker Clifton. He had been detailed by the First Lieutenant Rose to help an army officer carry his baggage to the jetty across the wreck to which *Jervis* was moored. Afterwards the officer ordered Clifton to continue along the jetty carrying the gear. The stoker, knowing of the speedy turn round, a fact unknown to the army, and worrying about missing his ship, heard his name called out of the darkness 'Stoker Clifton – ahoy'. That was enough for him. He dropped his load and rushed back, stumbling over the debris littering both jetty and wreck only to see *Jervis* moving and a widening gap of water appearing between him and the ship. He made a desperate leap. 'Jimmy and some of the lads were waiting to grab me when I jumped. With the swell lifting us up and down, it was no easy task I can tell you but I was dragged inboard.'

The ships were back safely in Alexandria at noon on the 24th. That afternoon *Jupiter* (Lieutenant-Commander N.V.S.T. Thew RN) which had rounded the Cape with a convoy for the Middle East, arrived on station to join the 14th DF. The flotilla now comprised of *Jervis*, *Jaguar*, *Jupiter*, *Kandahar*, *Kimberley*, *Kingston*, *Griffin* and *Gallant*.

The day after joining *Jupiter* sailed with the entire fleet to carry out a display of force intended to distract the enemy while a convoy was sailed from Gibraltar to reinforce and re-victual Malta. Operation Halberd was the first attempt since the July convoy of Operation Substance. Halberd turned out to be a successful venture, eight of the nine large, fast transports and store ships, carrying 81,000 tons of stores and 2700 troops arrived at Malta. One transport, ss *Imperial Star*, was torpedoed and sank after the troops and crew had been taken off. The Force H flagship *Nelson* was the only warship to be damaged, and she returned to Gibraltar without difficulty after the Italian fleet made a token and ineffective sally from its home ports.

The Mediterranean fleet, after carrying out its routine aggressive diversionary manoeuvres, returned to port on the 27th without incident.

In September's 'no moon' period the transfer of troops to Tobruk had been concluded. The eleven days of Operation 'Supercharge' had seen a further 6300 fresh troops and 2100 tons of stores carried to Tobruk by destroyers and the two minelayers, and 6000 troops brought out. While this was going on a gallant band of men manning ten 'A' lighters and tank landing craft had ferried from Mersa Matruh 2800 tons of stores, 55 tanks, artillery weapons and lorries. These unwieldy craft, armed only with light AA weapons, fought many battles with enemy aircraft and forced one U-boat to dive, by the end of October five of this 'lighter' squadron had been sunk.

For the first few days of October Captain Mack exercised his flotilla and its new units in gun, torpedo, anti-submarine and air defence skills. After the flotilla had returned to harbour on 10th October, it put to sea with the fleet that same night with the intention of bombarding enemy desert installation. The plan was abandoned and the ships were back in Alexandria in the early part of the first watch.

After *Jervis* had secured, Hugh Mulleneux was shaving in his cabin at 0730 when First Lieutenant Rose burst in to announce that his relief had arrived.

Lieutenant (G) M.A. Hemans had come out from the UK in one of the Operation Halberd ships to Malta. After a few days on the island, he had flown on to Alexandria in a Sunderland flying boat but, when he arrived, he was running a high temperature from sandfly fever contracted on the island, so he was turned into Mulleneux's bunk by Doc Hamilton. The flotilla, after refuelling, sailed with the fleet in response to a report that strong Italian fleet units were in the vicinity of Tobruk, gale force winds had developed from the west which gave the escorting destroyers a bad time, with deep seas washing down the upper-deck. At midnight *Jervis*, *Jaguar* and *Jupiter* with the cruisers *Ajax*, *Hobart* and *Galatea* were sent on ahead of the fleet to seek out an enemy contact reported by a Malta-based submarine. Then followed several hours of fruitless quartering of violent seas with gun crews hanging on for their lives at wave-swept action stations; it was a nightmare of darkness and huge head seas. The cruisers' radar failed to make contact and the squadron turned back and rejoined the fleet at dawn on the 13th just as a combined attack by German and Italian torpedo bombers developed. This was fended off by a fearsome barrage from the fleet.

Again that night, *Jervis* (without the cruisers) led her destroyers away to make a sweep, close inshore along the coastline of Crete, looking for enemy shipping, but again they drew a blank. When the destroyers rejoined the fleet at dawn it was being attacked by torpedo bombers, this time supported by dive bombers – no damage was caused by either side although many bombs, torpedoes and much anti-aircraft ammunition was expended. The fleet was back in its base, on the afternoon of the 14th.

Once Lieutenant Hemans had recovered, Hugh Mulleneux was able to depart from *Jervis*: he moved in with Admiral Wells and family whilst he waited for his passage home to be arranged. Lieutenant (T) C.R.L. Argles had also left *Jervis*, and later took passage in a transport with Mulleneux via Durban and Capetown.

In all some ten officers – ship and flotilla staff – had, within the two years of war service left the ship on relief, Captain Mack was of course still in command. From the lower deck only a minor proportion had been changed, and none allowed to leave the station.

The day after Hugh Mulleneux departed (17th October) Able Seaman Ronald Antony Bone also left *Jervis* on draft to another Mediterranean ship, *Hotspur*. Ron, as an ex-Wildfire training establishment Boy 1st class, had joined *Jervis* in November 1939 as one of the ship's complement of sixteen boy seamen. He was now 19, with two years of sea fighting experience under his belt. The majority of the boys on becoming ordinary seamen were retained in the ship but a few extroverts like Ron were drafted to other ships as trained and battle-hardened men. He was a slimly built 5' 9" with brown hair, blue eyes and a fresh complexion, and wore a tattoo on his right arm in memory of his sailor father. A robust individuality often had him in conflict with the ship's establishment, the coxswain, buffer, petty officer of his division and the first lieutenant, but his sunny exuberant personality created no animosity with those who strove to curb his antics ashore and the practical jokes inflicted on his shipmates. His draft to *Hotspur* brought him some luck; a few months later he got a draft back to the United Kingdom, for home leave and a course at the anti-submarine school, HMS Osprey, at Portland. Most of his *Jervis* shipmates were not to return to England until 1944 by which time Ronald Bone was back in the Mediterranean, to serve in the cruiser *Mauritius*.

Following the June failure of the Operation Battleaxe offensive in the Desert where the majority of the tank replacements brought out in the Operation Tiger convoy had been captured intact and the Guards Brigade extracted with great difficulty after being encircled, planning had been intensive for the next attack on the Axis deadlock. General Sir Claude Auchinleck had relieved General Sir Archibald Wavell as Commander-in-Chief Land Forces Middle East. General Auchinleck was putting the final touches to plans for the new desert offensive where his commander in the field was to be Lieutenant-General Sir Alan Cunningham, brother of the fleet Commander-in-Chief. Admiral Cunningham had moved to Cairo for October so as to be in close contact with his Army and Royal Air Force colleagues: the fleet was, for a time, under command of Vice Admiral Pridham-Wippell.

Following the fleet's unsuccessful sweep in bad weather to counter what proved to be false alarms, the 14th DF enjoyed a few days in harbour with only one more October excursion to sea in company with the battleships on the night of the 22nd/23rd, when positions round Sollum were bombarded. The last three days of the month were utilised by Captain Mack exercising his flotilla at sea, culminating with a whole day firing at air and surface towed targets. This last day was marred by the crash of an RAF Beaufighter, an incident described by Midshipman R.D. Butt in his journal.

> Beaufighters turned up to carry out dummy machine gun attacks and one of the pilots, swooping low over the ships to demonstrate his daring, fouled the top of *Kingston*'s mast and plunged headlong into the sea. It was a pity that the airman did not take better care of his craft, for it became a total loss and he and his gunner lost their lives . . . Some RAF officers in the flotilla had little sympathy for one who threw away his plane and crew in such a manner.

On Saturday 1st November Captain Mack inspected his ship's store rooms and magazines, then on Sunday following inspection at divisions the hands mustered 'By the open list', when each man came before his divisional officer and gave his name, official number, his rating and non substantive qualifications, number of Good Conduct Badges, in fact, every item for which he should receive payment. While the individual recited his entitlements, a Writer studied the ledger to check his fortnightly pay. Then came church parade after which Captain Mack announced a new Operation Glencoe. This was again a destroyer and minelayer ferrying of troops, this time to pull out the 50th (North Country) Infantry Division from Famagusta and replace them with units of the Indian Army and from West Africa and the desert. The ships were divided into three groups by Rear Admiral Glennie and were to run without a break between Haifa and Famagusta.

The task was completed in perfect weather conditions without a hitch or attempted interference by the enemy. The force was all re-assembled in Haifa at noon on the 8th having brought out the last of the 50th Divison. RA (D) referred to his ships as 'My grey painted removal vans' a remark that no doubt gave Philip Mack his idea. Next morning (Sunday 9th) when D14 led his flotilla through the boom of Alexandria harbour, every destroyer flew at the upper-yard a green and red flag with the words 'Carter Paterson Ltd', the livery colours and name of the well-known national removal firm – the minelayers following astern flew the rival 'Pickfords Limited' black flags.

Jervis berthed on *Woolwich* to have two additional oerlikon gun mountings fitted on No 3 gun mounting deck. On Tuesday 'paint ship overall' commenced and at Captains Requestmen's table one of the ship's original boy seamen, now an able seaman, had an important request granted; Victor Whitlock had asked for one of the Mediterranean fleet orders to be implemented; this was that elder brothers could ask for younger brothers serving in other ships of the fleet to join them. Victor Whitlock had a younger brother, a boy seaman, serving in the boys' mess-deck of the *Barham*. The younger Whitlock joined *Jervis* a few days later.

Jupiter left the 14th DF and departed from the Mediterranean fleet on 16th, passing through the Suez Canal on passage to join the East Indies fleet. A couple of days later *Griffin* also left the flotilla to become leader of the 2nd DF. On the same day it became general knowledge in the fleet that *Ark Royal* had sunk off Gibraltar after being torpedoed by *U-31* on the 13th.

Jervis sailed with the fleet on the 18th to bombard targets in the vicinity of Sollum but ran into gale force winds from the desert and a sandstorm of impenetrable visibility, which forced the operation to be cancelled. As the fleet reversed course to return to base, *Jervis* narrowly escaped being run down by *Galatea* which had failed to cease zig-zagging while the remainder of the fleet turned together through 180 degrees.

Back alongside the *Woolwich*, the depot ship's ordnance party commenced changing *Jervis*'s worn 4.7" gun linings.

The Western Desert Force renamed Eighth Imperial Army – with a new C-in-C, had since June been steadily reinforced by men and *matériel* arriving in great convoys from the United Kingdom via the Cape of Good Hope and disembarked at the Red Sea ports of Suez and Tewfik. There were strong rumours that a new assault on the Axis positions was imminent and soldiers had all but vanished from the streets of Alexandria. The Army commenced its advance on the 18th and there were reports of tank battles of considerable ferocity. The fleet sailed on the 24th to support the sea flank of the battle for Cyrenaica: the first stage was for the garrison at Tobruk to break out and link up with the Eight Army. *Jervis*'s gun lining change had not yet been completed when she sailed to lead the battle squadron's screen, so that No 1 gun mounting was out of commission. The cruisers had sailed 12 hours earlier and at high speed to intercept enemy supply convoys bound for Benghazi.

Throughout the morning and early afternoon of Tuesday the 25th the battleships *Barham, Valiant* and *Queen Elizabeth* with their nine screening destroyers steamed alternately east and west off the Gulf of Sollum, waiting for supporting bombardment to be demanded by the army locked in tank battles; it was a beautiful day, the brilliant blue of a cloudless sky reflected in a flat, calm sea. At 1600 the battleships were steaming a mean course due west, zig-zagging in line ahead. On the destroyer screen *Griffin* was ahead of the flagship, *Barham. Jervis* zig-zagged on the flagship's port bow and *Decoy* on the starboard bow, the remaining six destroyers were deployed to port and starboard on the screen astern of the leading three. Midshipman Butt wrote in his journal:

> It was grand weather and as we steamed close by the battleships many men were standing around on deck enjoying it; it might almost be a pleasure cruise . . . it was after tea that I strolled up on deck to enjoy the calm sea and the sunshine . . . I was idly watching the three great vessels when it suddenly struck me that all was not well, *Barham* had dropped back. I noticed a little cloud of yellow smoke puffing up on her side, she appeared to be listing to port. I felt convinced that she had been torpedoed.

At 1617 the asdic watch in *Jervis* reported a submarine contact: after a few moments, the OOW and duty staff officer considered that it was a 'non-sub' contact and ordered the asdic watch to resume sweeping.

At 1623 the battleships turned together 45 degrees and had steadied on the starboard leg of the zig-zag pattern, thus putting the three great ships into echelon formation.

At 1625 *U-331*, which had slipped through the destroyer screen, fired four torpedoes, three of which hit *Barham* amidships on her port side. As the submarine fired her torpedoes she lost trim and her conning tower broke surface 150 yards off *Valiant*'s starboard bow. The battleship was then beginning to turn under emergency port helm to get clear of *Barham* heeling over to port onto her beam ends. *Valiant*'s Captain Morgan arrived on the bridge to see the U-boat break surface and immediately ordered hard-a-starboard in an attempt to ram; the ship was slow to respond to the extreme change of helm and missed *U-331* which crash-dived 40 yards off, passed under the battleship and got clean away.

Captain Mack had turned *Jervis* and pointed at *Barham* which was still making way through the sea completely on her side, with water entering her funnel; he was preparing to go alongside the stricken ship to take off survivors: 'All along her starboard side and on the upturned bulge, hundreds of her men were abandoning ship.'

In *Jervis*, the TGM, Chief Petty Officer J. Edmunds, who had hurried aft when the submarine contact had been reported, was still on the quarter-deck (where he had gone to supervise the dropping of depth charge patterns) when he saw *Barham* hit:

> I saw 3 large explosions on her port side, in less than a minute she was on her side, then I swear I saw her bottom open up like a tin can followed by a huge explosion and smoke that went up a thousand feet. When the smoke cleared there was nothing left.

The 35,000 ton ship had disappeared in four minutes. John Ellis recorded in his diary:

> . . . heeling over she is still doing 20 knots and blows up like a huge bomb. Above the smoke I see a 15″ turret in the sky with the figure of a man above it.

Victor Whitlock and his brother watched the scene with a mixture of fear, distress and thankfulness for one boy seaman's escape from the holocaust in which so many recent shipmates died before his horrified eyes.

Jervis and *Jackal* were ordered to hunt the submarine while *Nizam* and *Hotspur* were detached to rescue the survivors; the remainder of the escort returned to Alexandria with *Queen Elizabeth* and *Valiant*. The rescuing ships picked up 450 men including Vice Admiral Pridham-Wippell but 56 officers and 812 ratings had died, including the battleship's commanding officer, Captain G.C. Cooke.

Jervis picked up one man a mile from where *Barham* blew up: he had been blown off the upper-deck when the torpedoes struck. D14 in *Jervis* and *Jackal* hunted all night, dropping many depth charges on suspected contacts, but *U-331* (Leutnant von Tiesenhausen) was no longer in the area. The two destroyers returned to Alexandria in the afternoon of the 27th and *Jervis* berthed again on *Woolwich* to complete her gun lining changes.

Lieutenant-General Cunningham's assault in the Western Desert was meeting fearsome resistance and the Eighth Army had not so far linked up with the Tobruk garrison. So, immediately after divisions and church on Sunday, the 30th, *Jervis, Jackal, Jaguar* and *Kipling* sailed at high speed to intercept three Italian destroyers reported to be approaching Derna. The same ships had previously made a round trip to that port carrying petrol and diesel oil for the Axis desert armour.

At 0300/1st December the destroyers went to action stations; for a light had been sighted on the starboard bow. The destroyers, in line ahead closed at 30 knots, altering course to place the target between themselves and the moon; then, as Captain Mack was about to order the destroyers to open fire, the light could be seen to be the starboard light of a hospital ship showing very dim lights and poor illumination of its International Red Cross identifications.

At daybreak, under cover of a torrential downpour, the line of destroyers closed the land. When the rainstorm suddenly cleared, the ships less than four miles off-shore could clearly see the houses of Derna, roads and vehicles moving along them but no sign of the enemy destroyers in the small port; the birds had flown.

Captain Mack knew that the sudden appearance of his destroyers off Derna would provoke enemy air activity. He did not have long to wait after the ships had turned back eastward in line abreast, zig-zagging, and at the same time carrying out an anti-submarine search. Five torpedo carrying Heinkel 111's came in at low level from the desert coast and released their torpedoes. Each destroyer took separate avoiding action. *Jackal*, having combed the track of one torpedo, was hit by a second on her stern, remarkably with no casualties but her quarter-deck was a mass of wreckage. The screws and shafts were relatively undamaged but her rudder was jammed hard a-port.

The other flotilla ships circled on anti-submarine and anti-aircraft protection patrol until *Jackal* re-centred her rudder; then steering by main engines she resumed her course eastward at 20 knots. At dusk, with the night closing in fast, the destroyers overtook a convoy out of Tobruk being harassed by low flying aircraft. The destroyers opened up with a low angle 2000 yard barrage which seemed to take the enemy by surprise and they broke off their attack.

Then came one of the tragedies which are the inevitable consequences of the war obscenity. After cease fire had been ordered by Captain D, the Gun-Captain of No 2 mounting in *Jervis* asked for permission to clear a shell remaining in one of his hot gun barrels. Authority was given to 'Clear gun' and he was ordered to train to port and fire his gun on the ship's dis-engaged side. Out of her station and unseen by the *Jervis* bridge lookouts, *Jaguar* was 2000 yards on the port beam when the gun fired. George Kean was one of the signalmen on the bridge:

> Captain Mack remarked that the shell burst was near her and told me to ask if she was all right. This I did and was stunned to get a reply that the Captain was killed. I think my voice was very small when I told our Captain and he asked me to get a repeat, which I did.

An able seaman had been killed with his captain, Lieutenant-Commander J.F.W. Hine, another able seaman was mortally wounded. It was a shattering and bitter blow to Philip Mack: he had had a special regard for Hine, who was the youngest commanding officer in his flotilla. The two men were buried at dawn on 21st December. In the four ships with ensigns at half mast, men stood bare-headed and silent while *Jaguar* buried her dead. In the swept approach channel to Alexandria a tug met *Jackal* to assist her into port whilst *Jervis* went on ahead with *Jaguar* – her first lieutenant in command – and *Kipling*, passing the infantry assault ship *Glenroy* which had been hit by an aerial torpedo. The assault ship was drawing too much water to enter harbour and was waiting for a salvage crew.

As soon as *Jervis* had secured to the oiler the motor cutter was called away to take a deeply moved Captain Mack, still in his sea-going gear, across to *Jaguar*, where he addressed the ship's company cleared from the lower-deck. Half an hour later when Philip Mack left to return to his ship, *Jaguar*'s men crowded the rails and cheered their Captain (D), a poignant and emotional moment in an endless war.

Jervis was again off Derna, this time with *Hero* and *Havock*, in gale force winds and heavy seas, looking for the elusive Italian destroyers

– only to encounter, for the second time, the Italian hospital ship which was now outward bound from Derna. Then, not long afterwards the destroyers passed the British hospital ship, *Somersetshire*. That night (5th/6th) as the ships returned to Alexandria and having passed Tobruk, U-boat, *U-81*, torpedoed the auxiliary naval transport *Chakdina* (Commander W.R. Hicky RNR) carrying prisoners of war and 380 wounded, British, New Zealand, German and Italian. Two hundred survivors were picked up including only 18 out of the 97 New Zealand wounded. One POW who survived was Generalleutnant Johann von Ravenstein, who was General Rommel's leading general and the first German general to be captured in the Second World War.

News that hostilities now existed between Japan and the United States of America and the Allies, and that America had declared war on the Axis partners was received with mixed feelings by the men in the fleet. Of more immediate consequence was to learn that on the same day, 8th December, the Eighth Army had succeeded in linking up with the Tobruk garrison. There were hopes that the supply commitment imposed on the navy might now be eased.

For those serving in *Jervis*, two days later, the 10th, brought a weary sense of being back at the beginning. The ship with others was again bombarding targets they had engaged exactly twelve months previously with the long since sunk monitor *Terror* and her 'Tiddler' river gunboats. This present bombardment however and a high speed dash by the cruisers to intercept an Italian convoy, M41 bound for Benghazi, was soon over after the Italians turned back their convoy to Taranto. As *Jervis* led the destroyers into Alexandria a signal came reporting that *Galatea* had been sunk by *U-557*. Captain Mack reversed course with his destroyers, but there was nothing that they could do. The cruiser had sunk in two minutes and the few survivors of her 450 ship's company had been picked up.

A fast turnaround, and *Jervis* was again heading west on 15th December as one of an escort with the task of fighting through to Malta the naval auxiliary *Breconshire* (Captain G.A.G. Hutchison) loaded with critically required stores and fuel. The escort, Force B, commanded by Rear Admiral Philip Vian were the cruisers *Naiad* (Flagship), *Euryalus* and *Carlisle*, in addition to *Jervis* the destroyers *Kimberley, Kingston, Kipling, Nizam, Hasty, Havock* and *Decoy*. The force sailed straight into a violent head sea and extremely poor visibility which persisted for the first twelve hours. To ensure the arrival of this vital supply ship Force K had been ordered to sail from Malta to join the escort and then later to take *Breconshire* into Malta after Force B had turned back to Alexandria.

Unbeknown to the Commander-in-Chief the passage of *Breconshire* coincided with a major effort by the Italian fleet to get a convoy through to North Africa where the Axis army was in difficulties because of supply shortages. November had been a disastrous month for the Italians. Nine merchant ships had been sunk, including the entire Duisberg Convoy of seven mixed Italian and German merchant ships plus one of its escorts. The convoy had been sunk by *Aurora*, *Penelope*, *Lively* and *Lance* operating as Force K from Malta, the new Strike Force. Later on in the month, Force K sank two escorted German freighters. Then in the early hours of 12th December four destroyers of the 4th DF, which had sailed from Gibraltar to join the Mediterranean fleet: *Sikh* (Commander G.H. Stokes), *Maori*, *Legion* and *Isaac Sweers* (Dutch) surprised two Italian cruisers off Cape Bon and sank them both with torpedoes. The enemy ships were carrying tons of cased petrol for Tripoli.

Admiral Vian was unaware that the Italian operation M42 – the passage of four ships in convoy – was underway; three ships bound for Tripoli and one for Benghazi. The close escort of the convoy consisted of seven destroyers with a heavy close cover of one battleship, three cruisers and three destroyers, the main fleet was also at sea to give distant cover, amounting to three battleships including *Littorio* (flagship of Admiral Iachino), two heavy cruisers and ten destroyers.

Force K and the 4th DF were to rendezvous with Admiral Vian (CS15) in position 33 degrees 45' north and 21 degrees 30' east – the two convoys, British and Italian, were destined to cross each other's tracks. From first light on the 16th the British convoy of one ship, *Breconshire*, and its escort of three cruisers and eight destroyers were having problems; during the night *Breconshire* had been forced to alter course south to effect repairs caused by the heavy head seas. Only *Carlisle* had seen the ship alter course, it took until 0750 for the remainder of the escort to find and reform round their charge. Because of this delay, Admiral Vian had to suspend the zig-zagging so that he could reach his planned west position by night fall.

The RAF on this occasion managed to maintain good cover over the force and prevented bombers or torpedo carriers breaking through, but they failed to supply reliable reconnaissance reports so CS15 had only sketchy knowledge of the large enemy units at sea. The Italian C-in-C was being better served by the many Ju52 transport planes flying to and from North Africa and Greece. These aircraft supplied frequent and accurate information on the passage of the British ships.

Twice in the late afternoon *Jervis* attacked submarine contacts with a single pattern of depth charges to force the suspected enemy to keep his head down; there was no time for a deliberate series of attacks. After dark CS15 detached *Carlisle* (because of her slow speed) and *Kingston* (who had developed engine defects) to return together to Alexandria.

The night of the 16th/17th passed without problems and only one incident when *Decoy* obtained a suspected submarine contact, which came to nought.

At 0830/17th Force K and the 4th DF from Malta linked up and the combined force of four cruisers and thirteen destroyers clustered round the solitary convoy ship. Since dawn, Axis reconnaissance aircraft were in continuous contact, then at noon air attacks started that went on through the afternoon. About 25 Italian SM79 torpedo bombers and 50 German Ju88's kept up a series of attacks; six times the British force made emergency turns together to comb torpedo attacks but only *Euryalus* and *Isaac Sweers* had very close near misses: the massed high and low angle barrages from the fleet held the attackers at bay.

Midshipman Butt's journal records the effect of these barrages: '. . . spent bullets and shell fragments pattered down on the decks and made the sea boil around us while great fountains of smoke capped spray rose into the air as bombs fell wide of their marks.'

At 1400, CS15 had altered course further south after being joined by three more ships from Malta, *Neptune,, Kandahar* and *Jaguar*. In the evening as the last of the attackers withdrew, a Cant flying boat was sighted, low on the horizon, dropping red flares in groups of four. These seemed to be signals to enemy fleet formations below the horizon; twice that morning Admiral Vian had received inconclusive reports from Malta indicating that large groups of Italian heavy ships were at sea to the north.

The red flares, did in fact, herald the approach of the Italian battle fleet; on the darkening horizon the grey shapes of battleships and heavy cruisers could be seen, followed by the sight of flickering red and orange flashes along the enemy line, indicating that fire had been opened on the British force. *Breconshire* shepherded by *Decoy* and *Havock* was ordered to steer south, then with the arrival of enemy shells among the ships of the starboard screen, eleven high level and five torpedo bombers delivered an air attack while other aircraft dropped lines of flares. It seemed that Admiral Iachino was about to deliver a set piece attack on the British formation. The enemy gun salvoes were very accurate and hits seemed to be inevitable, as CS15 ordered a 180 degree turn together away to the south while the destroyers on the engaged side laid a smoke screen. As they did so Philip Mack led his 14th DF boldly out through the smoke, straight at the enemy battle line ordering his destroyers to train their torpedo tubes to starboard.

At 1757 Admiral Vian made a recall signal to the 14th DF. The factors that influenced this order were; CS15's own forces were considerably scattered and he was out of contact with the 4th and 14th DF's; his priority was to get *Breconshire* intact into Malta, the Italian fleet was clearly deployed to contest an attack by his destroyers and it seemed obvious that it was shielding its own convoy; it was his task, therefore, if at all possible to cut out and sink the enemy convoy.

After dark the main Italian fleet units withdrew to the north; then at 2200 its convoy M42 was ordered south and later to divert the single ship *Ankara* for Benghazi escorted by the close heavy escort. *Ankara* docked in Benghazi at 0930/19th. The three ship section, escorted by the main Italian fleet, arrived at Tripoli at dawn the same day. *Breconshire*, escorted by Force K and two 14th DF destroyers, *Kandahar* and *Jaguar*, also arrived in Malta the same morning. Thus both fleets achieved their objectives at the same time avoiding serious confrontation in what was later euphemistically called the 1st Battle of Sirte.

The Mediterranean fleet did not escape unscathed. Admiral Cunningham ordered Force K to intercept the Tripoli section of the Italian convoy M42 and so *Neptune* (Captain R.C. O'Conor) led the Strike Force on its final sortie and to its demise on the night of the 18th/19th. At 0100 the force ran into a new, Italian offensive minefield laid off Tripoli in exceptionally deep water. *Neptune* sank, with only one survivor after hitting four mines; *Aurora* – badly holed, managed to get clear and return to Malta with *Penelope*, which also received mine damage but to a less serious degree. Whilst trying to help *Neptune*, *Kandahar* also hit two mines, then drifted for an entire day in worsening weather until *Jaguar* (Commander St J.R.C. Tyrwhitt) with great difficulty and daring took off her crew. 67 of *Kandahar*'s ship's company died in the mine explosions and in the rescue operation.

In the same night that Force K died in the enemy minefield, Admiral Vian's force was approaching Alexandria; on the bridge in *Jervis* the OOW was the ship's second lieutenant (Peter Aylwin) and the duty staff officer, Lieutenant Mike Hemans. Since the two encounters *Jervis* had had in recent months with submarines, at night and on the surface, Peter Aylwin frequently rehearsed in his mind the course of action he would take should a similar incident occur, when he had the watch.

He was going through this mental exercise when both he and the port lookout sighted a surfaced submarine fine on the port bow. Peter, standing at the polaris, leapt to his long rehearsed drill and pressed the alarm rattler button as he yelled down the captain's sea cabin voice pipe, then a helm and revolution order to the quartermaster and a dash to the after end of the bridge as Hemans took his place at the polaris. Fleet general orders discouraged destroyers and escort vessels from ramming so, as the unidentified submarine crash dived, Peter released a depth charge pattern, set to shallow depth. These exploded even as the ship went to action stations. As the other ships passed on their way into Alexandria harbour Captain Mack turned his ship and began a series of attacks on asdic contacts, breaking off when oil and wreckage was seen on the surface. Midshipman Butt was on the bridge when the submarine was sighted in the first watch:

> He crash dived as we reached him, but the conning tower was still awash as our bows ripped past him – I still saw his periscope above the water when he was abaft the bridge, so he must have been badly jolted by our port thrower. We returned to drop more charges on an asdic contact we obtained then fired starshell to try and spot him on the surface in case he was trying to escape at speed that way. We failed to find him after looking for some time, and so returned to Alex and went alongside the oiler, feeling fairly certain we had sunk him. . .

A probable kill was credited to *Jervis*, a fact which paradoxically was to haunt Peter Aylwin for many years – for the unidentified submarine could have been British or Allied. However no Allied submarines were reported missing in the area – or, for that matter, Axis U-boats. *U-371*, which was in the vicinity, returned safely to base after completion of its patrol; the only other enemy submarine operating close to Alexandria was the Italian *Scirè* Commander Borghese) and she did not report being attacked. *Scirè* was to reveal the reason for her presence to a startled fleet within a very few hours,

22nd March 1942. 2nd Battle of Sirte. *Kipling* next in the line.

2nd Battle of Sirte. The first division, *Jervis, Kipling, Kingston* and *Kelvin* prepare to attack with torpedoes.

(*Right*) Admiral Vian's destroyers return to Alexandria. (*Bottom left*) *Jervis*. Admiral Sir Andrew Cunningham visits Captain Poland after the battle. (*Bottom right*) – After Sirte *Jervis* cheered into Alexandria by men of the crippled fleet flagship *Queen Elizabeth*.

11th May 1942. *Lively* hit bombs, at full speed plung to her end.

Some of *Lively*'s men are rescued by *Jervis*.

(*Left*) *Lively*'s survivors climbing the side of *Jervi.* (*Right*) *Lively*'s survivors k helped into *Jervis*. Bill Skilling's head can be see the sea.

11th May 1942. *Kipling* at
dusk hit by bombs.

(*Left*) January 1942. *Jervis*
leave party waits for the Cairo
train. (*Below right*) Wardroom
steward – Zara.

(*Left*) February 1943. Frank (Nobby) Hall – ex-*Gurkha* survivor. (*Right*) Able Seaman Fearnough. 'Never fear, Rommel's here!'

(*Left*) *Jervis* ship's company cooks. PO Chef, Taffy and Slim. (*Right*) 30th June 1942. R. T. Taylor picked up by *Zulu* after he had rescued a *Medway* survivor.

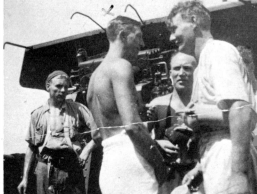

(*Left*) Janner Doxhall, Snowball and Petty Officer Mick Myers. (*Right*) September 1942 – No 6 mess. Standing on the right, Bill Skilling.

and at the same time that Force K struggled vainly for survival in a minefield off Tripoli.

Jervis entered harbour in the middle watch on the 19th, some two hours after Force B had returned to harbour; the flotilla leader made straight to the oiler *Sagona*, a short distance from the fleet flagship *Queen Elizabeth*, and berthed starboard side to, bow to stern. Everyone turned in except for the usual harbour watch-keepers and the duty stokers of the refuelling party.

Not long after *Jervis* had secured, the Commander-in-Chief, asleep in his quarters in the flagship, was called at 0400 and informed that two Italians, clad in rubber suits, had been found at 0325 sitting on a harbour mooring buoy and that they were being interrogated. At 0600 a large explosion under the stern of *Sagona* caused damage to the oiler and to the bows of *Jervis*. Stoker J. Clifton was one of the refuelling party:

> I was down below in the officers' cabin flat with another young stoker tending 5 and 6 tanks when we heard and felt a rumble, he said, 'What's that noise, Stokes?' I said, 'That's the force of oil going into the tanks, blowing the sides and the air escaping!'

John Ellis was turned in forward:

> I am asleep on the table of 13 mess, there is a terrific explosion, the ship shakes and vibrates, lights go out, cork and paint flakes drop off the deck head into my eyes. I cannot see. There is panic as I thought we had been torpedoed.

Ellis was not the only one to believe at first that the ship had been torpedoed. Michael Hemans the new flotilla gunnery officer, who had turned in before the ship had entered harbour was in a deep sleep when the explosion woke him. Disorientated with sleep he reached the upper-deck and for a few seconds could not understand how the ship was lying alongside a larger ship. 'I was quickly joined by other officers and under the direction of Captain Mack, set about saving the ship.'

George Kean was the signalman on watch on the bridge:

> I sat on the top of the signalman's table on the portside of the compass platform making a signal to the depot ship *Woolwich* by aldis lamp, a charge under the stern of *Sagona* hurled me across the compass platform on to the deck. Our bows had jumped up, as I scrambled to my feet they were dropping down again causing me to think for a second or two that

our end had come. The ship straightened up and for a pause there was dead silence then the noise of the crew pouring up from below. The captain came up at the double and called for damage reports . . . the communication messdeck received the force of the explosion. Forward of our mess-deck was the paint-store and, below, the compartment which contained the carbide used in practice torpedo heads. The explosion blew in the plates of these compartments, water entered and ignited the carbide which in turn set off the spirits etc., from the paint store and set us on fire. The boat alongside got away very quickly and then we went to our buoy and got the fire under control . . . there was a lot of noise in the oiler immediately after the explosion: they had a crew of Chinese and I remember the pandemonium as they poured out on deck jabbering away at the top of their voices.

There were no casualties and as damage control and fire fighting parties got to grips with the damage and fire a second loud underwater explosion rocked the harbour at 0620, and *Valiant* was seen to be settling by the bow. Four minutes later came yet another explosion and the *Queen Elizabeth* began to heel to starboard.

At a stroke, three human torpedoes of the Italian Light Flotilla had shifted dramatically the balance of naval power in the central and east Mediterranean. The effective fleet was reduced to three cruisers and ten destroyers, but fortunately for the Allies the Italian fleet never exploited their overwhelming advantage. The three human torpedoes, manned by three officers and three ratings of the Light Flotilla, had been launched from their mother submarine *Scirè* at 2000/18th and after waiting at the entrance, entered Alexandria harbour at 0030/19th when the boom gate was opened to allow entry of Admiral Vian's cruisers and destroyers. Through the brilliant exploit of this small Italian formation, the Mediterranean fleet was brought to the nadir of its existence.

Jervis entered Gabarri drydock on the 21st; a few days later *Valiant* was able to enter the floating dock, but it was to be some time before the more seriously damaged flagship could be moved for temporary repairs.

On 24th December the Eighth Army re-entered Benghazi, giving the crippled fleet a near impossible task to keep supplies moving along the sea flank in the face of increasing Axis submarine activity and at the same time to oppose the passage of enemy convoys to North Africa. Malta was undergoing the mounting ordeal of air raids, somehow supplies had to be fought through to the beleaguered island always under threat of invasion.

These problems notwithstanding, nothing seemed to interfere

with the celebration of Christmas in *Jervis* down at the bottom of the noisome Gabbari docks. Following the traditional rounds of the mess-decks by Philip Mack and his entourage, the wardroom relaxed with a hilarious game of charades. Captain (D) was in the midst of his impersonation of a German Tiger tank to a delighted audience when the wardroom door opened to reveal a flustered officer of the day announcing the sudden arrival of the Commander-in-Chief. On his heels entered the formidable and respected figure of Sir Andrew Cunningham to greet his old friend who was disguised in a cardboard costume created by Philip Mack and his indefatigable and lion-hearted steward, Petty Officer Quick. Quite unabashed Captain (D) introduced Admiral Cunningham to his officers and then asked him to take a seat to witness the end of the charade, before being conducted aft to the captain's day cabin where the hard pressed C-in-C relaxed for a while with his confidant.

Jervis remained in Gabbari dock for all but three days of January 1942. This was due to the slow progress made by the dockyard workforce; its men mainly Maltese – alarmed by the air raids and warning of raids – frequently fled from the bottom of the dock.

Every opportunity was taken to give leave to the ship's company. Those who during the last spell in drydock had not gone to Cairo now all went and enjoyed a break living in luxurious Nile houseboats. There were expeditions on the great river, a day at the races and picnics, all hosted by members of the Egyptian Royal Household. By a strange gentlemen's agreement between enemies, there was no bombing of either Rome or Cairo, nor was there any blackout in these cities. The horse-shoe bar in Jolly's hotel was a favoured rendezvous for the sailors on leave and the many New Zealanders who celebrated the navy's feats in pulling them out of Greece and Crete.

For those who remained in Alexandria leave was given for short stays in a rest camp at Sidi Bishr, while in the city, Pastrudi's and the Union Bar were favoured ports of call for the denizens of the wardroom. In Alexandria among the 'military' targets destroyed or damaged in the air raids were some of the 'approved' bordellos, notably two run by Mrs Mary – one in the Sister Street area for other ranks and the other – up town – for officers. Casualties were suffered by staff and clients, but with commendable speed replacement premises were commissioned and functioning to satisfy the 'frantic' needs of officers and men. In addition to their primary purpose, simple fodder such as fried eggs and cold beer could be obtained and the establishments were used very much as clubs to meet shipmates and friends from other ships.

Lieutenant (A/S) John Mosse who had relieved Lieutenant G.O. Symonds as the flotilla anti-submarine warfare officer visited the premises with two other wardroom colleagues after a local cinema show, seeking beer and eggs:

> We were sitting in the bar drinking beer when a young soldier descended the stairs strapping on his Sam Browne belt. As he reached the bottom step, he turned to his colleague and said, 'D'you know old boy I believe I could do that again? – My God I can!' and retraced his steps at full speed upstairs. The Eighth Army was obviously fighting fit and Mary's house was back in business.

The puppy Snowball had grown into adulthood, he was also enjoying the period in drydock and accompanied the ship's postman, Leading Seaman C.D.Jacobs, on his many walks through the dockyard to deliver and collect mail. Snowball also made many excursions alone into the yard seeking the bitches which strayed in from the city; his randiness became a byword, the emaciated pariah dogs of the port were no match for the well fed, groomed and pampered Snowball who was not particular about the sex of his temporary partner – he never failed to return on time for his meals or for 'pipe down'. He had acquired a further characteristic which delighted the sailors – he growled and showed his teeth at all officers.

On 7th January *Kelvin* returned to the 14th Flotilla after completing repairs in Bombay, and five days later, *Kimberley* left the flotilla and station via the Canal to have her torpedo-damage refit.

The situation in the desert was again deteriorating and, because of the near demise of the British Mediterranean fleet, the Italians were running regular supply convoys into Tripoli and other North African ports, bringing strong reinforcements to General Rommel's desert army. Malta, under constant aerial bombardment, was in desperate straits, supplies were only trickling in and then only during the new moon periods of each month. These came solely because of the heroic efforts of the men who manned the overworked *Breconshire*. Operation Crusader because of the shortfall of supplies had lost its impetus, the forward units of the Eighth Army west of Benghazi were once again in retreat.

This was the grim situation when *Jervis* undocked on 28th January in gale force NW winds gusting to storm force. Clumsy handling by the dockyard tugs nearly put the destroyer back into dry dock. In gathering darkness the helpless ship barged around the harbour, narrowly missing a violent collision with the stranded *Queen Elizabeth*, before the tugs finally berthed her on the coaling jetty where her repairs were to be completed. There were still many leaks forward, and engine-room defects outstanding, and when the dockyard hands were informed that unless these were made good they would have to *sail in the ship* to finish off their work, there was an immediate attempt to break out of the ship. This was stopped in the engine-room by Engineer Commander Ruddy who armed his stokers and gave them orders to shoot any workman attempting to leave. Captain Mack quickly endorsed this order and directed armed sentries to be placed with similar authority at the hatch leading down to the forward miscellaneous mess and paint store. As soon as he was advised of the situation, the C-in-C confirmed these stern and uncompromising orders. Captain Mack addressed the Maltese dockyard men: 'I am not satisfied with your work and no one is to leave this ship until it is done properly, the Commander-in-Chief has given me the authority to shoot any of you who attempt to leave my ship.'

In hurricane force winds which required the use of hurricane hawsers to hold the ship at her berth, *Jervis* completed repairs and re-ammunitioned. The wind was now coming off the desert: sand blacked out the sun and penetrated everywhere making breathing a problem at the same time causing suicidal despair to the 'Buffer', Petty Officer Fagg, as he watched the driving sand ruin the recently renewed paintwork of his ship. While in dock *Jervis* had been repainted in a new and experimental livery designed to reduce her visibility and silhouette, she now had a white painted superstructure and upperworks with a dark grey hull.

Jervis put to sea on 3rd February with every available destroyer to hunt submarines suspected to be in the vicinity of the seaward end of the swept channel. Then followed a day and a night in high seas attacking every suspect contact with depth charges but no positive results: one man was swept to his death from *Jaguar* in the turbulent seas.

On 13th February the cruisers and destroyers set off to escort three deeply laden ships for Malta and to bring back *Breconshire* and three empty supply ships. The Italians were passing convoys through to North Africa with less than a 9% loss of men and stores. The Allied convoy consisting of ss *Clan Campbell* and ss *Clan Chattan* both 7225 tons (convoy section MW 9A) plus ss *Rowallan Castle* 7798 tons (section MW 9B) came to be a 100% failure, none of the supply ships reached Malta. The following account of the five day operation is an extract from Able Seaman John Ellis's diary who was at his action station on No 3, 4.7″ mounting and without any privileged knowledge of the operation objectives or tactics, set down his experiences.

Convoy MW 9A escorted by *Carlisle,* one fleet and three Hunt class destroyers followed by MW 9B escorted by four Hunt class sailed ahead of Force B consisting of three cruisers with Rear Admiral Philip Vian's flat in *Naiad* and *Jervis* leading eight fleet destroyers. Ellis wrote:

Feb. 13th Friday. Slip and proceed to sea, at 0130 starboard watch close up to 3rd degree of readiness. Port watch closed up at 0400. *Jervis* in company with *Kipling, Kelvin, Jaguar, Griffin, Havock, Hotspur* and the cruisers *Naiad, Euryalus* and *Dido* covering a convoy to Malta, catch up with the convoy of three merchant ships, at 0600 .

14th February Convoy escorted by six Hunt class and the *Lance* and AA cruiser *Carlisle,* are being attacked by aircraft. One big merchant ship (*Clan Campbell*) bombed and taken into Tobruk with a near miss damage. We carry on with two merchant ships and an escort of 19 warships, enemy aircraft fly around shadowing us all day long.

We ping a Sub and drop depth charges, pass several floating mines on the starboard beam. Attacked by aircraft, Ju88's and Stukas, action stations from 1330 to 1800 dusk. Dive bombed all through the night aided by dropping flares, one merchantship (*Clan Chattan*) hit and set on fire, sinking fast. *Carlisle* and one Hunt stand by to rescue the crew, we carry on with 1 merchant ship.

Feb. 15th Sunday about 0530, sighted on the horizon, another convoy of empty ships coming from Malta. Four merchantships escorted by seven destroyers and 1 x 6″ cruiser *Aurora,* now 27 warships and five merchantmen. Malta force take the loaded one (*Rowallan Castle*) to Malta and use the four empties back to Alex.

Decoy and *Lance* come with our force. We are continuously being dive bombed whilst the convoys are changing over. The merchant ship that was on fire is torpedoed by *Decoy.* Shrapnel is falling down on us like rain, several are hurt, a stick of bombs from Stukas drops near our stern and shakes the ship from stem to stern.

When darkness falls the German bombers keep dropping some hundreds of flares and bomb us endlessly. The sea is all lighted up making a beautiful picture together with Ack-Ack fire especially the Breda colours.

We remain at action stations all night, *Jervis* repels and avoids several torpedo bomber attacks. We then fire at the flares and try to put them out.

The loaded ship with the Malta force is dive bombed and sunk. All next day attacked by Ju88's, one bomb drops near our stern again and when exploded sea water is showered all over our gun shield.

At 1600, three torpedo bombers come in very low and almost catch us by surprise. Captain goes full ahead, I saw torpedoes leave the plane, being the tray worker I cling to the grip and tray, for I thought we'd had it, but the torpedoes I think passed under us, could see planes and crews plainly, all guns in action. Very lucky that was.

Savoia bombers come in and machine gun us, but no casualties, we drive them off then our fighter planes arrive from Africa and shoot them down. The empty *Breconshire* together with some destroyers and the cruisers go into Alex, but we with *Jaguar, Kelvin* and *Kipling* pass by with the other empty merchantships to Port Said.

Monday 16th at 1640 arrive at P. Said, people waving to us. *Jervis* anchors by Ferdinand de Lessop's statue with bows pointing towards the canal. Watch ashore have meals in Piccadilly tea room then drinking in a cabaret.

The following day, the 17th, with *Kipling* in company, *Jervis* sailed at 1540 from Port Said escorting at 19 knots the fast ss *Princess Marguerite* carrying troops and stores to Famagusta. After a day in port, when the two destroyers played each other in a football match the ships were back in Alexandria on the 20th. Next day *Sikh* (Captain St J.A. Micklethwaite) left the 14th Flotilla to become the leader of the 22nd FDF.

From 0800/22nd *Jervis* took her turn as duty destroyer at 20 minutes' notice and secured to the duty destroyer buoy by a slip rope. Then at 1000 a stunned ship's company became aware that Captain Philip Mack was being landed as a sick man, sent to hospital by Doc. The flotilla navigating officer, Lieutenant-Commander J.B. Laing, assumed command, *Jervis* became a private ship and *Kelvin* assumed the role of 14th DF leader.

Fortunately for Laing the duty destroyer was not required, so he had 48 hours to settle in to his new responsibilities. On the 23rd *Jervis* put to sea with *Kipling* and the Greek submarine *Triton* for exercises with torpedoes.

All destroyers in the fleet received a copy of a signal date/time group, 1803B/24th from the C-in-C addressed to RAD Med. Headed – Destroyers Med, Allocation. The signal redeployed the available destroyers into three flotillas, the 14th DF from the 24th would consist of: *Jervis* (D), *Kelvin, Kipling, Kingston* (undergoing repairs in Malta), *Jaguar, Jackal, Kimberley*, His Hellenic Majesty's Ship *Queen Olga* and *Janus* (completing repairs in Simonstown). The

Queen Olga was commanded by a genial and courageous Commander Blessas who was in addition to being a highly professional seaman was also an international bridge champion. His destroyer was a British built H class of the 1934 programme, she had been armed by the Greeks with a German fire control system and four German 5″ guns. The ship had only two outfits of 5″ ammunition, one in her magazines and the other ashore in the ammunition depot in Alexandria. The expenditure of her main armament ammunition in action was to cause a long term headache for the flotilla gunnery department. It had to organise search parties who followed the ebb-and-flow of desert fighting, seeking overrun or captured enemy ammo dumps for replenishments for *Queen Olga*'s magazines.

The Greeks were to prove to be popular flotilla mates, their gaiety and somewhat casual discipline disguised what was in fact a highly efficient and courageous ship's company. In spite of their sufferings at the hands of both the Italian and German invaders and aching worries for families and friends left behind, the Greeks found it possible to find in laughter and song a way to ease their sorrow.

The 22nd Flotilla, under the leadership of *Sikh*, contained *Zulu, Legion, Lance, Lively, Havock, Hasty* and *Hero*. All the newly arrived Hunt class were formed into a recreated 5th Flotilla.

Between 25th February and 2nd March, *Jervis* made two round passages to Tobruk, first with *Queen Olga* as senior ship of the escort and the second with *Zulu* in charge. Both convoy runs were heavily bombed and a bad sand storm complicated navigation on the first run. A small coaster was near missed entering Tobruk but succeeded in being beached. Its cargo was later salvaged.

The Italians had successfully run three convoys between 1st and 9th March into Tripoli and the re-occupied Benghazi, bringing tank replacements to the German and Italian armoured regiments. An Italian cruiser was reported to have been damaged by the RAF so, on the 9th, Force B put to sea from Alexandria. *Naiad* (Rear Admiral Vian), *Euryalus* and *Dido* with nine destroyers including *Jervis*, the force was also required to meet the cruiser *Cleopatra* and the *Kingston* coming from Malta. The report of a torpedoed Italian cruiser proved to be false, so, after meeting up with *Cleopatra* the force turned back to return to Alexandria. In a position north of the Gulf of Sollum *U-565* (Lieutenant Jebson) torpedoed Admiral Vian's flagship *Naiad* which sank in very few minutes.

Jervis, Kipling and *Lively* were detached to pick up survivors while the other destroyers hunted for the U-boat, the other cruisers carried on at high speed for Alexandria. Laing brought *Jervis* – her sides draped with Flotta scrambling nets and ladders, her port whaler lowered to the waterline – slowly into the centre of the main group of survivors, dimly seen in the darkening, oily stinking sea.

John Ellis, had just come off watch having spent the 'last dog' at the wheel. He carried on down to the canteen flat when Petty Officer 'Duggy' Garrett raced past shouting: 'Come on, Ellis – life boat's crew immediately – in you go – bowman, *Naiad*'s been torpedoed and sunk.'

> I was only wearing overalls and no lifebelt, I had to go, did not want to face a court martial . . . we slip the whaler to pick up survivors in pitch black darkness . . . the skipper shouts, 'Don't pick up too many at a time, return to the ship and go back for more'. . . . This we do, our first load 25 or 30 or so. Duggy calls out, 'Come on Ellis, pull away' but heavy sea and so many coughing up fuel, groaning and grunting I had difficulty. I say to Duggy, 'Any water your end?', evidently the plug had been kicked out so we begin to sink, survivors clinging to gunnels. . . *Jervis* comes to find us and nearly rams. As we secure captain shouts, 'Cast off, sub being pinged in the area!' . . . I pull inboard an American commander, 3 rings and a star, the boat nearly overturns, he says choking, 'Thank God for the efficiency of the British Navy'. We row back to the ship again and get the survivors out of the boat and it hoisted, then help others up the scrambling nets. I am covered from head to toe with oil.

William (Bill) Skilling, a 'hostilities only' (HO) able seaman joined *Jervis* in December after she had entered drydock, and was witnessing his first sinking of a ship: 'I can never forget seeing the huge, dark shape of the tilting, sinking *Naiad* against the last light of the western sky.'

Bill Skilling with others climbed down the nets to help men out of the water and up inboard; struggling in the mass of oil and wreckage, he saw the fair hair of a boy seaman who seemed to be in a bad way. As he reached out to grab the boy the net gave way and a mass of grass rope and cork fell onto Bill and the boy whom he held in his arms. He struggled clear: other *Jervis* men roped the two and hauled them up the ship's side, but the young boy died in Bill's arms as they were lifted clear of the sea.

Standing on the iron deck, in the darkness, covered with black clinging boiler fuel, Bill was given a blanket and ushered forward, unrecognisable, to be given a tot of 'neaters' with the *Naiad* survivors. His leg was pulled mercilessly when his messmates later found him out.

Out of a ship's company of 620, *Naiad* lost two officers and 75 ratings. Admiral Vian was among the survivors, and immediately raised his flag in the newly arrived *Cleopatra*.

Captain Mack returned to *Jervis* on the 15th, but with the news that he was leaving the 14th Flotilla, he was to return to England and his relief was to be Captain A.L. (Patsy) Poland. In the four days left to him Philip Mack went the rounds making his farewells. The chief and petty officers of *Jervis* dined their captain at a restaurant in Alexandria and, on the night before he left, the staff and ship's officers 'dined him out'. It was a memorable wardroom evening of laughter tinged with regrets that a great seaman and leader was leaving the flotilla and the fleet. John Mosse, the most recently joined staff officer, wrote:

> Captain Mack was a giant among men. He simply exuded confidence among all who met him and did much to foster in the destroyer command a spirit of dedication that can only be compared to Nelson's celebrated 'Band of Brothers'.

His friend and Commander-in-Chief, Sir Andrew Cunningham, later expressed his feelings at Philip Mack's departure with a lengthy appreciation in his autobiography *A Sailor's Odyssey*, an extract is quoted which encapsulates the recollections of many who served under Captain Mack's command:

> Everyone was fond of Philip Mack and went to him for advice if in difficulty or trouble. I am not unduly sentimental; but few men have inspired in me such admiration and personal affection. In all respects he was a grand man, a fine officer, a fighting seaman of the very first quality with the supreme knack of making himself loved, respected and trusted.

Admiral Cunningham also recalled: 'At sea, while changing the destroyer screen, the *Jervis* often passed close down the side of *Warspite* and Mack's large weather-beaten face and broad smile acted as a tonic to us all.'

Philip Mack in May was appointed to command the battleship *King George V* and as such was Flag Captain to Sir John Tovey, C-in-C Home Fleet. Captain Mack handled *KG V* with panache and as if the great ship was a destroyer; something to be remembered by all who witnessed his manoeuvring at sea or in harbour.

He was promoted to Rear Admiral in January 1943, but tragically in April he was killed in an air crash, when flying out to North Africa.

CHAPTER FIVE

Failures – then Resurgence

Captain A.L. Poland, affectionately known as 'Patsy' by friends and colleagues, came to the command of the 14th Flotilla at a crucial time but supported by a wealth of personal professional naval experience and skills. Before the outbreak of war he had had a number of training assignments: there followed a testing sea appointment, command of the sloop *Black Swan* during the hideous trauma of the 1940 campaign in Norway. Then came the evacuation from the continent and patrols in the winter-blasted Western Approaches before arriving in the Mediterranean to operate off the Libyan coast.

He was a worthy though less extrovert successor to Philip Mack; he came to *Jervis* without a leave break or any kind of rest period from his previous appointment as Senior Officer, Inshore Squadron, which had consisted of a sojourn of many months in the port of Tobruk. His unflappable professionalism and modest personality had made a lasting impression on hundreds of soldiers of all ranks, Australian, New Zealand, Greek, Polish, Indian and men from many home regiments who had formed the garrison of the desert port.

Immediately on joining *Jervis* he sent for the flotilla staff officers and with his special brand of unassuming modesty, told them that as he was out of touch with destroyer operations, he would have to lean heavily on his staff for support. Forty hours later he was showing these same officers and the flotilla, the K's in particular, that he had not forgotten the principles of a fighting destroyer leader.

Throughout February and March the enemy had continued to pass – unhindered by an emasculated Mediterranean fleet – escorted convoys into their North Africa ports. The Italian Fleet, after its resounding defeat in the battle of Cape Matapan was showing an aggressive rebirth of confidence as each reinforcement convoy reached its destination. The sea between the Cyrenaica bulge, Crete and Greece was completely dominated by airfields from which operated Italian and German air squadrons, all expert in anti-ship attacks. Malta was in dire straits, civilian feeding stations had been set up and the island was under constant air attack. A much reduced Force H based on Gibraltar had succeeded in flying only sixteen Spitfire fighters off the aircraft carrier *Eagle* to assist the island's air defences. They were all shot down within 48 hours. No store ships had accompanied the air reinforcement operation so it was imperative that another attempt to bring in supplies should come from the east.

On the forenoon of 20th March, Convoy MW10 set off from Alexandria loaded with 26,000 tons of stores to feed the garrison and civilian population as well as ammunition replenishments and fuel. The convoy consisted of HMS *Breconshire*, ss *Clan Campbell*, ss *Pampas* and a Norwegian, mv *Talabot*, with a close escort, the veteran and expert anti-aircraft cruiser *Carlisle* and six Hunt class destroyers of the 5th Flotilla. In the evening *Jervis* (which had been berthed on *Jaguar* at 38 quay) sailed and, after passing the boom, proceeded at full speed leading the three K's, *Kelvin*, *Kipling* and *Kingston* to join Rear Admiral Vian and the 15th Cruiser Squadron.

When the 14th DF joined the covering force at dawn, Admiral Vian's ships and the convoy were under intense attack from bombers and torpedo-carrying aircraft arriving in relays from the desert airfields. The covering force consisted of *Cleopatra* (Flag), *Euryalus*, *Dido* and eleven fleet destroyers including the four 14th DF ships. In preparation against the possibility of an intervention by the Italian fleet, CS15 had divided the force into six divisions, the sixth being *Carlisle* and her Hunt class destroyers with the convoy.

Much to the surprise of everybody, a quiet night, 21st/22nd March followed, but from dawn Sunday, waves of aircraft attacked the convoy and escort. Five Stukas were shot down by *Carlisle* and the Hunts. The afternoon became overcast and stormy, the sea getting rougher by the hour as a gale from the south-east gained strength and severity. The air attacks continued; then a plane on the northern horizon was seen to be dropping groups of four red flares, a clear indication to Admiral Vian that units of the Italian fleet were in the offing; not long afterwards at 1510, three enemy cruisers were sighted. The 6th Division was ordered immediately to shepherd the convoy southward, deeper into the Gulf of Sirte making smoke as they went, while Admiral Vian also making smoke interposed his cruisers and destroyers between the convoy's line of retreat and the enemy ships. The Italians turned away intent on drawing the British ships from the convoy towards the oncoming Italian Commander-in-Chief, his flag in the battleship *Littorio*.

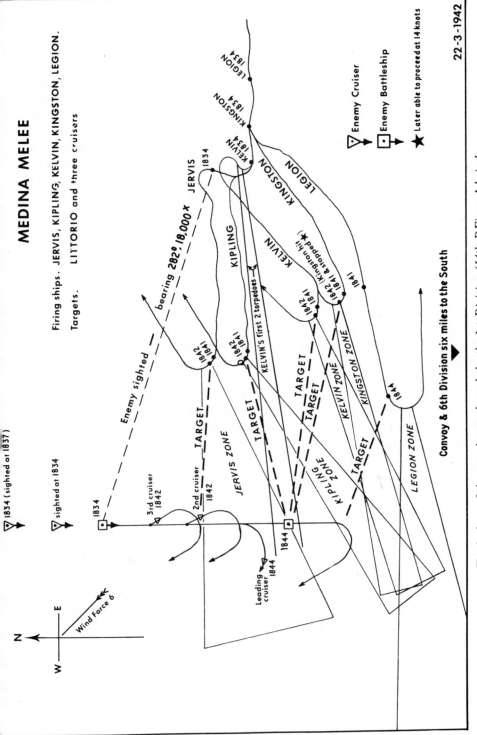

MEDINA MELEE

Firing ships. JERVIS, KIPLING, KELVIN, KINGSTON, LEGION.

Targets. LITTORIO and three cruisers

22-3-1942

1834 (sighted at 1837)

sighted at 1834

Wind Force 6

N
W — E

Enemy sighted

bearing 282°.18,000 x JERVIS

1834

LEGION 1834

KINGSTON 1834

KELVIN 1834

KIPLING

JERVIS ZONE

KIPLING ZONE

KELVIN ZONE

KINGSTON ZONE

LEGION ZONE

KELVIN's first 2 torpedoes

(Kingston hit)
(1842 & 3 stopped)

1842
1841

1842
1841

1842
1841

1842
1841

1842
1841

1841

1841

1844

3rd cruiser
1842

2nd cruiser
1842

Leading
cruiser
1844

1844

TARGET

TARGET

TARGET

TARGET

TARGET

TARGET

TARGET

Convoy & 6th Division six miles to the South

Enemy Cruiser

Enemy Battleship

Later able to proceed at 14 knots

Track chart of the torpedo attack made by the 1st Division (14th DF) on Admiral Iachino's heavy ships in what was called by those who took part, The Medina Mêlée.

At 1520 all the British ships had hoisted their battle ensigns to the masthead and while they pitched and yawed at high speed into battle, rather incongruously, John Ellis and others of No 3 gun mounting's crew were set to, painting a wide ring in red paint on their gundeck – identification for 'own' aircraft in the unlikely event of their appearance to assist in the convoy operation.

The Second Battle of Sirte has been well documented, praised and described in many works notably, in Roskill's *The War at Sea* and Admiral of the Fleet Viscount Cunningham of Hyndhope's autobiography, *A Sailor's Odyssey*. It will therefore serve if this account centres on the recollections of those who served in *Jervis* when she led the 1st Division and the three K's into battle.

It was a classic battle in which Admiral Vian's force was heavily out gunned by the 8″ gun cruisers *Gorizia* and *Trento*, the 6″ gun *Banda Nere* and four destroyers. These cruisers, commanded by divisional Admiral Parona continued to draw the British ships towards the nine 15″ guns of *Littorio* accompanied by three more destroyers.

The British ships were able to use the gale force SE wind to their advantage by laying a dense smoke screen that masked their movements and that of the convoy which the Italian Admiral tried to skirt, for he was fearful of entering the smoke and risking Admiral Vian's torpedoes. In this way the British held off the Italians for three remaining hours of daylight and until the Italian C-in-C eventually withdrew to the north. Before this happened, a critical phase developed at 1730 when the enemy ships got dangerously close to the convoy but were brilliantly headed off by the 5th Division, *Sikh* (Captain Micklethwaite) *Lively, Hero* and *Havock*. In the encounter *Havock* was badly damaged by a 15″ shell near miss in her boiler room forcing the destroyer to fall back onto the convoy. *Sikh* and her tiny division continued to engage the enemy with gun and torpedo at the same time extending the smoke screen across the convoy, forcing the Italians to turn away – but not before *Sikh* had been straddled by a salvo from *Littorio*'s 15″. Captain Micklethwaite was so certain that his ship would be destroyed by the next salvo that he ordered his last two torpedoes to be fired as he did not want to sink with any unfired: miraculously the shells did not come. *Littorio* had trained her turrets away to engage Admiral Vian and his cruisers coming out of the smoke to fire at the battleship at 13,000 yard range before falling back into the smoke barrier in support of the destroyers. The flagship *Cleopatra* had one 6″ hit on her bridge causing casualties including some killed.

At 1808 *Jervis* led the 1st Division, reinforced by *Legion*, toward the enemy at 28 knots. At this speed in the gale force wind and high seas, the destroyers were swept from end to end by breaking seas, guard rails went and boats were smashed as men clung for their lives at their action stations. At 1834 the range of *Littorio* was down to 12,000 yards and the destroyers were subjected to heavy gunfire but the sea conditions and dense smoke screen upset the accuracy of the Italian fire. *Jervis* closed the range to three miles before Captain Poland gave the order 'Turn to starboard to fire torpedoes'; the five destroyers turned together to present a combined torpedo broadside to a massed barrage of 6″, 8″ and 15″ guns from the enemy ships.

John Mosse recalls his part in the action:

My action station was on the plot, I was passed ranges and bearings of the enemy when visible and kept an estimated track of his movement when he was hidden by smoke. At speed and in rough weather there was a lot of vibration, and once when we fired a broadside all the lights went out including the projection compass rose on the underside of the glass table. There were frantic demands thro' the bridge voice-pipe for enemy movements and we had to improvise with a torch. Now it was our turn . . . the ship heeled over, everything rattled and a voice behind me said, 'Have a toffee!' It landed on the plot and I chewed it ravenously. The Padre had bought a bag of sweets from the canteen and was distributing them as tranquillisers to all and sundry. We discharged 25 torpedoes and beat a hasty retreat making more smoke. By all the rules we should have been blown out of the water – only *Kingston* received damage.

John Ellis later wrote in his diary:

As we came through the smoke I ask the officer on our gun, 'What is that great big thing?' He replied, 'A *Littorio* class battleship!' – What a shock. . . During the action the ship's tabby cat had kittens in the wardroom and for some reason she insists on carrying them onto the upper-deck . . . *Kingston*, second in the line is damaged. Our No 1 gun shield is battered in, all the guardrails and several washdeck lockers are swept over the side. Motor cutter shattered and upside down in her davits. Mess-decks flooded . . .

Euryalus and *Lively* had both received slight splinter damage before the enemy ships under the enveloping darkness, turned away north to return to base. On passage two Italian destroyers, *Lanciere* and *Sicorocco* foundered in the storm with heavy loss of life. Admiral Vian's force set course for Alexandria while the convoy resumed its course for Malta. Because of the three hours lost in taking evasive

courses it was now no longer possible for the convoy to arrive at
Malta and to berth under the cover of darkness which was the
original operation plan – the convoy was doomed; the Italian fleet
had indirectly achieved its objective.

At daybreak on the 23rd, bombers from the German Air Corps 11
FlK attacked the convoy; *Clan Campbell* was sunk right away,
Breconshire badly damaged and beached, capsizing later after further
hits. The Hunt class destroyer *Southwold* sank on an enemy mine,
Legion had to be beached after a near miss (later destroyed on the
26th after more attacks). *Pampas* and *Talabot* managed to enter
harbour but on the same day were hit by bombs and sunk at their
berths – only 5000 out of the original 26,000 tons embarked in the
convoy came ashore. The already badly damaged *Kingston* was also
hit by a bomb after entering harbour and some days later while
undergoing repairs finally destroyed in a raid on the dockyard.

The men in the ships returning to Alexandria knew nothing of the
convoy's fate; John Ellis's recorded in his diary:

> *Monday 23rd* – Full speed in heavy weather – air attacks off and on all day
> – baling out messdecks.
> *Tuesday 24th* – Entering harbour, tugs come out to greet us, all ships
> including the battleships (the damaged and immobile *QE* and *Valiant*)
> clear lower decks, sirens blowing, even the French battleship *Lorraine*
> gives us three cheers. Berth on No 38 quay – 'Guts' Cunningham comes
> inboard.

John Mosse also wrote:

> The force was greeted with heartening cheers and sirens from every ship
> in harbour. Hardly had we secured alongside and Captain Poland had
> started to relax in a well earned bath when Admiral Cunningham
> appeared at the gangway. I happened to be nearby and sent a panic
> message to the captain and tried to engage the C-in-C in conversation
> until Poland rushed up still buttoning himself up.

The flotilla had another loss on the 26th; *Jaguar* with *Queen Olga* were
escorting a small convoy to Tobruk when one of the convoy ships,
RFA oiler *Slavol* was torpedoed by *U-652*. The ship caught fire and
Jaguar went in alongside to take off the crew while *Queen Olga* carried
out an anti-submarine search. *U-652* struck again and fired two more
torpedoes; both hit *Jaguar* which broke into three parts, sinking
instantly. Only 53 of her ship's company survived and were picked
up by the Greek anti-submarine whaler *Klo*.

Boxing Day 1942. Malta.
Jervis's football team.

Some of 14 mess working on
the ship's cable.

(*Bottom left*) February 1943.
Captain Pugsley (wearing an
old jacket) and OOW
Lieutenant Lacey RNVR.

(*Bottom right*) 17th February
1943. *Paladin* having sunk
U 205 closes to report to
Captain D.

(*Left*) *Jervis* at rest in Alexandria. Note, wind scoops shipped.

(*Left*) March 1943. *Jervis* about to enter Tripoli for the first time. (*Right*) March 1942. Leading hand of the mess. Leading Seaman Sclater.

(*Left*) October 1943. *Petard* with *Jervis* carry Jeeps and trailers to Leros. (*Right*) Leading Seaman K. J. (Jock) Dare. Ship's 'Postie'.

John Ellis noted the sinking in his diary: 'Sadly my best pal Charlie Campbell from Glasgow is lost'.

In the month of April no convoys sailed from Alexandria to Malta, Axis air dominance of the central Mediterranean was total. Force H from Gibraltar did make a couple of successful sorties to fly in fighter replacements for the losses incurred in the heavy air raids, but no supply ships ventured to relieve the island. April proved to be the climax of air attacks on Malta, German bombers alone in the month made 4082 day and 256 night attacks. In the dockyard three destroyers *Gallant, Kingston* (both 14th DF) and *Lance* were bombed to destruction, a minesweeper, three submarines and an oiler were sunk, the cruiser *Penelope* damaged repeatedly. *Aurora*, her mine damage repaired, managed to sail and got clear to Gibraltar but *Havock* damaged in the 2nd Battle of Sirte and trying to escape westward ran aground and was torpedoed by the Italian submarine *Aradam*.

The Italian fleet, in spite of sinkings by British and Allied submarines, continued to convoy supply ships into Benghazi and Tripoli, supporting the continuing advance of the Afrika Korps.

The 14th Flotilla escorted a patched-up *Valiant* to Port Said from where the battleship passed through the Canal for onward passage to her repair port. Then followed several days of exercising and perfecting flotilla attacks by gun and torpedo incorporating lessons learned in the recent encounter with the Italian fleet. On 17th April *Janus* returned from her refit at Simonstown and rejoined the flotilla. From the 23rd *Jervis* and her flotilla were engaged on a further round of 'Carter Paterson' duties conveying troops between Haifa and Cyprus, a task made more hazardous because of minelaying activities by enemy submarines and destroyers off Famagusta. The week of non-stop ferrying duty concluded with the destroyers returning to Alexandria loaded with Cyprus potatoes for the fleet.

Into May the flotilla continued to observe a passive role. On the 4th *Jackal* with repairs completed rejoined the flotilla. Then on 10th, *Jervis, Jackal, Kipling* and *Lively* were sent off on Operation MG2 to intercept a reported southbound Italian escorted convoy of three German and one Italian supply ships bound for Benghazi. Captain (D) had orders to turn back if his ships were sighted by enemy aircraft. The destroyers had an escort of four Beaufighters for part of the 11th but in late afternoon when the last flight of Beaufighters had returned to base and the destroyers had steamed beyond the range of a relieving patrol, Captain Poland's ships were being closely shadowed. Obeying his operational orders, D14 at 1640 reversed course and with his destroyers in a loose diamond formation, set course at high speed for Alexandria.

Then came Stuka Ju87's from their Crete airfields, especially trained and expert in anti-ship attacks. John Mosse:

> We were moving at high speed . . . and *Lively* was first to be hit for'ard. Her speed drove her under, bows first. The sea was warm and calm and all the men in the water were picked up by the other three ships, mostly by scrambling nets. Her CO, Cdr Bill Hussey, a personal friend, floated off the bridge and thus he became separated from the rest of his ship's company who jumped from aft. I saw him waving and waved back, also gave him some encouragement by loud hailer, but it was some minutes before we were able to move over and pick him up. He was unconscious but not visibly injured. I had previous success in restoring the apparently drowned, but sadly all efforts failed, despite attempts by our hard pressed doctor to give him oxygen.

Several of *Jervis's* men including Bill Skilling went over the side to help their exhausted flotilla mates, Bill back inboard covered in oil fuel was spotted by his petty officer, Mick Myers, and given a ribald warning not to queue up with survivors for an extra tot ration. Boy Vic Merry had helped to pull in survivors, his oilskin had been taken to cover injured, lying on the iron-deck, waiting for attention from the Doctor and his tiffy.

John Mosse continues with his recollection of the incident:

> Further waves of bombers came shortly after sunset, *Kipling* (Cdr Aubrey St Clair-Ford) was sunk and then *Jackal* was hit and disabled. Once again the sea was covered with survivors and despite many near misses *Jervis* was unscathed. We called to the men in the water to remain in groups and told them by loud hailer that we would return and pick them up after dark.

These men were then subjected to repeated machine gun attacks. John Moss continues:

> Meanwhile we withdrew to a short distance taking violent evasive action until the last of the bombers went home. Later we returned and picked up the survivors, some of whom had been sunk twice. A few of the carley floats and ship's life belts had phosphorescent flares attached – these were an embarrassment because they could not be extinguished. It was necessary to weight them. When all survivors had been picked up including the COs, we took the stricken *Jackal* in tow, we made very slow

progress and could not get under the air umbrella by daylight, so we took off her crew and torpedoed her. We had lost 112 men in the three ships. *Jervis* was now heavy and sluggish* in the water with her 630 survivors in addition to her ship's company of 220 plus.

John Ellis in his diary notes one special and personal cameo:

We pick up *Kipling* survivors after about 2½ hours in the water, amongst them are previous survivors from the *Lively*, whilst they were in the water German aircraft dropped bombs amongst them. Scrambling nets are down, all *Jervis*'s sailors available are jumping in the water assisting them up, one survivor I pulled out was an old school mate. I didn't know until the oil fuel had been washed off him. I rig him out with a set of clothes at about 2400 . . . so we slip the tow and proceed away roughly two miles and torpedo poor *Jackal* (very sad) she goes up in flames and settles down to the sea bed. Meanwhile help has been sent for, about 0400, two Hunts arrive to protect us then later another Hunt. *Sikh* and *Hasty* join the escort with *Jervis* in the centre. Lots of survivors die on board us, our ensign at half mast all day, ever more are dying and are buried during the forenoon. Captain Hussey of *Lively* receives artificial respiration from us but dies and is buried; everyone in tears, it's been such a bad time. Captain Jellicoe of the *Kipling* was picked up and conducts the services . . . We arrive Alex pm Tuesday 12th May go alongside 46 shed; crowds are waiting on the jetty, lots of ambulances and nurses, mainly South African. The police form a barrier to keep the onlookers away.

Previously in the middle watch, Boy Seaman Vic Merry went along the crowded iron deck to retrieve his oilskin which he had lent to cover a survivor, he found it under the torpedo tubes covering a shape, as he bent down to claim it Coxswain Mortimer's voice came out of the darkness, 'Leave it there, son. He'll not want it much longer now.' It was covering Commander Hussey, waiting for burial. John Mosse's comment on their return to harbour, 'No hero's welcome this time, but *Jervis* had cut another notch in her claim to immortality.'

After working for several hours cleaning ship of oil and debris, Vic Merry recalls that the ship moved to a buoy at twenty minutes' notice for steam, *Jervis* was the duty destroyer. While at the duty destroyer's buoy one member of the ship's company wrote a letter to his father describing his latest experience at sea, which appears in its entirety as Appendix 1 to this book.

*The loss of stability would allow only 5° of helm to be used.

Janus had the misfortune to damage herself on an acoustic mine on 4th June and was taken under repair at Alexandria where it was established that it would take until November to patch her up sufficiently for her to sail to the UK for a complete refit. Her place in the flotilla was taken by *Javelin* (Commander H.C. Simms) which had arrived on station on 9th June after having been almost completely reconstructed.

The flotilla was now down to four active destroyers – *Jervis*, *Kelvin*, *Javelin* and *Queen Olga*. *Kimberley* was still undergoing repair. The Commander-in-Chief was Acting Admiral Sir Henry Harwood, the victor of the River Plate Battle on 13th December 1939. He had hoisted his flag in *Queen Elizabeth* on the 20th May. Admiral Sir Andrew Cunningham, his formidable predecessor – 'Guts' Cunningham to the men of the fleet – had departed secretly and unwillingly to plan the forthcoming Anglo-American landings in French North Africa. He had gone secretly in early April because the Chiefs-of-Staff were fearful of the effect on the morale of the fleet if his departure had been known in advance. The appointment of Admiral Harwood with his River Plate reputation was an attempt to counter this possibility but very soon events would prove to the sailors that the new C-in-C was not in the same league as 'old Guts'.

When it became known that *Janus* was going to be out of action for many months, Michael Hemans organised the stripping-out of her radar equipment which had been installed by the dockyard in Simonstown. *Jervis* at long last possessed a gun-ranging set with its aerials fitted to the DCT, an aircraft and surface warning set with a rotating aerial at the top of her foremast, capable in good conditions of giving a bearing and range of the approaching enemy. Snowball now had an electronic system to back up his acute hearing and sixth sense that had given so much confidence to the ship's veterans.

By the end of May, aircraft carriers, including USS *Wasp*, had flown in 77 fighters to Malta from the west Mediterranean. Of the 47 flown in during April, only six remained serviceable and these new reinforcements were soon to be reduced to dangerous levels. The enemy were laying fresh minefields at night with great frequency off the approaches to the harbours, two submarines of the 10th Flotilla had been sunk by these mines and others sunk or damaged in harbour, and it was decided to withdraw the flotilla to Haifa and Beirut. This action completed for a while the neutralisation of Malta, allowing the Italians to pass convoys just 25 miles to the east of the island; between the 1st April and 13th May the enemy sailed

23 convoys southward without loss and a similar number returning with empty ships. It was imperative that supplies and reinforcements should reach Malta, otherwise the island would be forced to surrender without the need of a full-scale landing by a sea-mounted invasion from Sicily.

Two cruisers had recently arrived in the east, *Arethusa* and *Birmingham*, plus a few destroyers including some from the 12th Flotilla, the P class, to play a part in joint operations from the east and western ends of the Mediterranean sea, Operations Vigorous and Harpoon, both with the objective of fighting supply ships through to Malta.

The eleven ships making up the Vigorous convoy sailed from the ports of Alexandria, Port Said and Haifa in time to be formed up as a single convoy at dawn on 12th June under their commodore R.A. England. The convoy had its own close escort of nine Hunt class of the 5th Flotilla and the AA cruiser *Coventry*. Rear Admiral Philip Vian, with his flag in *Cleopatra*, commanded a covering force made up of eight cruisers and fourteen fleet destroyers of the 7th, 12th 14th and 22nd Flotillas. He had also the old battleship target-ship *Centurion* disguised to represent a modern ship with dummy funnels and turrets but whose main armament consisted only of massed numbers of close-range AA weapons. There were also four MTB's towed by merchant ships in the convoy, destined for Malta.

The convoy soon came under attack south of Crete by Ju87 Stukas of I/KG 54 and one freighter, *City of Calcutta* (8063 tons) was damaged and had to be detached with a corvette as escort and ordered to put into Tobruk.

The convoy from Gibraltar, subject of Operation Harpoon, consisted of five freighters and one oiler. The close escort was on the same scale as for the Vigorous convoy; the AA cruiser *Cairo*, four Hunts and five fleet destroyers, four minesweepers and six motor gunboats. The covering Force W was made up of the old battleship *Malaya* (Flag Vice Admiral Curteis), two ageing aircraft carriers, three cruisers and eight fleet destroyers. The western operation ships passed through the straits of Gibraltar on 12th June; two days out on the 14th, the convoy and covering force came under attack by Italian S79 torpedo bombers, one freighter ss *Tanimbar* (8619 tons) was sunk and the cruiser *Liverpool* hit in the engine-room, had to be towed back to Gibraltar.

Away to the east Vigorous had another set back, as the freighter *Aagtekerk* (6811 tons) developed engine trouble and had also to be sent into Tobruk with two corvettes. On the way the little group was jumped by 40 Ju87 and 88's; the freighter was sunk and one corvette, *Primula*, badly damaged. Meanwhile Ju88's from Crete continued their assault on the convoy, ss *Bhutan* (6104 tons) was sunk and ss *Potaro* (5410 tons) damaged.

After dark six boats of the German 3rd MTB Flotilla attacked the covering force with torpedoes: John Ellis recorded the attack:

> as darkness falls 6 E-boats come in on the port bow and are driven off, but they sneak up to the convoy, torpedo and sink *Hasty*, survivors picked up by a Hunt class. Then the cruiser *Newcastle* is torpedoed making a big hole in her bows.

While this attack was still going on with a night sky filled with drifting flares dropped by enemy aircraft to assist the E-boats, Admiral Vian learned by signal from his C-in-C that the Italian Commander-in-Chief was at sea with two battleships, two heavy and two light cruisers and twelve destroyers steering a course to oppose the advance of his Vigorous convoy.

In the west the Harpoon convoy came under attack from the Italian Admiral Zara's 7th Division of two cruisers and three destroyers. The AA cruiser *Cairo* is hit twice by Italian shells. The cruisers then sank the Tribal class destroyer *Bedouin* and badly damaged the 12th Flotilla ship *Partridge*. While the surface action continued in the Sicilian narrows the convoy was attacked by Ju88's which sank ss *Burdwan* (6069 tons). SS *Chant* (5601 tons) and the American tanker *Kentucky* (9308 tons) were so badly damaged that they were abandoned. The remaining ships of the convoy and escort then ran into a new enemy laid minefield in the Malta approaches. One of the two remaining merchant ships, mv *Orari* (10,350 tons) was damaged, the Polish destroyer *Kujawiak* sunk and another Hunt class *Badsworth* was badly damaged, as was the fleet destroyer *Matchless* and the minesweeper *Hebe*. Just two ships from the six that set out in the Harpoon convoy reached harbour at great cost in men and ships but their arrival was to prove crucial for the island's survival.

From the east none of the eleven ships were to get through; the approach of the Italian fleet and its subsequent manoeuvres, lack of reliable air reconnaissance reports, the worsening weather and sea conditions influenced Admiral Harwood to order Admiral Vian to embark on the intricate evolution of reversing course from west to east. The great armada of merchant vessels and warships reversed course in a night confused with falling flares and under attack from E-boats and torpedo-bombers. The manoeuvre was again repeated at 0655/16th when the C-in-C had decided that the possible threat from the Italian fleet was less than the risks involved by remaining in 'Bomb Alley' between the Cyrenaica bulge and Crete. He hoped optimistically that the Italian fleet would be weakened by attacks from British submarines. However as the enemy fleet remained intact and his own ships were still under intense air bombardment, Admiral Vian for the third and final time turned his force and convoy 180 degrees to retreat eastward. The turn was achieved, using the Admiral's own words, 'Subjected to all forms of attack'. All his ships were low in ammunition: it was to be a humiliating and bloody retirement. The destroyers *Airedale* and *Nestor* were sunk by air attacks; then in the early hours of the 16th before the ships reached Alexandria, the cruiser *Hermione* was sunk by *U-205* (Lt Cdr Reschke) with the loss of 88 officers and men.

Dive-bombing and torpedo assaults were constant and fearful: John Mosse:

> At one stage a torpedo-bomber attacked *Jervis* from the quarter. John Stodart was on the quarter-deck at the time and later described how he was hypnotised as a torpedo chased the ship from astern and passed up along the starboard side – deflected by our wake?

From a total of seventeen merchant ships which had set out from both ends of the Mediterranean, only two reached Malta. The Allies lost one cruiser, five destroyers and six merchantmen. Three cruisers, one AA cruiser, three destroyers, two corvettes and two merchant ships were badly damaged. The enemy lost only one cruiser, *Trento*, initially damaged by a torpedo from a Wellington bomber and then sunk by the submarine *P-35*.

It was an awful period for the long serving *Jervis* ship's company and for all the men who had spent two years or more with the Mediterranean fleet; they had only sketchy knowledge of conditions at home, where air-raids still caused alarm, there was little mail and what did arrive was weeks – often months – old. News that filtered through to the lower-deck of the war with Japan was doom-laden; the Germans continued to advance into Russia; in the Atlantic the battle with U-boats raged and in the West Atlantic, the Caribbean and Gulf of Mexico – where the Americans had not learned from the experience gained by the British in two bitter years – the loss of shipping was horrendous, a virtual killing ground for the U-boat commanders. Closer at hand, the Axis desert army had driven back the Eighth Army from its Gazala/Bir Hacheim line and on 21st June the South African General in command at Tobruk surrendered his garrison and the enemy reached El Alamein by 1st July, where his advance was checked.

Yet, because of the potent chemistry of a close-knit community, professionalism, faith in their ship and its reputation, few men had doubts about their ultimate survival as a fighting unit. Aware that the next departure to sea or the current stay in harbour could end in sudden or horrible death and terrible wounds, most regarded the congested, comfortless messdecks and primitive conditions as an oasis of comradeship and security within the context of an endless and merciless war.

A few days in harbour now followed for the fleet destroyers, which enabled men to find some kind of relaxation in the cosmopolitan atmosphere of Alexandria where the population did not seem unduly alarmed or concerned at the prospect of occupation by the advancing Afrika Korps; if anything they welcomed a probable cessation of air raids.

In contrast, the Fleet's Shore headquarters at Ras el Tin was in a highly disturbed state because of that threat: then followed a precipitous evacuation by rail and road to the southern end of the canal to set up shop at Port Tewfik. In the scramble to clear Alexandria of shipping, *Jervis* and her flotilla became involved, escorting the large ships to the Canal. The first to get away was *Queen Elizabeth* which undocked from the floating dock where the battleship had had a narrow escape from a second attempt by Italian human torpedoes on the night of 14th/15th March to destroy her. This time the 'Sea Devils' launched from the submarine *Ambra* were dazzled by searchlights and swept away from their target by an unexpected westerly set. After seeing *Queen Elizabeth* safely into the Canal on passage to 'Yankee Land' for permanent repairs, the flotilla escorted the 8750 ton destroyer depot ship *Woolwich* to Port Said and on the following day collected *Resource* (12,300 ton fleet repair ship) and four merchant ships carrying priceless armament and electrical stores. The evacuation had – perhaps predictably – one disaster. *Medway* (14,600 ton submarine depot ship) carrying the entire stock of spare torpedoes for the submarines operating in the command was sunk by *U-372* as she approached Port Said. Able Seaman R.T. Taylor who had been sunk in *Gurkha* was now serving in *Hero* as part of the escort graphically describes his experience of the sinking before he joined *Jervis*:

> an officer who had been in *Medway*'s sickbay with hernia trouble was shouting for help, he was way off so I dived in and brought him alongside. He was hauled aboard but I had to submerge and swim away as a Jumbo boat was bearing down on me. When I regained the surface *Hero* was underway, she had a ping and was off to investigate, leaving me and my mess-mate L/S Jackson to swim around, we only hoped that they had plotted our position. Eventually *Zulu* picked us up and transferred us to *Jervis* and back to *Hero* at Haifa to be greeted with 'off caps' for deserting the ship!
>
> Although my first stay in *Jervis* was short I had a feeling that here was a real fighting ship that would overcome any obstacle – what a difference in the two ships *Hero* and *Jervis*. The former had her 'bluebell and polishing rags' and her captain's irritating training-ship orders. I dipped my hook when I and my seamanship training class changed into overalls to re-lay and splice our spring. I hadn't permission to change, I think he had it in for me when I trained the boy's whaler crew and beat the arse off the ship's officers. The *Hero* went home and to my delight I found myself in *Jervis* once more. She was a real fighting ship. Just to look at her riding at anchor filled me with pride and I was part of her . . . the crew did their duty, they were satisfied, no bullshit and gaiters. We were treated like men not like a load of nozzers as in the *Hero*.

Jervis and her reduced flotilla began, for the third time, bombarding familiar targets around Sollum Bay; a depressing factor for the original hard core of her ship's company and something which was not fully appreciated by the wardroom, who had all changed, and by Captain Poland himself. The situation became tense as raids on Port Said became more frequent and heavy, mining of the Canal from the air was also critical, until a plan formulated during Admiral Cunningham's time as C-in-C was adopted. This was to spread nets over the canal at night so that mines dropped from the air could be pinpointed by the rips in the netting.

Jervis then returned to Alexandria where the ship had to endure the torment of successive formal inspections, first by Rear Admiral (D), Rear Admiral I.G. Glennie, followed a few days later by the new Commander-in-Chief, Acting Admiral Sir Henry Harwood.

In the midst of the preparations for the inspections, turning the ship into an object of pristine peacetime naval beauty while maintaining at the same time fighting efficiency, a strange apparition appeared at the shore-end of the ship's brow as she lay at

No 38 quay. The tall, massively built and bearded figure was clothed in a stained army greatcoat of vast proportions and, on his close-cropped head, as if to establish his naval connection he wore a scruffy sailor's blue cap with the letters HMS crudely painted in white paint. He stalked inboard before the astonished eyes of a new and inexperienced officer of the day and his gangway staff, proclaiming loudly that he was Able Seaman Fearnough, recently liberated by General Rommel. He later repeated to an affronted coxswain that General Rommel's advance to El Alamein had forced the authorities to release him and his fellow detainees from the notorious Royal Naval Detention Quarters at Agami.

Fearnough, from Stoke, was one of a special product of the Royal Navy, a senior seaman with twelve or more years of service, a three badge-man (when he had not forfeited them for misdemeanours) from a section of generally highly skilled sailors, who recoiled from the prospect of accepting the responsibility which accompanied promotion, possibly because of idleness or – more frequently – because they were rugged individualists and rebels against the constraints of King's Regulations and Admiralty Instructions, while paradoxically remaining total patriots with a consuming pride in their service.

Many were highly talented, creative and articulate. Fearnough quickly established a court of admirers because of his talent as an actor, his obvious seaman-like skills and as an independent soul existing within the confines of a disciplined service in a war situation. A cork sea-boat life-jacket he always wore at sea instead of the smaller issue inflatable variety was a badge of this independence and eccentricity. He was a tonic to the lower deck – he quickly had a 'Crown and Anchor' board layout inscribed inside his oilskin, his schools became a legend. He showed newly arrived HO seamen how to splice, to throw a heaving line and how to survive within the fetid confines of a destroyer's messdeck. He was the source of every shipboard attempt to produce a concert party or a 'Sods Opera'. When the ship went into action, his cheerful face followed by his great tattooed torso, emerged from the nearest hatch or opening, preceded by his cry, 'Never fear, Rommel's here!' or 'There's blood on the moon'. He had, however, the Jack-ashore appetite for alcohol – rum in particular.

Fearnough's popularity and personality were, however, resented by some in the ship, none more so than the officer who had been present when the 'jail bird' rebel arrived to join *Jervis*. The Potteries man's excursions ashore had been for some time sheltered from the awareness of shipboard senior authority through a conspiracy of collusion by his messmates and some duty petty officers when receiving returning libertymen. Nemesis was nevertheless inevitable: returning from an especially alcoholic based run ashore in Port Tewfik, Fearnough and friends, loaded with Stella beer but in good order and humour – were lined up for inspection by the same OOD. All went well until the diminutive officer reached Fearnough's massive presence gently swaying with eyes closed tight. The little officer yelled in his distinctive accent, 'Are you all right man' – The large seaman replied, 'Yes, sir, but the sun is too bright.' It was midnight in a moonless period. The officer lost all control and screamed that the seaman was being abusive, showing dumb insolence, etc; he was to be placed under open arrest. It rapidly became a situation of no return. Fearnough in one silent movement took a step forward, gigantic and powerful, wrapped his trunk-like arms round his tormentor, carried on to the opposite guardrails and held him, impotent over the harbour water. Nothing worse happened; the duty petty officer took calm charge, and he and the QM staff persuaded the gentle giant to release his hysterical opponent. Then still silent, and showing no resistance he permitted himself to be led away and to be put below under guard in the tiller flat.

Three days later the processes of naval law had taken their irreversible course, a Warrant, recommended by Captain Poland and confirmed by the C-in-C, was read to Fearnough standing in a similiar situation, bare-headed before his lower deck shipmates, standing at attention, also bare-headed. He was sentenced for another long period, but this time to an army run detention camp well away from a possible rescue by his benefactor, General Rommel. A few hours after his departure from *Jervis* under escort, the cause of his latest downfall left the ship for the shore base, HMS *Sphinx*, to await a new appointment.

In July, while no operations were conducted by the Mediterranean fleet's surface ships, its submarines inflicted many sinkings on Italian escorted convoys.

Jervis, based with her flotilla ships, at Port Said, endured the inspections by senior officers and the nightly air raids on the port and Canal. This continued until the 19th when the flotilla sailed to escort the cruisers *Dido* and *Euryalus* for further bombardment attacks on targets and enemy shipping at and near to Mersa Matruh. This was repeated on successive nights in terrible weather and sea conditions, then *Jervis* entered the Canal on her way, to Port Tewfik, for a period in dock which she entered on the 26th. While in this 'fly blown' dock, the opportunity was taken to give as many as possible of the ship's company 48 hours' leave to Cairo. A number could not take leave, because they had been laid low with dysentery and for those who remained aboard to take care of the ship came the alarming experience of being bombed and of very near misses to the drydock – something well known to other ships of the flotilla which had been docked in Malta.

The flotilla gunnery officer, Michael Hemans, had a rare opportunity to have a couple of days' leave with his army brother in Palestine while other members of the wardroom took their leave in Cairo and followed some of the tourist routes to visit the ancient monuments; an unreal expedition for those in the vortex of a world war.

Hull repairs were soon completed; leave over and on 3rd August, *Jervis* was back at Port Said, whence she departed in company with *Coventry* for Beirut. A few days later, off Haifa, the Italian submarine *Scirè* and her specialist crew of torpedo riders was sunk by the anti-submarine trawler *Islay* before they could repeat the mayhem caused in Alexandria in the early hours of 19th December 1941.

The fleet still only consisting of the cruisers *Dido*, *Arethusa*, *Euryalus* and destroyers, recently reinforced by the arrival of the 12th Flotilla Leader *Pakenham* (Captain E.B.K. Stevens), *Jervis* with her depleted flotilla which included one remaining seaworthy 'K', *Kelvin*, sailed as part of Operation MG23, escorting a diversionary convoy of three merchant ships from Port Said on 10th August towards Malta. The departure had been observed and the Italian fleet on the 11th was reported to be leaving Taranto in strength. The MG23 diversionary force, once the Italian fleet had sailed, turned back after dark so that *Jervis* and her group berthed again in Port Said on the morning of the 12th.

Meanwhile the main Operation Pedestal; which was to escort a convoy of thirteen transports and one oiler to Malta, had passed through the Straits of Gibraltar. There followed a tremendous battle over three days, with only three freighters and one oiler reaching Malta after one aircraft carrier, two cruisers and other ships had been sunk, but the arrivals were sufficient to ensure the island's tenuous survival. So while the Mediterranean fleet had made a demonstration, uncharacteristically free from casualties or loss of shipping, their colleagues and friends serving in the Home Fleet and Force H had succeeded in forcing the Italian Navy and Axis air blockade of Malta, after five months.

Immediately prior to this bloody and momentous operation, on 7th August small changes occurred within *Jervis*. Of her original 1939 complement, Ordinary Seaman Albert Stoker was rated up to able seaman, remaining in the ship, and Lieutenant Peter Aylwin departed as a highly skilled and experienced destroyer watch-keeping officer for courses in the United Kingdom, and then to await a new appointment. Peter was the last of the original wardroom officers to leave the ship.

On 20th August, whilst on passage to Cyprus, *Princess Marguerite* loaded with troops was torpedoed. There were very few casualties and *Jervis* and *Hero* picked up the survivors. They hunted the U-boat without success for many hours before returning to Port Said, where a new member of the ship's company joined; Leading Seaman Jack Dare took over as ship's postman from Leading Seaman Jacobs. Dare quickly established an experienced destroyerman's imprint in *Jervis*. Within the small caboose allocated as the ship's mail office, every libertyman returning from shore and a visit to a bordello left his numbered ticket, identifying the girl he had been with. This was stuck to the bulkhead with others in numerical order so that every shore-going libertyman with a special objective in mind had only to stick his head into 'Postie's' caboose to see which were the most popular girls. His selection could often be supplemented by Dare's expert knowledge culled from conversations with his flotilla and fleet postmen colleagues.

Off El Daba, bombarding, the destroyer *Eridge* was hit and badly damaged by an Italian-manned E-boat. Then followed a ten-hour succession of dive-bomb attacks as the crippled ship was towed back to Alexandria, its survival entirely due to the skill of Captain Poland, *Jervis* and his 14th DF destroyers. And so into a September of uneasy patrolling and preparing either to counter an Axis advance into Egypt or then to support an Eighth Army assault. Enemy convoys were under increased pressure from attacks by submarines of the 10th Flotilla but continued to bring supplies and reinforcements to Benghazi and Tripoli. On the Allied side a succession of huge troop convoys had arrived at Port Tewfik and Port Suez but, so far as the Mediterranean Fleet personnel were concerned their arrivals increased the sense of unease as rumours of changes in the Middle East and Desert Army commands grew, coupled with the aftermath of the inexplicable fall of Tobruk. The fleet was missing the firm implacable grip of its previous Commander-in-Chief.

Then came a new disaster. For many days Alexandria had been rife with rumours of a joint Army-and-Naval raid on Tobruk, nobody could see the sense of it, but the bazaars were alive with details of the plans. Laundry and felucca men brought back the dhobying for payment and collected fees for boat trips earlier than usual and explained to their astonished and fearful clients that their ships were to take part in an operation and their eventual destruction.

The background and bloody account of this incompetently planned and senseless operation has been described in other works. It will suffice to quote from one of *Jervis*'s staff officer's objective comments on Operation Agreement. John Mosse wrote:

> Attempt to recapture Tobruk, September 13th 1942. (Garrison 30,000 – the force to recapture 500 Royal Marines plus 400 Desert Raiding Force – author's note.) . . . General Auchinleck – relieved by General Montgomery August 13th – urgently needed a diversion to relieve pressure on the Eighth Army now feverishly rebuilding its strength at El Alamein, whilst at the same time fearing an attack on Alexandria.
>
> To meet this requirement, what can only be described as a desperate plan – approved in advance by Montgomery – was made to recapture Tobruk by frontal assault. Marines were to be landed from *Sikh* (Captain Micklewaite) and *Zulu*, supported by the AA ship *Coventry* and Hunt class destroyers.
>
> This proved to be a disastrous failure in which *Sikh*, *Zulu* and *Coventry* were sunk and the landing force were either killed or captured, as were the crews of the sunken ships.
>
> The choice of two Tribal class ships, rather than *Jervis* and her J and K class, was because the Tribals had two funnels which – it was hoped – would make the enemy think they were Italian. This ruse did not succeed and indeed it appeared that the enemy was expecting the attack.
>
> Thus *Jervis* and the 14th DF were relegated to the relative safety of a diversionary operation in which they escorted the cruisers during a night bombardment of Mersa Matruh. Intercepted messages told us of the fate of our colleagues at Tobruk.

Following this disastrous operation, for a time, few men could muster enthusiasm for light-hearted runs ashore, but one member of *Jervis*'s ship's company recalls a craze that swept the ship and, for a while, superseded the demand for Tombola. This was the simple game of 'battleships', where opponents tried to block out squares on ruled scraps of paper that represented battleships, cruisers, destroyers and submarines. The prize for the winner was a portion of the loser's dinner ration; this became especially popular when the flotilla returned to be based on Malta, where food was short. The game was played everywhere, closed up at the guns, magazines, boiler and engine rooms as well in the messes off watch and the ship at midday became a scene of losers scurrying round the ship with their dinner plates to offer a portion to the victors.

On 4th October, *Jervis* berthed in Alexandria dockyard for a boiler clean and a short self refit. She was immediately required to organise her crew into armed boarding parties with the objective of taking over designated ships of the French squadron. Since the British takeover of the French colony of Madagascar in May, relations with officers and men manning the demilitarised ships had deteriorated, there were reports that clandestine supplies of fuel and war stores had been embarked during the period that the fleet had evacuated Alexandria. The tension lasted for several days forcing the somewhat supine naval headquarters staff hurriedly to organise scratch boarding parties from men in the desert naval holding camps of HMS *Nile*, for each ship of the French squadron.

There were lighter moments while *Jervis* refitted, there was night leave for the non-duty watch and most nights the non-duty part of the duty watch frequently got a 'beer run' until 2230. Petty Officer Mick Myers had joined *Jervis* from the *Queen Elizabeth* before she left the station. He was an easy-going individual who fitted well into a small ship environment and was popular with the troops. When he was duty petty officer checking in returning libertymen and handing back the watch cards, many would whisper to him, 'two behind the right hand crates', 'a couple between the two crates on the left' and so on. These whispered codes ensured that certain individuals next morning got 'a guard and steerage' hammocks lie in after Myers had stepped ashore to collect the concealed bottles of beer. 'I had more bottles of beer than if I had gone ashore.'

Snowball became enormously attached to this genial rascal; when action alarm rattlers went he would wait at the bottom of the ladder leading vertically up to Myers' action station in the DCT, leap on to his back, and then holding on with his fore-paws, would be carried piggy-back up and into the DCT where he remained coiled up at his hero's feet. Snowball did cause some problems, Myers's sleeping berth when he had the middle watch, was on some locker cushions in the petty officers' mess, Snowball slept on his shoes, and beware any unfortunate detailed off to give Myers a shake for his watch. The dog would not allow anyone to touch the petty officer, but snarl and attack, so Myers had to put up with his caller rousing him with hurled missiles or a long distance prod with a broom handle.

Quite suddenly everything changed. The fleet was at sea – except for *Jervis* completing her refit – and was off the desert coast on the night of 23rd/24th October when the whole sky blew up with an eruption of hundreds of field artillery battery guns. This was the opening of the Eighth's Army's new field commander's assault on the Axis Alamein lines and the start of a meticulous step by step rolling back of the enemy out of Cyrenaica for the final time.

Jervis was still in Alexandria completing her refit on 8th November when news came through of the start of the Anglo-American landings in French North Africa, Operation Torch. *Jervis* with every other ship and shore unit in the port stood to for 48 hours, expecting a hostile reaction from the French squadron but nothing happened. When *Jervis* sailed for Port Said on the 12th the French ships exchanged pipe and bugle courtesies with the departing flotilla leader. At Port Said D14 found *Nubian* waiting after her arrival from a refit at Bombay, and the Tribal class destroyer rejoined her old flotilla and her chummy ship.

When *Jervis* sailed on the 17th with her flotilla from Alexandria she was piped again by the French squadron. Outside Alexandria the destroyers joined four ships of Convoy MW13, (two American, one Dutch and one British); Operation Stoneage was an attempt to supply Malta from the east. The Eighth Army was in powerful conflict in the Western desert, the Allied landings in French North Africa were firmly established, the Axis was at full stretch, creating conditions auspicious for the operation and lifting the siege and blockade of Malta.

The task of fighting the convoy through was in the hands of the new CS15 (Admiral Vian had been relieved by Rear Admiral A.J. Power) with three cruisers and ten destroyers of the 12th and 14th Flotillas. The force was heavily attacked at noon on the 18th without damage but with the ships heading into strong winds and seas from the west. At dusk the Ju88's returned to deliver a torpedo attack; *Arethusa* was hit under the bridge and suffered 155 killed. The cruiser was taken in tow by *Petard* (12th Flotilla) and stern first, made for Alexandria escorted by *Jervis* and *Javelin*. Passing the tow and then turning the cruiser, broached to, in what was now a full gale, called for seamanship of the highest order from *Petard*'s captain, Lieutenant-Commander Mark Thornton. Once he was on course for

Alexandria, Mark Thornton – realising how vital it was to get the convoy to Malta – signalled that he could manage alone with the crippled ship and the two J's returned to the convoy.

For the whole of Thursday, the 19th, the convoy battled westward towards Malta in mountainous seas but free from further air attacks – fighters appeared overhead from the island – a reassuring sight for the storm tossed ships below. Unfortunately one aircraft crashed and *Kelvin* picked up the body of its 23-year-old pilot. In the afternoon, with fighters giving firm protective cover, the 14th DF ships turned back to Alexandria. In a perilous manoeuvre turning across the huge steep seas, *Jervis* flooded her messdecks and smashed her boats, *Javelin* very nearly capsized and lost four men over the side, only one being rescued. *Nubian* also lost one man over her side. *Javelin* flooded her empty fuel tanks in an endeavour to improve stability but had to seek shelter in Tobruk. *Jervis, Nubian* and *Kelvin* entered Alexandria at 0500/20th.

Meanwhile *Petard* with her huge tow – still going astern – made slow and immensely difficult progress toward the port, the ships had fought off two air attacks by three Ju88's. Off the approach channel *Petard* was unable to turn her charge into the swept channel and had to hand over to two large tugs. Later in the day when the crippled cruiser had berthed, *Kelvin* embarked some of her dead, then sailed for a burial at sea.

The other cruisers of the 15th CS returned to Alexandria on 23rd, and the whole force was given permission to give 24 hours' leave to each watch. The break was to be short-lived. John Ellis with his messmates booked in to sleep in the Fleet Club Annexe but they were given an unexpectedly early shake and told to report back to their ship immediately. They found the 14th DF at two hours' notice for steam. With the 15th CS, the flotilla sailed for Malta where the force arrived at 1830/27th and somewhat to everyone's surprise and pleasure the ships were cheered into harbour by Valletta's population, lining every available vantage point of the honey-coloured ramparts and battlements. It seemed that the citizens knew something, as yet not revealed to the men in the ships.

The drill for warships arriving at Malta was to empty their store and cold rooms of all victuals while refuelling. The ships, having added their provisions to the island's larder, would then return to Alexandria or Gibraltar, subsisting on their emergency 'hard tack' rations. This time, *Jervis* and her destroyers sailed to meet the incoming Convoy MW14 escorted by D12 *Pakenham* (Captain

E.B.K. Stevens) and his flotilla, Operation Portcullis. This second successful convoy arrived intact on 1st December ensuring the basis of a sound build up of strength in the island fortress. Much to their surprise the ship's companies of the 14th Flotilla found themselves back in Malta – berthing in French Creek and, only then, told that they were to remain based on the island as part of Force K and a reconstituted Malta Strike Force. Their task was to be the same as in 1941, to seek out, intercept and sink enemy convoys. These convoys were making frantic efforts to bring fuel to the Axis desert army falling back towards Tripoli.

A British Force Q was already operating out of Bône: on the night of 1st/2nd December, three cruisers and two destroyers had attacked one convoy 40 miles north of Cape Bon and sank the four merchant ships and one of the escorts. Force Q lost one destroyer by an aircraft torpedo.

On the night of the 3rd/4th *Jervis* led *Javelin, Nubian* and *Kelvin* towards the Gulf of Gabes where aircraft from Malta had sighted and attacked, with torpedoes, a convoy of three supply ships and two escorts. At midnight the four destroyers in line ahead could see tracer AA fire being directed upwards and the glow of a ship on fire. The 14th DF using their radar advantage over the Italians who had none, came silently at speed and undetected upon the scene, closing to under 2000 yards when *Jervis* opened fire and simultaneously exposed her 40 inch searchlight onto her target, the escort destroyer *Lupo*. The first salvo demolished the small warship's bridge and the second plunged into the victim's engine room. The enemy escort was caught helpless, engaged in picking up survivors from her convoy. None of her three 3.9" guns was manned, only her AA armament. Captain Poland led his ships in a half circle round the doomed ship held in the relentless, blinding, unblinking, merciless beam of his searchlight and each of the flotilla poured a terrible holocaust of 4.7" broadsides into the helpless ship, pounding it into grotesque destruction – 24 guns of 4.7" calibre versus an unmanned battery of three 3.9" – before the flotilla disappeared into the night, returning to Malta.

It was a terrible end for a gallant ship and a ship's company who had a fighting record the envy of many of her opponents; she never abandoned her charges, and fought to the end in the defence of her convoys.

The destroyer was known to the long serving ratings in the Mediterranean, so the 14th DF ships returned to Malta in a sombre mood prevailing in the lower deck.

The destroyers were back with a vengeance into the 1941 routine; they waited in harbour at immediate notice while air patrols from the island's airfields scoured the Sicilian channel and to the east and west of Sicily for enemy ships. When a report came through to the Combined Headquarters, two or three destroyers sailed in the Dog Watches and made for the estimated position of the enemy ships at high speed. The destroyers were required to engage and destroy the targets and then get back in darkness, so that at first light they were under the outer umbrella protective limits of fighter aircraft patrols from Malta.

In the night of Tuesday the 9th, *Jervis* with *Kelvin* and *Nubian* swept deep into the Gulf of Gabes, then between Ras Turgeuness and Kerkenak, but the reported shipping had disappeared.

On the 12th, while *Jervis* remained in harbour, the 15th CS with the other three 14th DF ships intercepted a convoy and sank the three supply ships and one of the escorts. Next morning as the successful force entered harbour the island was under the heaviest air attack for some time. Forty Ju88's directed their effort on the islands airfields.. large fires and explosions could be seen inland as the ships berthed in dispersed locations within Grand Harbour and Sliema.

In the evening of Tuesday the 20th, *Jervis* and *Nubian* (Commander D.E. Holland Martin) sailed in company at high speed to intercept a single 2000 ton ship sighted by Malta reconnaissance patrols. Soon after midnight the destroyers located the merchant ship hugging Cape Ras Turgeuness steaming towards Tripoli. In a short, clinical action *Jervis* sank the ship and the destroyers returned to base.

Life was becoming tougher than usual in the destroyers at continuous short notice for steam and with sparse shore going opportunities or facilities, rations were short and monotonous. For three weeks there had been no variation from corned beef and ship's biscuits, the rationed flour could allow fresh bread only every three days and then only in small quantities.

The rare opportunities for men to stretch their legs ashore revealed a city with streets choked with bomb debris, very few cafes or bars were able to function because, even from 'Black Market' sources, beer was in short supply; it was rare for a libertyman to locate more than a couple of bottles. For officers, one small and remarkable haven had survived the countless air raids, two elderly English spinsters still ran their small establishment known universally as 'Auntie's' from their Edwardian-furnished sitting room with a large window overlooking one of the harbour creeks. By some special magic these gentle eccentrics were still able to serve modest quantities of bottled beer; how and why this unlikely pair were able to obtain stocks against fierce competition from the island's small time 'Mafioso' was a baffling mystery.

D14 took his ships to sea early on Christmas Eve for high angle/low angle gun and torpedo firing exercises and returned in time for the flotilla to berth in the First Dog Watch, and then to pipe evening leave.

Next day (Friday), Christmas Day, dawned overcast and raining in torrents; the low cloud guaranteed freedom from air raids but it was a gloomy day. Bill Skilling wrote, 'This is the worst Christmas of my life – no beer, no grub, only bully beef, spuds and biscuits – and everyone is chocker.'

Boxing Day, *Jervis* entered drydock for a boiler-clean and the ship fielded a football team to play *Kelvin*. Each watch was given 48 hours' leave, there was nothing to do, but accommodation was arranged to give men a rare opportunity to sleep in a bed, between sheets and free from the constant hum of shipboard fans and noises. While in dock the ship's company, on the initiative of the wardroom officers, gave a party to some of the many children of service families who had remained on the island during the siege and shared the bombing with the islanders. In the evening of the 30th the flotilla attended a hilarious concert party staged by *Kelvin* in one of the deep shelters.

January 5th 1943, *Jervis* with *Nubian* in company sailed on another 'Club Run' seeking one of the last enemy convoys making for Tripoli. The area of search was between Lampedusa and Kerkenah. The destroyers deployed on the Club Runs always, after dark, proceeded in close order in line ahead, one and a half cables astern of each other. Total W/T and R/T silence was maintained, the few signals for speed changes or 'Enemy in Sight' alarms were passed by a small blue light, the OOW's of the ships astern of the senior ship steered on a shaded blue stern light of the ship ahead – something requiring tremendous concentration especially when action was joined and the night was riven by gun flashes, bombs and aircraft flares. It became a skill that the enemy, Italian or German, could never match. With these skills and radar to seek out and range on targets the 'Club Run' cruisers and destroyers became irresistible and devastating raiders on the enemy's sea lines of communication to North Africa.

Captain A.F. Pugsley arrived in the ship on 7th January to relieve Captain Poland as D14. That night the club run was carried out by

Javelin and *Nubian* who found and sank three schooners off Kuriat.
Next morning *Jervis* put to sea, acting as anti-submarine cover for
Euryalus. Both the new and outgoing captains were still in the ship
and it was immensely rough: on return to harbour that evening Patsy
Poland, who had been a well respected Captain (D), was rowed
ashore in a whaler crewed by his officers. He flew home that same
night for an overdue and deserved rest. For his services he was later
in February to receive from King George VI, at the same investiture,
the Distinguished Service Order for his courage and resource during
the Norwegian Campaign, a bar to that DSO for his leadership and
bravery when he commanded the Inshore Squadron from Tobruk
and the insignia of CB for the part he played in the Battle of Sirte. It
was unusual – if not unique – to receive so many honours at the same
visit to Buckingham Palace.

CHAPTER SIX

One Year and Four Captains (D)

After the shattering damage to his command (*Javelin*, torpedoed in 1940 with Captain Mountbatten, D5, embarked) Commander A.F. Pugsley had had a very short spell of leave before being appointed to command another destroyer, *Fearless*. Then followed an action-packed six months of operating mainly with Force H, out of Gibraltar, until – in Operation Substance to re-supply Malta – *Fearless* was torpedoed by an Italian aircraft on 23rd July 1941. In October he took over a new 'P' class destroyer *Paladin* at John Brown's yard. After completion of trials and working up, *Paladin* joined Admiral Somerville's Eastern Fleet at Colombo in March 1942. The new destroyer had an alarming time but avoided destruction by the Japanese fleet commanded by Admiral Nagumo. On 5th April Commander Pugsley first located and subsequently with a sister 12th Flotilla ship, *Panther* and the cruiser *Enterprise*, picked up over one thousand survivors from the cruisers *Cornwall* and *Dorsetshire* both of which had been sunk by carrier-borne aircraft of Admiral Nomura's fleet.

Not long after this incident *Paladin* formed part of an Eastern Fleet contingent of cruisers and destroyers sent north via the Red Sea into the Mediterranean to take part in the ill-fated Operation Vigorous. When the Eastern fleet ships returned to their station, *Paladin* and her 12th Flotilla Leader *Pakenham* were held back at Port Suez and ordered to stay with the Mediterranean Fleet, thus Commander Pugsley had been operating with the fleet and in close association with the 14th Flotilla since June 1942.

On New Year's Eve two signals had been received in *Paladin*; the first to the effect that Commander A.F. Pugsley had been promoted to captain, the second instructed him to take over as temporary Captain (D) of the 14th Flotilla in *Jervis*. This was so that Captain A.L. Poland could be sent home – 'after the gruelling time he had had from the beginning of the war'. Captain Pugsley's promotion had come at a convenient moment to relieve 'Patsy' Poland 'while his permanent relief was swanning his way round the Cape', as Pugsley wrote some years later.

Pugsley was immensely proud to be in command of the leader of the flotilla in which he had served when in command of *Javelin* and to have followed two men whom he so much admired. 'Mack was my ideal of what a destroyer leader should be.' He also had the advantage of having come to know, since he had arrived in the Eastern Mediterranean, a number of *Jervis*'s ship and flotilla staff officers, including Commander (E) H.C. Hogger the flotilla engineer – who in March had relieved the resolute and inimitable Engineer Commander J.A. Ruddy; J.C. Stodart who since the departure of Laing and Rose had held the triple responsibilities of Second-in-Command, first lieutenant and flotilla torpedo officer. He also knew N.M. Mules the ship's and flotilla navigator, John Mosse, anti-submarine specialist, Mike Hemans, the flotilla gunnery officer and 'Flags' G.H.H. Culme-Seymour the 'signalman'.

On Sunday, 10th January, *Jervis* was at sea steering east with *Nubian* and *Kelvin* in company, to meet an incoming convoy from Alexandria at a position north of Benghazi. The convoy consisted of five merchant ships escorted by nine Hunt class destroyers, led and commanded by Commander Blessas in *Queen Olga*. The weather was appalling with a gale and huge seas from the west, and the escort reinforcements were in serious trouble as soon as they started to turn across the sea to take up their screening stations. *Kelvin* lost one man over the side and then almost capsized as she searched in vain for the missing crew member. *Jervis* also had a near fatal tragedy: someone was seen to go over the side while the iron deck was covered by a deep mass of broken water. Captain Pugsley turned his ship to search – *Jervis* rolling to her beam ends – but could see nothing in a maelstrom of confused seas, before resuming the convoy course. Not long afterwards, an insensible body was found under the torpedo tubes; it was Midshipman Moberly who had been swept back inboard unseen, with injuries to his head and crushed ribs. The midshipman survived and was landed for treatment at the Royal Naval Hospital in Malta, after the ship returned in suddenly calm seas, to harbour at 2000, Monday.

Jervis was preparing to sail pm Wednesday with *Nubian* and *Kelvin* for another Club run but at the last minute developed an engine-room defect and had to remain behind while the other two ships sailed to investigate an air reconnaissance sighting of an enemy convoy. With *Kelvin* leading as senior ship the two destroyers located the convoy and after a short brisk action the 14th DF ships sank an enemy escort destroyer and two merchant ships. One of the merchantmen had 5000 troops embarked. The raiders returned to Malta at dawn full of survivor prisoners of war and many stretcher cases.

That night 19th/20th *Kelvin* sailed again but this time as leader to *Javelin*, then during a long night north of Tripoli, the two destroyers sank no fewer than eleven enemy small ships in convoy including four minesweepers, three auxiliary minesweepers, three smaller craft and the convoy's escort destroyer. While her flotilla ships slaughtered the dying effort by Axis naval forces to re-supply its defeated desert army, *Jervis*'s engine-room department struggled to rectify its defects. These were cleared in time for the flotilla leader to sail with Force K at 1300/20th for a patrol between Cape Ras Turgeuness and the approaches to Tripoli. At 2100, CS15 detached *Jervis* and *Nubian* with orders to sweep deep into the Gulf of Gabes. At first they drew a blank, a salvo of star shell over Gabes showing that the small port was empty; then at midnight, as Captain Pugsley withdrew to return to Malta, they came upon two small steamers apparently making for Sfax. These were quickly despatched in an overwhelming avalanche of gunfire, coming at short range out of the blackness of cloud blanketed night.

After a few daylight hours at the destroyer berths in Sliema creek refuelling and stocking up ammunition replacements, snatching at sleep, the 14th DF sailed again with the Force K cruisers for a night bombardment of Zuara and the road to Tripoli along which Panzer units and regiments were retreating westward towards Mareth. The bombardment produced large fires and explosions which shattered the night but, when the destroyers moved inshore to probe the harbour of Zuara with searchlights and star shell, all the shipping had gone. Enemy shipping was also being sunk by Malta-based aircraft and submarines and yet there was no sign of any major units of the Italian fleet emerging to challenge the Allied Strike Forces.

Shortly after Force K and the 14th DF returned to harbour on Saturday the 23rd, signals were received announcing the fall of Tripoli to the Eighth Army which had passed on through the city in pursuit of the retreating Axis army. The city had apparently received little damage from British bombing or demolitions by the departing enemy.

It was a different story in the harbour and port area. Few buildings remained, dockside machinery and berths not already bombed had been blown up by demolition parties, the harbour was choked with ships scuttled and sunk in air raids; the entrance had been systematically and very professionally blocked with six scuttled ships and a number of barges sunk loaded with cement and booby-trapped. The task of clearing the obstructions and bringing the port into operation fell to Captain Poland's successor in command of the Inshore Squadron, Captain C. Wauchope, and his naval parties who had followed hot on the heels of the Eighth Army throughout its advance from El Alamein. They had opened up every port as it was captured and poured in supplies by sea to sustain the advance, they had also made beach landings of stores and men immediately behind the front line. Benghazi – the last major port before Tripoli – badly damaged, had been cleared to handle 3000 tons discharged per day. It now was to take two days for the naval parties to open a small passage into Tripoli, sufficient to allow landing craft to pass through. It was the 29th before the first supply ship could squeeze into the harbour to discharge cargo.

Meanwhile the first convoys from Alexandria, XT1, and from Benghazi, BT1, had arrived and lay at anchor outside: this left them vulnerable to attack from submarines and they also suffered losses in the violent storm which so damaged Benghazi harbour that its function was reduced to a fair weather port.

The Italian battle fleet – short of fuel – continued nevertheless to be a potential threat and so *Orion* screened by *Jervis*, *Kelvin* and the Hunt *Tetcott* departed from Malta to reinforce the escort of a convoy from Alexandria. The convoy contained an important troop carrier, ss *Antwerp*, three large storeships and a tanker, all – with the exception of the tanker – bound for Tripoli. The reinforcements from Malta joined the convoy in rough and overcast weather conditions at 0630/25th, then at noon *Jervis* and *Kelvin* were detached to take the tanker to Malta while the remainder of the convoy carried on south-west to Tripoli.

A similar routine was repeated when *Cleopatra*, screened by *Jervis*, *Kelvin* and *Javelin*, sailed next day (27th) to meet another convoy from the east and again bound for Tripoli. The rendezvous was made at 1815/29th in rough sea conditions – a feature which had, with only rare lulls, persisted for weeks. After juncture with the convoy *Jervis* continued on alone at high speed to Alexandria where she arrived at noon on the 30th. Following the usual practice of warships reaching port, *Jervis* proceeded across the harbour to berth on a tanker to refuel. The nominated tanker was the *Sagona* which still lay immobile at the berth where she had been damaged by the 'Sea Devils' in December 1941. It was an awkward berth close to the entrance to

Gabarri drydock, in the high westerly wind gusting to gale force *Jervis*, much to Captain Pugsley's chagrin because of his justifiable pride in ship-handling, crunched heavily into the Norwegian tanker. *Jervis* suffered four buckled 'rigols' forward and some minor plate distortions and leaks.

Jervis remained at Alexandria until 6th February and like all the other ships in the command learned with special regret of the torpedoing of the fast minelayer *Welshman* by *U-617* off Sollum on 1st February; *Tetcott* picked up the survivors but the fleet mail from the United Kingdom was lost. This included letters for the 14th Flotilla and would have been the first since before Christmas 1942.

In high seas and a strong westerly gale *Jervis*, with 50 ratings embarked for passage to Malta, departed from Alexandria with Captain Pugsley, the escort commander, screening an 8-knot twelve ship convoy which included a troopship with a Scottish regiment embarked. The escort comprised *Jervis*, *Kelvin*, *Javelin* and three Greek-manned Hunts. The route was close inshore to obtain protection from RAF fighter squadrons operating in strength from recaptured desert airfields; German Ju88's and to some extent Italian S79's were still active from bases in Crete and southern Greece.

The convoy passed within sight of Tobruk and then off Derna, the damaged town and harbour could be seen clearly from the ships; the whole sea area was littered with mines that had broken free from their moorings in the current and prolonged rough sea conditions. Ships were continually taking avoiding action from mines in daylight hours and there was not a man in the convoy and escort ships who did not view the night hours with intense alarm. Lieutenant Lacey RNVR from *Jervis*'s bridge, opened fire on one mine surging in the broken waves 20 yards from the ship; the rogue mine exploded driving splinters into the ship, fortunately causing no damage but a considerable amount of nausea to the entire ship's company, and for a few days afterwards Lacey's popularity slumped.

Off Benghazi the convoy's progress came to a near stop in the night 8th/9th as the ships ran into torrential rain and squalls of near hurricane force bringing confusion to the formation of deeply laden ships. At dawn 9th with the wind reducing in strength, *Jervis* and the escort started rounding-up the scattered convoy and were helped in this task by the arrival of *Euryalus*, *Nubian* and *Paladin* who joined the escort for the last leg across the central basin to Malta. Apart from damage caused by the elements the convoy arrived safely at 2200/11th, unopposed by enemy naval or air units.

After only one night 'in', *Jervis* sailed into the still turbulent and storm-racked central Mediterranean in command of the escort of Convoy ME17 made up from two empty tankers, *Erinna* and *Yorba Linda*, and a troopship *Egro*. Those of the ship's company who had seen service in the Atlantic and Arctic convoys to Russia consoled their tooth-sucking belly-aching long serving Mediterranean shipmates by describing the facts of life in the ships on passage for two weeks or more in the freezing mountainous seas of the North Atlantic and Arctic. Here, passages lasted rarely more than three or four days and the rough seas were at least warmer than the northern waters; there was always an opportunity to clear up and clean chaotic messdecks every few days and, as Captain 'Barry' Stevens, D12, remarked, 'The Med had far better bathing facilities'.

On the second day out (Sunday) the ships – rolling and yawing eastward in huge following seas – were joined by two Beaufighters. Shortly afterwards for some inexplicable reason one fighter skimmed over the violent sea and struck a wave top, the plane cartwheeled and broke up in a confusion of spray, flame and smoke, not far from *Jervis* at the head of the convoy.

Captain (D) turned *Jervis* across the sea and stopped engines so the destroyer, rolling through many degrees, drifted downwind forming a lee for the wrecked plane; the bodies of the crew could be seen in the broken water held up by their inflated jackets. The pilot was helpless and unconscious and there was great difficulty in grabbing hold of his life-jacket and danger that the violently rolling ship would ride over him, but a young Australian, Jack (Digger) Godson, leapt into the sea with a lifeline paid out by his shipmates. With his help Sergeant Pilot Turner was hauled inboard. Meanwhile one of the Hunts had picked up his crew member.

Unhappily during the night, while a single enemy aircraft – no doubt working in co-operation with a submarine – dropped lines of flares over the convoy, the 21-year-old airman died. At dawn he was given a sailor's burial. Shortly after this, *Jervis* left the convoy and made for Tripoli. Off the port on Monday the 15th *Kelvin*, *Paladin* and *Queen Olga* arrived to escort three merchantmen which had discharged their cargoes and were to return to Alexandria, the sea was still very rough as the convoy set off. During Tuesday the wind died away and the seas began rapidly to moderate, visibility improved and the tawny outline of the African coast could be seen to starboard. Dawn came on Wednesday over a flat calm sea, everyone began to relax in the sunshine of a glorious Mediterranean morning but the grim reality of the ever present war menace returned with a rush when dull thumps of underwater explosions were felt on the ship's hulls and Captain Pugsley's 'old ship' *Paladin* was seen to be turning under full helm and increasing speed having fired a pattern of five depth charges. While *Jervis* and the remainder of the escort herded the convoy away from the danger area, *Paladin*'s signal light began to blink: 'D14 from *Paladin*. Sorry false alarm!' The signal lamp had barely completed its morse message when in an eruption of foam and spray, the black hull of *U-205* (Lieutenant Bürgel) came boiling to the surface and set off at 9 knots, but, with its steering gear jammed, the U-boat could proceed only in a wide circle.

The guns of *Paladin* and *Jervis* crashed into action and on target, straddling the hopelessly out of control U-boat. Hits could be seen on hull and conning tower as the submarine crew tried to retaliate with their single gun.

At the moment that Captain Pugsley ordered 'Cease fire' an aircraft of the South African Air Force roared in and dropped two depth charges, banked round and returned to rake *U-205* with machine gun fire. The plane then flew off returning to its base where the crew promptly claimed a U-boat kill! John Ellis' diary records:

> *Jervis* speeds ahead and opens up with 4.7″ and hits the conning tower with 1st salvo. An aircraft then sweeps in on it and kills the crew who have manned their gun, their bodies hang over the rails – dead.

Jervis proceeded on with the convoy leaving *Paladin* to pick up the U-boat survivors and to endeavour to secure the submarine as a prize. The boat was badly damaged and obviously letting in the sea but *Paladin*'s new captain, Lieutenant-Commander Rich, and his men managed to secure a tow and set off towards the coast to beach their prize. It was not to be; *U-205* sank two miles offshore.

After arrival at Alexandria Captain Pugsley learned from Commodore (D), Percy Todd, that he was soon to take command of all the fleet destroyers in the Eastern Mediterranean when Captain Barry Stevens left *Pakenham* for a staff appointment. In his turn Pugsley was keen to interest the commodore in an adaptation of an evolution successfully used by the Italian fleet to confuse air attacks on their formations. This was the use of smoke, the formation when under attack, particularly by aircraft carrying torpedoes, would turn into the wind, every ship making smoke from funnels and canisters leaving only two or three destroyers at the head of the formation exposed to the air attackers. This defensive manoeuvre frequently confused Allied airmen and, on occasion submarine commanders. It was particularly effective at night and at dawn when the natural conditions, off the desert coastline, was hazy.

Commodore Percy Todd was persuaded to embark in *Jervis* to witness D14's scheme being practised in daylight with a convoy making an emergency turn into the wind, every convoy ship making smoke with the escorts and two destroyers zig zagging across the front of the convoy. The commodore was convinced and thereafter escorts and convoyed ships were all well supplied with smoke canisters. The scheme was an immediate success and, while Captain Pugsley remained in *Jervis*, he never lost a ship to air attacks.

Still in Alexandria at the start of a boiler clean and docking, a new first lieutenant joined and relieved Stodart of the appointment that he had been temporarily covering. The new 'Jimmy' was Lieutenant C.E.M. Thornycroft, a tall, fair, blue-eyed and athletic individual, ambitious and full of exuberant enthusiasm who was quickly to make an impact on a war-weary and somewhat jaundiced ship's company. With the ship in drydock for a few days for underwater inspection and repairs, 48 hours' leave was given to each watch. Many made their way to Cairo for a further taste of the unreal 'peacetime' atmosphere. Even Captain Pugsley availed himself of the opportunity of taking a short rest and booked into the Mena Hotel. 'Though I was rather repelled by the place itself with its teeming crowds of "back area" uniforms, I shall always remember the bliss of being able to really relax for the first time in many months.'

There was surely a need for him to re-charge his batteries. The new Captain (D) had impressed everyone in the flotilla with his stamina – John Mosse who served with him for only a short time, wrote of Captain Pugsley:

> I marvelled at his incredible stamina. He seemed to need no sleep at all. He would be on the bridge all night during a strike from Malta and on returning to harbour, he would have a few gins and some lunch and then, still alert, would send for his staff officers and confront them with the problems of the day. A run ashore with him could indeed be a fierce undertaking.

John Mosse left *Jervis* on 26th February to become the Fleet Anti-Submarine Officer on the staff of Admiral Harwood.

With the boiler clean completed and everyone refreshed by the short leave and a few evenings ashore in Alexandria *Jervis* sailed on 6th March escorting a convoy of four troopships, filled with reinforcements for the Eighth Army's attack on the Mareth line. The escort included *Nubian, Petard* and *Isis. Petard* had just completed one round trip to Tripoli and she had entered the port in company with D12 in *Pakenham* and their convoy ships. While the ships refuelled the port came under a heavy air attack by German aircraft; in addition to bombing the enemy launched a new weapon, circling torpedoes, which rampaged round the harbour in ever widening circles watched by the hypnotised and helpless crew members and even distracting the AA gun crews from their tasks until the torpedoes ran their course and then bobbed with warheads pointing skywards, like grotesque phallic symbols. In this attack the erratic torpedoes hit only wrecks and other obstructions but bombs did considerable damage including setting fire to a tanker that was discharging her fuel. Two bombs hit the Hunt destroyer *Derwent* and she had to be beached in a corner of the harbour. In a later attack she was irreparably damaged by a circling torpedo.

On this current run *Jervis* brought her convoy of fast troopships, ss *Malayan Prince*, ss *Princess Katherine*, mv *Ergra* and one supply ship safely through recurring rough sea conditions but with no opposition from the enemy. After the convoy ships had negotiated the narrow entrance through the blockships, *Jervis* followed into Tripoli to find the harbour filled with Liberty ships discharging war cargoes. It was very, very warm with a sand-laden hot wind blowing from the desert to the south of the city.

The remainder of the month was spent taking convoys to and from Tripoli, Tobruk and on one occasion to Port Said, and as if to stop the ship's company getting bored, two days were spent on gun and torpedo exercises with *Orion*; the cruiser had recently returned to the Mediterranean, following repairs to the terrible damage and slaughter she had suffered during the final stages of the Crete evacuation in 1941.

High seas and sand storms plagued most of the month, climaxing on the 20th when waves were gigantic, menacing and impenetrable, like deep blue mountains of water with foamed crests that crashed in roaring cascades upon the slender destroyers. In *Jervis* guard-rails were distorted, boats smashed and No 1 gun mounting shield was forced back onto the guns so that they could not be brought into action. The immense seas seemed to discourage enemy submarines;

only one suspect contact was made after *Paladin*'s sinking of *U-205*, *Nubian* was left behind to worry the contact until the convoy had passed on out of the danger zone. The wind eventually moderated, the great seas passed under instead of over the escorts. *Jervis* with her destroyers and a three ship supply convoy arrived at dawn on the 29th off Malta's Grand Harbour, as nine Ju88's appeared overhead to bomb Valletta. The ships moving along the swept approach channel had a grandstand view of 16 Spitfires and 5 Beaufighters diving into the enemy formation which they broke up, forcing the Ju88's to flee back towards their Sicily bases, some jettisoning their bombs across the island as they went.

Fighter patrols continued in strength for the rest of the day while the convoy's ships commenced discharging their cargoes and the destroyers in Sliema Creek fuelled and followed the lead given by *Jervis*, piped 'Hands to bathe' in the creek's clear water. That evening Captain (D) received his copy of the signal to the fleet announcing that the Eighth Army had breached the Mareth line after a nine-day siege.

Next morning *Jervis* departed early, in charge of the escort and a convoy of one empty store ship and three troopers filled with 'time expired' men. This was a singularly inappropriate misnomer for the Army and RAF units which had been part of the garrison during the long months of siege, enduring innumerable air raids while living on short and hard tack rations as well as bolstering the morale of the civilian population. They had been replaced by fresh units and were going only as far as Egypt to rest, prior to re-training. The troops included the Territorial 4th Battalion of the Buffs – volunteer citizen soldiers. They were destined, within a few short months, to suffer grievous casualties without the consolation of being able to defend themselves.

The first two weeks of April produced little excitement for *Jervis*, the time was occupied in escorting convoys from Alexandria to Tripoli and on to the newly-captured ports of Gabes, Sfax and Sousse. Only on one occasion did the ship encounter signs of the enemy, just two shadowing aircraft which, a few weeks earlier, would have heralded the arrival of Italian or German air squadrons or the appearance of Italian fleet units. For a while there was to be a lull from air attacks on central Mediterranean convoys.

Jervis made her fifth entry into Tripoli on the 16th and, for the first time gave afternoon leave to one watch. The men who went ashore into the city were impressed by the immaculate state of the Italian neo-colonial city, a marked contrast to the devastation of the dockyard and harbour.

John Ellis ventured beyond the outskirts of Tripoli to where fierce fighting for the city had taken place: 'I picked a poppy from the battlefield of damaged and burnt out tanks . . . I met an old *Jervis* shipmate, Jack Salzer, now in Combined Ops.'

While *Jervis* paused and spent the 16th/17th night in Tripoli harbour, *Pakenham* (D12) and *Paladin* on an offensive patrol out of Malta encountered two enemy destroyers *Cassiopea* and *Cigno* covering a convoy passing close to the island fortress of Pantellaria. In the ensuing action *Cigno* was sunk whilst *Pakenham*, hit four times in the engineroom was immobilized. *Paladin* took her flotilla leader in tow while *Cassiopea* picked up the *Cigno* survivors and beat a hasty retreat from the scene: her convoy was the last to reach Tunisia intact. At dawn *Paladin* and her tow were under air attack beyond the range of fighter cover from Malta, so Flag Officer Malta ordered *Paladin* to sink *Pakenham*. This was done and the destroyer returned at high speed to Malta without further problems.

When *Jervis* put into Sliema Creek briefly on the 18th to fuel, Captain Pugsley had time to go across to congratulate his old ship's company. He then departed for Alexandria only to spend 48 fruitless hours assisting two Hunts, *Dulverton* and *Exmoor*, hunting a submarine that had attacked their 15-ship convoy off Tobruk. While the long hunt went on for an elusive and skilful adversary, Pugsley heard that the men he had trained had again been in successful action. *Paladin* with *Petard* led by *Nubian* (Commander 'Pinky' Holland Martin) located and sank a large supply ship loaded with ammunition, vehicles and men, together with its escorting destroyer *Perseo*.

Captain Pugsley, impatient for action, returned to Malta in a thick fog on 21st to learn that with the sinking of *Pakenham* and the demise of the 12th Flotilla, *Paladin*, *Petard* and *Queen Olga* were to become part of his 14th Flotilla. It was the second time that *Queen Olga*, the popular Greek, became a 14th DF ship; she had been transferred to the 12th DF soon after *Pakenham* arrived in the Eastern Mediterranean, and while with the 12th had formed a successful sub-division with *Petard* which had already established a reputation after taking part in the boarding and sinking of *U-559*. *Queen Olga* and *Petard* had also shared in the hunting and surrender of the Italian submarine *Uarsciek* which they very nearly succeeded in towing triumphantly into Malta's Grand Harbour. All three newcomers to the flotilla had

May 1943. Operation Retribution, German POW's crowd *Jervis*'s QD.

May 1943 – General Rommel drinking in Tobruk (in happier times) with a successful Italian submarine captain. Photo taken from a POW by R. T. Taylor.

December 1943. *Jervis* escorts HHMS *Adrias* after her escape from the Dodecanese.

December 1943 – *Janus*.

(*Top left*) May 1944. Skerki with two of her three pups, Anzio and Whisky.

(*Top right*) March 1944. Snowball, ship's veteran and proud father to be. Posed in Gibraltar.

July 1944. *Jervis*'s wardroom and Midshipman Loveday.

June 1944. Off Normandy beaches. Daniel Geluyckens, Tony Casswell, Frank Peters, Captain Trevor Keightly RA, Midshipman Selman.

their successes sinking ships in the Sicilian Narrows which increased their new Captain (D)'s desire to add to *Jervis's* reputation as the scourge of the enemy.

The night after the new ships joined, Captain Pugsley – to improve his luck – took *Queen Olga* with him to seek shipping reported in the early afternoon off Kelibia and in the Gulf El Hammamet. It proved to be an elusive target and a frustrated Captain (D) wrote, 'but my luck seemed to be dead out around this time and I drew a blank.'

As April drew to a close the Eighth Army's advance had come to a halt near Enfidaville while the First Army, which had been attacking from the west since the 22nd, ran into extremely stubborn resistance. There was a short stalemate until General Alexander transferred strong forces from the Eighth Army to the First Army's front and restarted the final push into the Tunisian hump. It seemed possible that major units of the Italian fleet would be forced into a desperate attempt to succour some of the Axis army which was being compressed from both the east and west. So on the night of the 2nd May, *Jervis* set off with *Nubian* and *Petard* on what was rumoured to be a highly dangerous mission – to locate large enemy units suspected to be at sea and about to make a high speed sortie into the Gulf of Tunis or to Kelibia.

With his ships closed up at action stations and at full alert Captain (D) set off to patrol between Pantellaria and the Gulf of Tunis; the first alarm came within a known British submarine patrol area, when *Nubian* sighted a conning tower and flashed the day's challenge signal, but there was no reply. The submarine dived – no time to stay and hunt, the destroyers were after bigger game. Captain Pugsley turned his ships back at a position west of Cape Bon and then, at 0300 steering east at 25 knots a large vessel was first picked up by radar and then sighted; it could only be an enemy cruiser. The destroyers increased speed to 30 knots, but – out of character for Italian fleet units at night – the target must have been keeping a good lookout system or, perhaps, also had radar for the unidentified ship increased speed and quickly outstripped the stalking destroyers and disappeared into the night. When the destroyer strike group returned to Malta in the late forenoon, the destroyer crews – still unaware of the probable extra risks of the patrol – were surprised to find the upper-decks of the cruisers and destroyers in harbour crowded with men who cheered them in. Later, libertymen ashore learned, from *Paladin* and other flotilla friends, that all ships in Malta had been at immediate notice for steam, to make a high speed dash to come to their rescue; rumours had abounded that *Jervis* had been sunk and *Nubian* badly damaged.

The First and Eighth Armies on 7th May achieved their final objectives: Bizerta and Tunis had been captured, the enemy's land forces in North Africa were in an impossible situation with the only option an evacuation by a less than resolute Italian fleet which was also short of fuel. However the possibility had to be anticipated that an attempt would be made to bring some of the Axis army back to Sicily, for their fleet was still intact and considerable air strength was operating out of Sicilian and Sardinian air bases. Admiral of the Fleet Sir Andrew (Guts) Cunningham, who had returned to the Mediterranean in the wake of the Operation Torch landings as the Allied Naval Commander-in-Chief, set in motion Operation Retribution with his historic signal to all the ships operating out of Bône, Malta and the captured Tunisian ports: 'Sink, burn and destroy – let nothing pass.'

When the signal was received in *Jervis*, D14 had with him *Nubian* and *Paladin* carrying out what was known on the nightly Club runs, as the Kelibia regatta. The ships had just concluded bombarding positions in and around Kelibia and had started to withdraw so as to be under the Malta fighter umbrella by dawn when an open boat under oars and sail, towing a rubber dinghy was sighted. When *Jervis* stopped alongside, the boat was seen to contain thirteen German Panzer troops, one British airman and four Italians crouched in the small dinghy.

The Spitfire pilot, who had been shot down, later explained that after he had got into his dinghy the boat containing the Germans and Italians approached and took him inboard; they were trying to make for Pantellaria. The predominantly German crew then forced their Italian allies to get into the RAF rubber dinghy to make adequate space for Sergeant Pilot Carver.

Landing their passengers at Malta, D14 reinforced by *Petard* returned the following night to repeat the bombarding of Kelibia; as the ships in line ahead, shrouded by the night, neared their bombarding position the area around and behind the target area was ablaze with gun flashes and other explosions, indicating that the final battle to overcome Axis resistance was in full swing. Assistance from 14th DF gunfire seemed an unnecessary extra, spotting the bombardment fall of shot was an impossibility because of the massed pyrotechnics which enveloped the coastline as far as the eye could see, the night sky reflected the titanic finale. A few shells from shore fell harmlessly among the watching destroyers.

To allow any of the enemy north African armies to escape to fight again in the European battlefields would have been an act of folly, so – to fulfil the 'let nothing pass' directive of his operational order – Admiral Cunningham ceased temporarily all coastal and Malta convoys and deployed his eighteen destroyers of all classes to patrol in the Sicilian Channel, west of Marittimo and off the African coast each side of Cape Bon. The only casualties to the patrolling ships came from half trained and ill-led American airmen. Allied airmen were having a field day shooting down Junkers transport planes striving to lift vital units out of the Cape Bon areas; many were also shot down by the destroyers as the great lumbering planes flew low over the sea to escape the fighter aircraft.

The American airmen seemed unaware that the sea between Tunisia and Sicily was dominated by the Mediterranean fleet, and attacked any ship they sighted, so Admiral Cunningham ordered all ships in the Sicilian Channel to paint their funnels and bridge structures with red paint during the night of the 10th/11th. In a rising wind it became a night of anger and for most of the cursing seamen and many of their officers, final confirmation of the incompetence of their tardy and boastful ally.

When dawn came, all the ships – destroyers, Fleets and Hunts – in line abreast plunging into a sea knocked up by a brisk westerly wind, had had their bridges painted red, but at a cost to bridge staffs who were splattered and spotted as if all had been struck down by a sudden plague.

The task proved to be of little avail; the ships were all tuned into bridge loudspeaker watch of the fighters R/T, which were flights of Spitfires piloted by Americans. The destroyers listened in delight to Lieutenant-Commander S.W.F. Bennett (*Bicester*) giving full uninhibited vent to his renowned command and range of naval and English oaths while his ship repelled strafing by the Americans. The amazed eavesdroppers hugged themselves with delight when they savoured Bennett's unrepeatable retort to an overheard American pilot's drawl, 'I guess this guy is friendly'.

Over the next 72 hours, groups of two and three destroyers maintaining patrols in specific and designated areas, carried out search and counter search for signs of any last minute desperate sea moves by the enemy. Admiral Cunningham kept his cruisers at Bône and Malta at immediate notice for steam should the destroyers require back up or assistance.

Jervis, *Petard* and *Nubian* throughout the 12th to 15th patrolled continuously between the towering lump that is Pantellaria and Kelibia; from early on the morning of the 12th they began picking up Germans and a few Italians out of the sea. The scene is described by John Ellis:

> We pick up Germans all day long, about 100 of them, they are searched and taken aft to the quarter-deck. They have all tried to get away in small boats, floats and inner tubes. One of them pretends to be dead in a motor inner tube, some of those we pick up are AA gunners and air crews. They wave white flags as we approach them and some smiling but to make others come inboard we have to fire pistol and rifle shots . . . French flags are hoisted over Fort Kelibia, one officer picked up did not know that Tunis and Bizerta had fallen. One soldier I searched could speak good English and was a German international footballer who had played against England in Berlin, 1936.

Leading Stoker Albert Gore observed the collection of water-logged Germans:

> One prisoner coming inboard spat on the deck only to be punched in the mouth by one of our seaman petty officers. This caused quite a rumpus but nothing came of it.

Able Seaman Taylor wrote later:

> Some were obstinate like one high ranker, but a few bullets through his canoe made him change his mind. They were all interrogated and searched; all had some photographs of their families but much of it porn. I have one photo of Rommel* drinking with a U-boat commander at Tobruk – I must have filched it off a prisoner.

Also during the day *Jervis* sank ten mines and the others in her group sank many more by rifle and machine gun fire. When the night closed in, *Orion* with her 14th DF escort *Kelvin*, *Javelin* and *Paladin* bombarded Pantellaria's coastal defences. Later, at 0200/13th, MTB's entered the small port and damaged shipping and installations. Then all day Wednesday, disturbed only by the

---

*See facing page 192.

sighting of a few wary Ju88's, *Petard* and *Nubian* continued to pick up escapees. *Jervis*, with 96 crowded together aft, living on the open deck under guard, could not accommodate any more. It was a strange experience patrolling these waters which for so long had been under Axis control, in full daylight with the ship full of prisoners, the ship's company at action stations. On Thursday the 13th came the news that all enemy forces in Tunisia had surrendered.

Jervis returned with her group to Malta two days later, the ships more than anxious to land their prisoners who were becoming a serious embarrassment and a strain on the ship's organisation. John Ellis recorded their departure:

> Prisoners disembark and wave to us as they leave, the Maltese try to get at them, booing, throwing stones, all singing the National Anthem and shouting 'Down with Mussolini'. Scotch soldiers escort them away – one officer and eight sergeants.

Jervis remained in harbour until the 18th while the flotilla and destroyers from Bône continued the final stages of sweeping up the small numbers of Axis troops who tried to cross the Sicilian Channel, and maintained the blockade of Pantellaria and other small Italian-held islands. At midnight on the 18th with her usual flotilla companions, *Nubian* and *Petard*, Jervis sailed to continue patrols round the embattled Pantellaria. The ill-armed garrison was in a bad way and short of fresh water due to damage to the supply system caused by bombing. Cruisers *Orion* and *Penelope* accompanied by 14th DF destroyers had made several heavy bombardments to soften up the coastal gun batteries. In spite of the close investment of the island it was learned later that a small Italian naval water tanker had twice run the blockade and brought in fresh water from Trapani and then made a third run carrying a water purification and distilling plant. The damage inflicted on the small port made it impossible to offload the equipment so the intrepid crew took their ship back to Trapani carrying with them a large number of Germans who had been sharing the garrisoning of the island.

On patrol *Jervis* sighted a large ship which made off at high speed when challenged and ordered to heave-to. The destroyers set off in hot pursuit with Captain Pugsley signalling to the unknown ship 'You are standing into a minefield'. However the destroyers soon overtook their quarry which submitted to D14's order to stop; the ship had international markings of a hospital ship but the upper-decks were filled with lines of fit looking men all wearing inflatable jackets; this was hardly the expected appearance of a hospital ship bearing wounded from the North African battlefield. *Nubian* and *Petard* circled the ship and the now stopped *Jervis*, on anti-submarine patrol at the same time keeping a keen lookout for E-boats that might attack from Pantellaria which towered over the scene. There was an initial delay to allow a boarding party into the ship, but the sight of the 4.7" guns of the three destroyers training round and the guns crews loading shells into the breeches hastened the lowering of an accommodation ladder.

Very quickly the officer in charge of the boarding party signalled that there were few signs that the ship, an ex-Greek, was a genuine hospital ship. Pugsley ordered the ship to make for Malta then to his concern it got underway and immediately steered direct for Pantellaria. *Jervis* chased after her and coming up alongside they could see the boarding officer on the bridge: Hailing him, Captain (D) asked him where the devil did he think he was going? A few minutes' delay and the sheepish young officer called back that the rifles of the boarding party had been stacked alongside the binnacle – inducing a large error in the magnetic compass!

Jervis with her consorts shepherded the bogus hospital ship into St Paul's Bay, Malta where a search party soon located a complete and heavily armed company of special troops with their technical support units.

Next day *Kelvin* and *Javelin* left harbour, cheered out by the remainder of the flotilla, the fortunate ships were on their way home for refits and leave. *Kelvin*, which had seen so much action as part of the 14th Flotilla, was the last of the K class operating in the Mediterranean.

The long serving hard core of *Jervis*'s ship's company who had been in the ship since 1939 and some of the more recently joined, who in the main were survivors of other ships lost on the station, watched the two ships departing, torn with mixed emotions. The ship was now commanded by the third Captain (D), had its fourth first lieutenant and a wardroom which had a complete change of its members. They retained a fierce pride in their ship and its achievements but were often naturally irritated by new officers who had not been present during the ship's earlier vicissitudes.

Whenever the ship entered or left harbour her men gave a lead and example to the flotilla and fleet with her appearance and men lining the upper-deck in the appropriate rig of the day, no matter that the ship had been in action or struggling through high seas to the very entrance to the port. In winter months, men cursing the demands of a 'pusser' navy scrambled in crowded, flooded out, fetid, messdecks to 'clean' into serge No 3s, then – after arrival and berthing – changing back again into working rig to re-store and ammunition, repeating the process over again when the ship sailed. In spring and summer when the rig was tropical dress, white shorts and singlets, the task was marginally less demanding and frustrating. Able Seaman Frank (Nobby) Hall recorded his feelings and those of his shipmates:

> Where does discipline end and bull-shit begin? When coming into harbour weary and the deck covered in cordite cylinders, hands are piped into 'rig of the day' and we are made to stand like chorus girls on the Fxle and QD and then back again into overalls to ammunition and store ship? A good job that we are young and feel indestructible.

More night Club runs and bombardments with *Orion* and *Penelope* in the continuing task of softening up the grim, barren, cliff-encircled Pantellaria island. Captain Pugsley was becoming somewhat frustrated and anxious that he might not experience surface ship-to-ship action before his tenure as temporary Captain D14 came to an end. He was constantly pressing Flag Officer Malta for permission to take *Jervis* and the flotilla along the coast of Sicily and the toe of Italy to seek enemy shipping.

He finally got his chance. *Jervis* and *Queen Olga* had completed refuelling after an all night Club run, at continuous action stations, up the east coast of Sicily. Reconnaissance aircraft reported that an escorted convoy was on passage along the Calabrian coast making for the Strait of Messina.

With *Queen Olga* in company *Jervis* set off at high speed in mid-afternoon 1st June steering north back over the route covered on the previous night making for the south eastern approaches to the Strait of Messina. The two ships, *Queen Olga* keeping close station astern in the wake of *Jervis*, sped through the night – ship's companies closed up at action stations.

At 0100/2nd, the ships were 1¼ miles off Cape Spartivento. The black outline of the coast line was sharp, clean cut against the night sky, when the ships came to full alert and tension with the cry from the plot, 'Alarm Port'.

Michael Hemans at his flotilla gunnery officer's station in the action plot had spotted blips on the 286 RDF screen that indicated shipping between the destroyers and the precipitous coastline. The convoy had been located.

Mike Hemans' recollection of 'Our battle of the Glorious 2nd June' includes:

> *Queen Olga* was hanging on to our stern like a terrier and radar came into its own as we went into the old standard well tried gunnery action routine. Director and guns trained onto the alarm bearing, star shell gun ready to open fire with the searchlight at standby to expose the target, guns loaded. Then one premature hiccup, the searchlight operator momentarily exposed his beam, but the enemy did not appear to notice.
>
> Starshell gun opened up and the flares fell exactly right followed by the blinding beam of the searchlight exposing the convoy in all its glory, 4 or 5 store ships and a small tanker escorted by a sloop and 2 or 3 smaller escorts.
>
> We were so close that our shells scored immediate hits, the sloop – we raked her decks and bridge with oerlikon fire, I saw men manning her forward gun jumping into the sea, we sank about 50% of the convoy.

An extract from John Ellis' diary describes:

> We open fire and put our searchlight on a troop and merchantship and set them on fire. *Olga* also scores direct hits, we sink them both, soldiers in the water are screaming for help as we pass them. We then open fire on an escorting destroyer hitting her hard, she immediately blows up. We sight another destroyer which comes out of the smoke screen to ram us, we pump salvo after salvo into her with our 4.7″, she passes close down our port side with the crew jumping into the water, pom pom and close range kills all her bridge crew, she begins to settle.

R.T. Taylor, Captain of No 3 mounting recalls:

> All hell broke loose as the searchlight came on and the enemy are in range, they were taken completely by surprise and did not know what had hit them. How many shells we fired, how long the engagement took or how many we sank I do not know. We had not much time to admire our handiwork. No one talked much and even back in port information is very sparse – nothing on the ship's noticeboards.

Taylor's opposite number on No 2 gun mounting, Frank Hall, remembers:

> They didn't know what had hit them as we raced thro' the screaming swimmers. Someone shouted out, 'You shouldn't have joined, you spaghetti waffling bastards'. He wasn't being cruel, he felt as we all did

that things at last were going our way after taking a hammering for years
– his cry was a sign of our jubilation.

Captain Pugsley could not remain in the area longer to destroy the
convoy entirely, he had barely time left to reach the outer limits of
fighter cover and range of the special air escort laid on from Malta,
but the two 14th DF ships had sunk half of the convoy and its escort.
The store ships *Vragnizzia, Postumia* and escort destroyer *Castore* were
sunk and a smaller torpedo boat had been driven ashore on fire.

Racing south through what was left of the night, towards air cover
and Malta *Jervis* could overhear on the R/T, German pilots of
aircraft conferring and gathering to take revenge: as dawn
approached the Ju88's were waiting to attack as soon as they could
see the jinking, speeding destroyers. Bridge staff and gun crews gave
a great cheer when the lovely shapes of three Spitfires were sighted –
it was later learned that the fighters were down to their last five
minutes of patrol duration before having to turn back to base – it was
enough, the 'Spits' tore into the Ju88 formation and put the enemy to
flight. Every sailor below took back many of the hard things that they
had said in the past about the RAF!

Under a deep blue sky and extreme visibility, with no fighters left
in sight and with enemy airfields in close proximity *Queen Olga*
suddenly came to a stop with condensoritis. While *Jervis* circled the
stopped destroyer every eye was strained anxiously to the north and
towards the Sicilian mainland for signs of enemy aircraft while the
imperturbable Greek captain, Commander George Blessas, assured
his Captain (D) that the engine-room staff only required a little more
time to get his ship under way again and refused several offers of a
tow. It took a very long hour and only moments before Captain
Pugsley was about to order Blessas to take the tow, the Greek started
to move again. At reduced speed the ships made Malta safely, and a
rare 'Make and Mend' afternoon was piped.

The Italian Fascist press reacted violently to these latest sinkings
by *Jervis*, headlines screamed that there was a price 'Dead or Alive'
on each of the ship's company. 'Murderers' who had also sunk the
'heroic' *Lupo* while she tried to rescue survivors of her convoy (3rd
December 1942).

A few days afterwards Captain Pugsley heard that he had been
admitted to the Distinguished Service Order, as was Commander
George Blessas. This splendid Greek officer and seaman already had
an impressive chestful of colourful 'Ice cream' decorations – all these

he removed and henceforth, until he died with his ship a few months later, he wore only the British DSO on his uniform.

The awards received in *Jervis* had a mixed reception. When the captain ordered the lower deck to be cleared so that he could read out the names of the recipients, he had to admit to a failure in the system. Among the decorations, the captain had received the DSO but, sadly, the engine room department had not received even a 'mention.'

One captain of a gun mounting was also overlooked. Not long after the action R.T. Taylor, captain of No 3 mounting, broke a bone in his wrist and was discharged into 94th General Hospital then to the Algiers naval barracks. When *Jervis* appeared in the port during the later stages of Operation Husky, Taylor visited his old shipmates:

> With my arm still in plaster I managed to visit her, Lieutenant Thornycroft was at the gangway. I remember him greeting me with, 'Sorry about your hard luck Taylor', I thought he was referring to my wrist, but it seemed that DSM's had been awarded to the other captain of guns but I had not qualified. It was because as the First Lieutenant's action station was aft, he was therefore senior on my gun, so he got the DSC. He laughed when I replied, 'Maleesh'. It would have been nice to have got the DSM; think of all the extra matches I could sell with it on my chest.

This 'Second Battle of Spartivento' issue of medals caused no more or less lower deck cynicism than had occurred in the follow up to the second Battle of Sirte – then ratings were invited to draw lots for a spare DSM. The draw was won by a Maltese steward named Zara, whom everyone agreed deserved it as much as anyone else. A tailor-made citation followed later with the ribbon.

The rest in harbour proved to be brief; overnight, the weather deteriorated and by dawn a howling gale was blowing and the Vice Admiral Malta learned that a flotilla of nine tank landing craft equipped only with primitive navigation aids were in dire trouble; a destroyer had to go to their assistance. Captain Pugsley detailed his own ship to venture into the turbulent sea to find the lost and dispersed TLC formation. With the aid of the RAF, the storm battered TLC's were found and rounded up, restored into a semblance of a flotilla formation and given a course to their north African port, Sousse.

Remaining at sea *Jervis* set off eastwards to a rendezvous off Tobruk with a recent arrival from the Eastern Fleet. The cruiser

Mauritius, since being first commissioned two years previously, had not seen any action during her escort duties of great troop convoys on long ocean routes. She had spent some days in Alexandria loading many tons of ammunition for the ships based in Malta. *Jervis* waited for many hours off the approach channel, to Tobruk, only to receive a signal that *Mauritius* had run aground and badly damaged herself while leaving Alexandria. The cruiser had a fortuitous escape from becoming a total loss, her repairs were to take until late July to complete.

After refuelling in Tobruk, *Jervis* steamed west and took charge of six destroyers screening the cruisers *Newfoundland* (Rear Admiral Harcourt), *Penelope, Orion* and *Euryalus* off Pantellaria as part of the force making a final assault on the island, scheduled to take place at noon on 11th June. With her destroyers *Jervis* was present to witness their first mass bombing raid, a hundred or more American bombing aircraft flying, in close formation, dropped tons of bombs onto the small island port. The island disappeared from sight of the men watching from their ships, in a giant eruption of flame, smoke and dust, this dense cloud blew out to sea enveloping the ships standing-off in a filthy choking fog. It seemed impossible that anything could survive the American-created holocaust, so it was with considerable surprise that when the destroyers, preceding the cruisers, moved close inshore, they found themselves subjected to sporadic gunfire from some of the gun battery emplacements. The ships suffered nothing worse than some splinter damage. It was a last act of defiance.

In mid-morning *Jervis,* still very close inshore and engaging one of the last batteries to show fight, reported to Rear Admiral R.R. McGrigor, in command of the landing force, that white flags were appearing at many locations inshore. Capitulation by the island's C-in-C was made at 1237/11th and the British Army HQ accompanied by tanks were ashore by 1600; with very little trouble from a few isolated pockets of remaining resistance and one very half-hearted Ju88 raid, all was quiet ashore by late evening.

For the next two days the 14th DF was involved in the surrender of the smaller islands of Lampedusa, Linosa and Lampione. At Linosa, *Nubian* covered by the guns of other flotilla ships closed the tiny port and sent in a landing party which accepted the surrender of the island. After spiking the coastal and anti-aircraft battery guns, the landing party brought off 140 Italian naval and army prisoners of war. Three more days followed on mopping up operations and giving anti-submarine and anti-aircraft cover to landing craft ferrying army units to clear up and garrison the islands. *Jervis* then made a high speed dash to Tripoli with her somewhat mystified ship's company engaged in washing paintwork, repainting blistered gun barrels and other spit and polish evolutions. On arrival with *Nubian, Lookout* and *Eskimo* in company they found that they were to escort the cruiser *Aurora,* with HM King George VI embarked, to Malta.

Aurora preceded the destroyers into the Grand Harbour with King George standing on a platform, constructed on the top of 'B' turret, taking the salute and receiving a tumultuous welcome from the Maltese population crowding the barrakkas. That evening of the 20th, *Aurora* and her escort returned the King to Tripoli from where he continued his tour of the north African battle area. (See Appendix 5. Orders of the Day. 19th and 20th June 1943.)

When *Jervis* re-entered Sliema Creek next morning, Captain Pugsley found Captain J.S. Crawford waiting to assume command of his ship and flotilla. This was the man for whom he had been appointed to substitute on a temporary basis, his arrival having been much delayed. Captain Pugsley was extremely reluctant to leave but, because he had been at sea since the outbreak of war, commanding four destroyers, it had been decided that he should have a rest and some leave before a new appointment. That evening he was pulled away from *Jervis* in a whaler, crewed by ship and staff officers, to the fast minelaying cruiser *Adventure* for passage home. That same evening (21st), *Jervis* moved into drydock for an overhaul and boiler-clean and to give three days' leave to each watch, sending men to a rest camp, set up near to St Paul's Bay.

Men in the 14th DF, or for that matter, in any of the ships operating on the station, were not privy to the next phase of the war in the Mediterranean. It was, however, obvious that preparations were under way on a vast scale for an attack planned to be directed on either Crete, the Aegean islands, mainland Italy or Sicily. The men in *Jervis* had already seen and escorted special Combined Operation Ships *Bulolo* (flagship of Rear Admiral T.H. Troubridge), *Largs* (flagship of Rear Admiral R.R. McGrigor) and their attendant flotillas of large landing ships respectively to Tripoli and Sousse and start training for landing operations. They knew too, that a third headquarters ship, *Hilary* (Rear Admiral Sir Philip Vian), and her landing ships were based on Sfax.

Moreover vast convoys of British and American troop and store ships were arriving in the central Mediterranean from both the east and the west. Flotillas of British manned infantry and tank landing ships, built in America and sailed direct were also arriving at frequent intervals at Bône and Bizerte.

The 14th DF ships shared the task of shepherding and protecting these great movements of shipping, but with only rumours to sustain and to give a meaning to the ceaseless maritime activity.

Captain Crawford, in *Jervis*, sailed from Malta, 2nd July, with P class destroyers (ex-12th Flotilla) *Petard, Penn, Paladin, Panther* and *Pathfinder* deep into the western Mediterranean bound for Oran. This was an area unknown to the men in *Jervis* who had spent their entire three years at the eastern end of the inland sea. The flotilla stayed at Oran for little more than half an hour, long enough to have its first sight of a large force of the US Navy, three cruisers and thirty destroyers dominated by the huge bulks of three major ships from their own fleet, the battleships *Nelson, Rodney* and the aircraft carrier *Indomitable*. It was an awesome and thought provoking sight for men who since December 1941 had operated with nothing larger or more powerful than two or three cruisers.

Following the short visit to Oran and with new orders, *Jervis* and her P's continued westward to Gibraltar, where the battleships *King George V* and *Howe* waited for them to be screened into the Mediterranean. Both ships had been completed and commissioned after *Jervis* had left home waters in 1940. There was no time for a quick run ashore in Gib, just refuelling, and Captain Crawford led the destroyers reinforced by *Tyrian* and *Arrow* out of the harbour to organise the screen while the battleships made their stately and menacing departure. With *Jervis* in the van, the force started out at 0500/5th on passage to Algiers: off Oran *Nelson, Rodney, Indomitable* and seven more destroyers joined. The sight and presence of the five mighty ships of war inside the screen prompted Bill Skilling's understatement which reflected what his shipmates felt, 'Christ, I think that something must be up!'

The great ships were seen safely into Algiers harbour without problem on the 8th. During the day a general message to the fleet and ships serving on tbe station was issued by the headquarters of the Allied Naval Commander-in-Chief. This brought the first awareness that they were part of an Anglo-American armada of 2500 war and merchant ships, poised to land American and British troops along the southern coastline of Sicily, the Americans in the west and the British in the east. Next day *Jervis*, with her destroyers, accompanied the capital ships moving into the central area of the Tyrrhenian Sea and patrolling south of Sardinia to discourage or fend off intervention by the Italian fleet.

The British and Americans landed on their allocated beaches in the early hours of 10th July and, within a few hours, were firmly established ashore and pushing inland to planned objectives. In the west the Americans experienced only moderate resistance from the Italians but in the east, after landing round Cape Passero and capturing Syracuse on the first day, the British Eighth Army ran into stiff opposition from the German defenders.

After bombarding Trapani and the Egadi isles, *Jervis* returned to Algiers with *King George V* and *Howe* which had carried out the unopposed bombarding; she sailed immediately after completing refuelling to join *Nelson* and *Rodney* which were steering to challenge what turned out to be a false American reconnaissance sighting of the Italian fleet. It was a short-lived panic, a classic tail chasing alarm, the aircraft had mistakenly reported *KGV* and *Howe* returning from their bombardment as the enemy – so *Jervis* was out looking for herself!

The flotilla saw the leviathans back into the safety of Algiers and then sped off to the east to back up cruisers bombarding the Sicilian coastal road running north from Syracuse to Catania. Syracuse had received a terrible pounding from *Warspite* and several 14th DF destroyers so men and armour were escaping north along the road when *Jervis* arrived to take charge of her flotilla ships. *Petard* and *Penn* were with their leader when *Echo* and *Ilex* joined. These later destroyers, who had been with part of the fleet patrolling the Ionian Sea, flushed out the Italian submarine *Nereide*, which they sank after a short hunt; *Echo* had picked up 32 members of the crew so she was ordered into Malta leaving only *Ilex* to stay with Captain D and his two P's.

The attack on the highway started soon after first light on 14th, at a point where the road carried a heavy flow of traffic, most of it military traffic from the Hermann Goering Division but some seemed to be civilian refugees mainly in lorries. The destroyers approached in line astern, *Jervis* leading from the east at 90 degrees to the road.

Turning to starboard in succession, each destroyer opened fire in turn as they took up a course roughly parallel to the congested highway, until all four ships were saturating the road and its verges with rapid salvoes for a distance of about a mile. In a few minutes the vehicles were a shambles. A few were hit and on fire, others abandoned by the crews and passengers running to take cover in fields away from the sea; many others crashed into the roadside ditch, while in portions of the road back to Syracuse not receiving attention from the naval guns, lorries, tanks and cars were frantically trying to turn back away from the area under attack from the sea.

Before Captain Crawford reversed course back to the east, at least two tanks had recovered from their surprise and were returning fire on the ships less than 4000 yards from the shore-line, firing solid shot that they used for anti-tank conflict. One shell hit *Petard* above the water-line forward of the boiler-room, passing out of the starboard side after drilling a neat hole through intervening bulkheads without causing casualties or damage to vital ship equipment or services.

The tanks had retired when D14 turned the destroyers back for a second run at the highway and the created congestion point nearest to Syracuse, setting fire to many heavy war vehicles causing a succession of violent explosions, and many fires.

The attacks on the coastal road were repeated by day and night. From time to time the destroyers came under accurate counter-fire from Italian manned shore batteries stiffened by German support and Tiger tanks. While her flotilla suffered superficial damage and some casualties, *Jervis* continued her charmed life, all the while leading from the front.

Captain Crawford came from a different mould than produced his 14th Flotilla predecessors, he was less robust and forceful, complementing a smaller physical stature and chiselled features. He had a kind, gentlemanly nature and mannerisms which soon gave him a sensitive appreciation of the problems of his veteran ship's company. He was quick to sense the motivating spirit of the men who had been for so long in the Eastern Mediterranean, and an awareness of their needs, fears and superstitions. He gave evidence of this when the ship entered Malta to refuel on 22nd July.

On completion of refuelling, *Jervis* berthed alongside in the dock-yard to re-store and to top up with ammunition during which, follow-ing his usual alongside routine, Snowball trotted ashore to exercise his four legs and to seek out the local 'bitch' talent. Whether it was because there were no longer any dogs left in the dockyard and island after the long siege or he had wandered far beyond the boundaries of the yard to find a female with which to assuage his doggy desires when the time came near for slipping and sailing, Snowball was adrift – and, what is more, the ship's company were approaching total shock and panic. Captain Crawford, fully aware of the effect on his men if the ship sailed without its 'proven' symbol of success and survival, delayed his departure for an hour, sent the Petty Officer Myers (the mongrel's minder) ashore with helpers to search and call amongst the bomb-shattered dockyard buildings.

When the disconsolate search party returned empty-handed, their captain sent a signal to the Malta SDO* asking for a general signal to be made to all ships and establishments in the command to keep a lookout for the white mongrel, well-known to many in the fleet, and to hold him until *Jervis*'s return to port.

The ship was destined to be away from Malta for some time, patrolling off Algiers and Bizerte, then into Algiers to collect three of the P's on the 30th, sailing direct to Bône, whence on 31st July *Jervis* and her destroyers screening *Euryalus*, *Dido* and *Sirius* departed with orders to bombard the Italian west coast mainland at Vibo Valentia on the southern shores of the Gulf of San Eufemia. Here during a long night into 1st August the ships without encountering opposition, pounded railway marshalling yards, creating fires and explosions. The force then withdrew east into the Tyrrhenian Sea before turning north under brilliant sunshine and in calm seas – perfect for air attack – until dusk then steering east to strike a bridge south of Naples at Castellamare.

Under the light of star shells fired by the cruisers, the vital supply route bridge was picked out, then in advance of the cruisers, the destroyers opened fire with SAP (Semi-armour piercing projectiles) and set pine woods beyond the bridge on fire, improving the cruisers target by silhouetting it against the fires. After 1½ hours in the area the bridge was destroyed and, as the force withdrew, they sighted then passed at close range a brilliantly lit Italian hospital ship. At 0600/1st August eight Ju88's made a half hearted attack on the speeding and retiring force throwing up a massive AA barrage, as they retired.

At Bône the returning bombarding force were ordered to refuel while taking in ammunition replenishments from lighters alongside – ship's companies stripped to the waist – toiled under a broiling sun to re-stock magazines and ready use lockers with 4.7″ SAP and close-range weapons ammunition. On completion and with some surprise *Jervis* was ordered to Bizerte where on arrival the flotilla leader was ordered by the King's Harbour Master to berth in the lagoon away from the main harbour, which was full of shipping

* Signals Distribution Office.

left) Captain Keightly, the , indicates new targets.

right) *Jervis* bombards ts ashore. No 3 nting in action.

ust 1944. Anthony swell points to the landing on the 'Plateau des hes D'Ouvres'.

ed boat's crew approach slet suspected to be still by the enemy.

29th January 1946. The ss *Gradisca* aground on Gavdo island.

(*Left*) 27th January 1946. MTBs sink while on tow from Malta to Alexandria. (*Right*) 25th May 1946. Illegal immigrant ship *Symri* stopped by *Jervis*.

June 1946. *Jervis* departs from Malta for the last time, to pay off.

serving the Husky operation. It was a scene that made many in *Jervis* feel uneasy: it was a period of the full moon; the nights were cloudless and the harbour was crowded.

Jervis and all warships in Bizerte, whether American or British, maintained a third-degree AA armament watch, which in the 14th DF was one major gun mounting and all close range AA weapons, plus a continuous radar watch (in *Jervis* the 286 RDF).

The middle watch, 6th August 1943, had nearly run its course; the bosun's mate in *Jervis* and many other British warships in the port were moving quietly through darkened and hammock congested messdecks and spaces, arousing the morning watch. In *Jervis*, a wild scream of a shout up the RDF voice pipe galvanised the OOW and bridge staff, warning them that enemy formations were rapidly closing the port. As the OOW pressed the alarm rattler button, sirens began to wail ashore, and searchlights flicked on in rapid succession to start criss-cross pencil thin probing of the night sky.

Action alarm rattlers sounded their stomach-churning cacophony, above which could be heard the scream of the bombers diving down onto the ship as men still drugged with sleep struggled to clamber out of their hammocks. Bombs fell ahead and close down the starboard side, causing *Jervis* to leap and writhe with grotesque convulsions in time with the underwater explosions. Within the ship, messdecks were thrown into blacked out confusion; mess tables collapsed and men sleeping on them crashed onto others sleeping below, and from slung hammocks above, occupants were tossed out to fall into the shambles of broken tables, stools, bedding and struggling shipmates; it was a maelstrom of darkness pierced only by dim emergency lighting. Overhead, No 2 mounting crashed into life, adding to the nightmare.

There was no panic, almost casual calm born of long action experience, as the ship's company scrambled to their action stations. Bill Skilling was the bosun's mate of the middle watch: he recorded in his 'black book' diary; 'This was the worst raid I have ever experienced in harbour.'

The attack went on for 1½ hours, searchlights picked out single raiding planes and groups of four or five aircraft. The barrage put up by the massed shipping was tremendous and menacing in its unco-ordinated and undisciplined fury. When it was over *Jervis* was found to have only minor damage from the near misses and falling shrapnel, and no casualties. Knowing wise-acres in the ship swore that Snowball's protective influence was still with them and that he must surely be alive. While the air raid was at its height the cruisers *Aurora* and *Penelope* entered harbour no doubt preferring the air raid to the menace of patrolling enemy submarines.

Bill Skilling no doubt was reflecting the mood of the ship when two days after the raid, he wrote: 'Chocker, not been ashore for many days – some lads swimming alongside but not me.' The following day, 9th August, was Bill's birthday and *Jervis* sailed with *Panther*, *Pathfinder* and *Paladin* screening four cruisers *Aurora*, *Penelope*, *Sirius* and *Dido*. The ships made a fast passage through flat calm, deep blue seas under a broiling sun disturbed by only two air alerts that came to nothing.

At a position ten miles due north of the island of Stromboli the ships split up into two groups at 2130. One group, *Jervis*, *Paladin*, *Aurora* and *Penelope* , shaped a course to bombard Castellamare for the second time while the other group carried out a sweep, seeking out enemy shipping – two Italian cruisers were suspected to be in the area.

At 0130/10th the bombarding cruisers opened fire at 15,000 yards targeting on a German troop concentration camp located behind a low hill. Two very large explosions resulted from the cruisers' efforts. Meanwhile *Jervis* and *Paladin* closed to 8000 yards from the shore and engaged a shore battery. The battery opened fire with star shell and then replied with big calibre guns and began to straddle the destroyers until Captain Crawford prudently retired behind a dense smoke screen. 'What an end to my birthday,' noted Bill Skilling.

The entire force returned safely to Bizerte. After refuelling, *Jervis* sailed again with her group and, on her way through the boom, met *Penn* inward-bound, carrying mail for the 14th Flotilla. She sent across a boat with Captain (D)'s and *Paladin*'s mail; Bill got twenty airmail letters and a photograph of Lily.

The force entered Palermo (captured by the Americans 22nd July) for a few hours and *Paladin* was able to collect her share of the mail. By midnight the ships were off Vibo Valentia which had been bombed earlier by Allied aircraft; a harbour warehouse was still on fire, giving a good aiming mark for the cruisers and destroyers, there were also aircraft co-operating with flare dropping. For an hour the ships subjected the harbour, the town and railway station to a continuous cannonade – *Jervis* fired 300 rounds of high explosive shells.

When the force returned to Bizerte to refuel and ammunition the ship's company were informed that Italian and German forces were pulling out of Sicily across the Strait of Messina. *Jervis* and *Paladin*, still with *Aurora* and *Penelope*, were off again to bombard the Italian mainland south of Naples, a town and road junction named Scalea where little opposition was encountered and likewise the nights bombardment produced no evidence of serious damage having been caused to the nominated targets.

During the night of 17th August the Axis completed its evacuation of Sicily, 40,000 German and 75,000 Italian troops had escaped with much of their armour and artillery.

The ships remained in Bizerte for three days and – much to the indignation of his men – Captain Crawford nominated his own ship to be duty destroyer for two of them. Their disappointment was mollified somewhat when they learned that a boiler clean had been scheduled for the end of the month.

The same group, two cruisers and two destroyers including *Jervis*, returned to Palermo in the evening of the 22nd and during the night a nasty short sharp air raid developed. One bomb near missed *Jervis* aft as she lay at her alongside berth and the ship suffered its first casualty due to enemy action. This was George, the wardroom's pet chameleon which had joined *Jervis* soon after the ship's first appearance in Alexandria in 1940, George died, squashed flat by one of the WR deadlights dislodged from its open position by the underwater bomb explosion. George who spent most of his time motionless hanging from the chains that held the wardroom table lampshades must have made one of his rare perambulations and was looking out at the outside world through the port-hole glass when he met his end. He was not mourned universally by the afterguard: Michael Hemans positively disliked the long-tongued lizard which was always threatening meals with its droppings.

Before getting her next boiler clean *Jervis* and her group sallied forth once more in response to an American reconnaissance report that an Italian task unit of two cruisers and four destroyers was heading south, but it proved to be an abortive search, the ships – if they ever were at sea – must have returned to base.

In the forenoon of 27th, *Jervis* left Bizerte docks passed through the canal and across the lagoon to Ferryville for her boiler clean and to give 48 hours' leave to each watch. Accommodation had been found ashore so that libertymen could benefit from a couple of nights in beds sleeping away from the confined and machine noisy messdecks; several enterprising individuals exploited American flamboyant generosity, laxer discipline and lavish quantities of transport. They hitched lifts from the 'doughboys' who proved willing to show them the sights including the very recent battle areas, and scrounged accommodation in Army camps and supplies from 'Aladdin's Cave', PX stores.

Michael Hemans had last seen his elder brother, John, shortly after joining *Jervis* in the Eastern Mediterranean. By now he was a major in the Gunners and had come through the desert with the Eighth Army. Having spotted the flotilla leader's distinctive black funnel band as she lay alongside in Ferryville, the sighting enabled a close liaison to be set up between the Gunners' H/Q and the wardroom team.

The short boiler clean leave was soon over, the men were rested; but paradoxically it made many more aware of the fact that they had not had home leave for more than three years. Their first contact with the bemedalled Americans who had comparatively recently entered the conflict and had been away from their homeland for only a few weeks, emphasised their battle weariness and homesickness. Captain Crawford understood this mood and its symptoms, did his best to soften the dictates of King's Regulations and Admiralty Instructions and the special strains of those serving in a flotilla leader, which had always to give a lead and example in dress, drill and deportment. He did what was possible to improve the conditions in the confined messdecks of a ship at war.

On 2nd September, *Jervis* was back at sea and in command of the escort of five large troopships – it seemed clear that, after a three week breather since the Axis abandoned Sicily, the Allies were about to carry the fight to the Italian mainland. The troopships carried reinforcements for the Eighth Army and the Canadian Corps which were about to cross the Straits of Messina in Operation Baytown next day.

Enemy mainland coastal batteries and defence positions were currently being eliminated by the 16″ and 15″ guns of the battleships *Nelson, Rodney, Warspite* and *Valiant* backed up by the monitors *Abercrombie, Erebus* and *Roberts*. Still at sea with her troopships *Jervis* learned that the straits had been successfully crossed by the Eighth Army, using 270 landing craft of all types, protected by the army's own artillery stationed on the Sicilian coastline and under a strong Allied fighter aircraft umbrella. Then off Malta in the afternoon of the 3rd as destroyers from the island took over the escort, a firm submarine contact was established.

An hour's search and several depth charge attacks produced no results and the contact was lost so *Jervis* and her four P class destroyers (ex-12th DF) turned west and set off for Algiers. *Jervis* ship's company were beginning to feel uneasy; since they had lost Snowball six weeks previously, they had had two very near bomb misses which had shaken up the ship badly; this submarine attack had not been successful, and they felt that their luck could be running out and were losing confidence in the ship's invincibility. Then everything changed; the unexpected happened.

Jervis led the way in through the boom gate at Algiers early in the morning of the 4th; the great bulks of *KGV* and *Howe* dominated the alongside berths and harbour: the battleships had not moved for five weeks. As the destroyer slid past the great ships with her men assembled at their stations for entering harbour any temptation to whistle or sing out the derisive chorus of the song about ships which were 'dockyard wallflowers' died in many throats as they learned the portent of a signal which had started to be flashed from *KG V*, the moment that *Jervis*'s bow appeared at the harbour entrance, namely:

To *D 14* *from King George V*

Have your dog, absent over leave – please send escort.

Abreast of the battleship, cheers from *Jervis* broke the disciplined silence of her men fallen in ranks when the small white absentee was sighted, restrained by his Royal Marine minder, barking an excited greeting and trying to jump from the great ship's forecastle.

As soon as *Jervis* berthed ahead of the battleships, Petty Officer Myers ran to be re-united with the delirious mongrel. Back inboard, Snowball's white shampooed coat was soon back to its usual grubby state, firstly from the many hands which patted the ship's mascot, then later tired, sated with titbits and the uninhibited affection of his shipmates the small dog retired to sleep in his old, oil stained refuge under No 2 gun mounting, to appear later covered with oil and gun grease.

Snowball had been found in a distressed condition in Malta dockyard: for about ten days he had been passed from ship to ship in an attempt to catch up with his ship's movements. As this failed, he was placed in the care of *KG V* as the battleship was rather more of a harbour fixture, and was held there to await the next appearance of *Jervis*.

Events began to accelerate for *Jervis* and her destroyers: on the night 5th/6th September she led a half flotilla to cut the railway line which followed the coast line from Taranto, round the foot of Italy to Salerno. The point selected for the operation was on the west coast, north of Cape Vaticano in the Gulf of San Eufemia. The destroyers in line astern of *Jervis*, under the cover of darkness, had closed to a point about 5000 yards from the railway where the permanent way was cut out of the side of the towering coastal cliffs. The plan was to bring down the cliff-face and bury the track – 'just as *Jervis* was about to order the ships to open fire the lights of a goods train were sighted.' There followed a grim game of cat and mouse as the train ran into and out of the numerous tunnels which are a feature of this spectacular coast railway. A salvo from *Jervis* struck the electric locomotive as it emerged from one of the tunnels, causing a tremendous explosion accompanied by an impressive display of sparks as the overhead power-lines collapsed and short-circuited. Searchlights from the ships revealed that the train was carrying freight, including ammunition, the resulting explosion had partially destroyed a tunnel bringing down the track and cliff-face. It would be some time before the line could be re-opened.

After a few hours in port *Jervis* with her four P's departed from Algiers on the 7th, screening *KG V* and *Howe* to join five aircraft carriers and a strong screen of Hunt class destroyers. The united force passed north about Sicily and through the strait of Messina. *Jervis* with her P's entered Malta to refuel while the battleships remained off the island; while fuelling the news flash 'Italy has surrendered' was received in the ships. *Jervis* with three of the P's, sailed on fuelling completion to rejoin *Howe* and *King George V. Howe* was now wearing the flag of Vice Admiral Arthur J. Power. The Vice Admiral Malta had been ordered by Admiral Cunningham to hoist his flag in the battleship, to collect four cruisers of the 12th CS and to take with him the American cruiser *Boise* and fast minelayer *Abdiel* which had embarked 400 troops of the 1st Airborne division. Vice Admiral Power's orders were to proceed with all despatch to the Italian naval base of Taranto, to seize it by sudden descent with light forces and to hold it until the Eighth Army reached the city and base. The operation succeeded brilliantly but not without losses. *Jervis* entered the outer harbour – Mar Grande – in the very early hours of the 9th and anchored, but was immediately ordered to shift berth to allow *Abdiel* to take her place and begin landing her troops. The men in *Jervis* had a grim confirmation that their legendary luck had returned when the unfortunate *Abdiel*, anchored in the position vacated by D14, swung to her cable and detonated a magnetic mine.

She sank in minutes suffering large casualties among her ship's company and the 400 troops. In what remained of the night the destroyers strove to rescue men from the minelayer.

Meanwhile, on the west coast of Italy, strong American and British forces were being put ashore in the Gulf of Salerno in the face of stiff German resistance. The objective of Operation Avalanche was to land forces which would then link up with the Eighth Army advancing from the south, to cut off and capture a large part of the German Army in Italy. *Nubian* of the 14th DF with other destroyers was highly committed at Salerno. She was in continuous action with enemy batteries, infantry units and tanks, for the Germans were strongly contesting the landings.

In her dash to Malta with some of the seriously injured survivors, *Jervis* overhauled and passed two Italian battleships, *Andrea Doria* and *Caio Duilio* which obeying the orders of Admiral Cunningham had left Taranto and were making their way to Malta wearing their black flags of surrender.

On arrival, *Jervis*'s men observed, with considerable and derisive emotion, an Italian fleet of four battleships, seven cruisers and six destroyers assembled off Malta and lying to their anchors under the guns of the fortress and the battleships *Warspite* and *Valiant*.

Jervis was not long in harbour. She left Malta during the first Dog Watch of the 14th taking with her *Penn*, *Pathfinder*, *Petard* and *Ilex* to screen *Warspite* and *Valiant*. The battleships had been ordered to proceed at their best possible speed to the Salerno beach-head where a serious crisis had developed. German panzer counter-attacks down the Sele river valley had driven troops in the main British sector to within 1000 yards of the water's edge and threatened to drive an unbridgeable salient between them and the United States Rangers in the town and outskirts of Maior who were also pinned down.

Admiral Sir Andrew Cunningham had despatched three additional cruisers from Bizerte to the beach-head to increase the invasion force's fire power. *Jervis*, her destroyers and the battleships drove hard through the night; Mount Etna glowered red and menacing away to the west as the ships entered the tide ripped narrows of the Strait of Messina with no regard for obstacles or darkened shipping. The task force arrived off the beaches at 1100/15th and the battleships without delay manoeuvred into their bombarding positions.

The Gulf was crowded with shipping, over all hung a thick pall of smoke, the air was heavy with the stench of fires and cordite and ears suffered the assault of gunfire of every kind. Inshore, close to a scene of smoke, flame, gunfire and explosions, Allied cruisers and destroyers steamed a few hundred yards out weaving a passage through a constant stream of incoming and outgoing landing craft. *Jervis* and her destroyers joined the line of warships engaging enemy positions ashore, in many places gun-layers aiming and firing over open sights at targets only a few hundred yards distance, over the heads of British troops hanging on to a strip of beach above the high water mark. The whole area along the length of the beach head had been turned into an inferno of attack and counter-attack with ships responding to calls from the army to break up concentrations of infantry, tanks and artillery.

The hills surrounding the Gulf reflected and multiplied a pandemonium of explosions, bomb blast and gunfire, palls of smoke and dust drifted, its density increased with frequent eruptions coming from shipping hit by bombs and enemy artillery. Wrecked landing craft and vehicles covered the beaches and foreshore, many burning and exploding. Enemy aircraft constantly harried the invasion shipping, and *Jervis* shot down three Me fighters.

Fifteen-inch broadsides from *Warspite* and *Valiant* thundered out with dreadful and magnified fulmination, overwhelming the obscene battle orchestra. *Warspite* smashed enemy concentrations in the Sele valley while *Valiant*, in the American sector, pulverised the town and road junction of Nocera. The devastating impact of the battleships' armament had by noon on the following day, the 16th, stabilised the situation for the army ashore. Then followed the first attacks from a new weapon developed by the enemy that made an immediate impact on the invasion fleet. Bombers carrying radio-controlled glider bombs scored several successes then started to concentrate on *Warspite*, the prime target. There were several very near misses followed by a hit which knocked out four boiler-rooms, causing much other damage and heavy casualties. Escorted by *Jervis* and the 14th DF the gravely damaged Mediterranean veteran was extracted from the Gulf under her own power; then, with the aid of first two American naval tugs later a third, *Warspite*, passed crabwise through the Messina Strait making Malta on 19th hampered by 5,000 tons of sea water in the ship.

After one night in *Jervis* left with her five P's, this time to escort the fleet aircraft carriers *Illustrious* and *Formidable* to Gibraltar: the ship was seething with feverish 'buzzes' that she was going home with the carriers. But it was not to be: six hours in the base and the destroyers returned to Malta arriving in the late afternoon on the 24th. Then followed an unexpected and pleasurable four days in Sliema Creek for *Jervis* and *Petard* while Captain (D) and his staff received a briefing for new operations in the Adriatic, supporting the Eighth Army.

From the 29th *Jervis* with *Petard* commenced extended patrols ahead of the Eighth Army advance looking for German-controlled shipping, probing inlets and islands on both sides of the Adriatic, men in both ships revelling in the glorious sunshine, free from air attacks and with only a remote possibility of U-boats in the area. On the last day of September the destroyers entered Brindisi, which the Eighth Army had captured a few hours earlier. Bill Skilling wrote in his black book, 'Cleaned ship – shore leave but no grub to be found but plenty of wine.'

The Italians in the city, particularly members of the armed forces, were dazed and wary, they had escaped massacre by the Germans following their surrender to the Allies, and were slowly coming to terms with the capture of their city. *Petard* departed next day under orders to join the Levant Command (Vice Admiral Sir Algernon Willis) to be sucked into an incredible débâcle taking place within the Aegean Sea. In Alinda Bay, off Leros island, a 14th DF ship, *Queen Olga* had been sunk, and her gallant commander, George Blessas, and many of his men had been killed. With awful inevitability *Jervis* was also to be drawn into this senseless operation but for a while she was joined by *Offa* of the 17th Flotilla. Captain (D) was heavily engaged in supporting the army's right flank which had practically reached Termoli. On 6th October the two destroyers spent every hour of daylight bombarding the town's railway, gun positions, concentrations of enemy troops and transport.

This sort of support on the army's flank was to continue by relays of destroyers for many months. On the next two days these two ships crossed to the Yugoslavian side and co-operated with liaison officers working with the partisans, shooting up a wide variety of targets ashore as they were identified. This free-lance operation came to a sudden end when D14 received orders to proceed to Alexandria and take command of the destroyers carrying out a hopeless operation among the Dodecanese islands deep in the Aegean sea. When *Jervis* arrived Bill Skilling noted: 'A run ashore after we arrive, everything dearer now that the Yanks are here – got drunk as a lord, but escaped Jankers.'

Captain Crawford conferred with Percy Todd (Commodore Destroyers, Levant Command) on the situation which had developed as a consequence of the Italian surrender in September. The Germans who had shared with the Italians the garrisoning of the larger Dodecanese islands had disarmed – and in some cases killed the officers – of their recent ally. A few of the islands, including Samos, Leros, Kos and Kalymnos, had only Italian garrisons. The British government decided that this was an opportunity to attack the German 'under-belly' in the Balkans via the Aegean Sea; it was however a proposal strongly resisted by the Americans who were now the dominant partner in the alliance. They very much suspected the British Prime Minister's concept of grand strategy and his desire to liberate the Greeks. The American Supreme Commander in the Mediterranean, after the first few days' attempt to secure all the islands for the Allies, had withdrawn air support and in particular their Lightning fighters, an act which was the origin of the catastrophe to follow.

In Rhodes the Germans had overpowered a larger force of Italians and a few British troops landed on the island to stiffen the Italian resolve. The enemy reacted strongly and transferred large numbers of aircraft from the Balkans and the Russian front and used troops from Crete and Greece backed up by paratroops, to take the islands of Kos and Kalymnos.

Instead of allowing the garrisons to remain, draining German strength from Italy and the Balkans and thus to gradually 'wither on the vine', British politicians forced the field commanders into a continuation of an insane venture in the very area where in 1941 hundreds of men were killed and a host of proud cruisers and destroyers were sunk or damaged at the hands of overwhelming air power. Once again, German air superiority was making the appearance of surface craft suicidal in daylight hours and pinned down troops defending the remaining islands of Leros and Samos.

Intrepid had been sunk with *Queen Olga* on 26th September, dive-bombed out of existence in Alinda Bay. *Panther* was also sunk by dive-bombing and the old AA cruiser *Carlisle* with a matchless fighting record, was irreparably damaged in the same attack.

The commanding officers of destroyers, being sent in time and again to take men and supplies to the remaining two islands deep in the Aegean Sea, were becoming restless and highly critical at the senseless futility of the operation. Elsewhere in the Mediterranean, at long last, the Allies had adequate and frequently dominant air power and it seemed inconceivable that the Chiefs of Staff, to satisfy political expediency and vanity, were allowing men's lives to be squandered in a situation that was a repeat of the disasters of Norway, Dunkirk, Greece, Crete and more recently at Tobruk in Operation Agreement.

Jervis with her reputation as a formidable and experienced flotilla leader, was now in Alexandria to stiffen the resolve of the destroyer captains and for the Commodore (D) to have a senior captain afloat. While *Jervis* loaded for her first run to Leros at the jetty used many times on the Tobruk 'Carter Paterson' runs, a new officer joined the ship. He was Daniel Geluyckens, a Belgian naval officer, appointed in the rank of lieutenant RNR. Daniel had been a naval cadet on a cruise in a Belgian training ship when Germany invaded his homeland. With a number of his brother cadets he had made his way from Freetown to England and entered Dartmouth Naval college to complete his cadet and midshipman training. Then followed a strenuous war before being appointed to *Jervis* as the Gunnery Control Officer (GCO).

Jervis and *Penn* fully loaded, slipped out of Alexandria at 0500/16th, allowing the two ships to enter the Aegean after dark. The cruiser *Aurora* and two Hunts accompanied them as far as the southern extremity of the island of Scarpento to give extra fire-power should an air attack develop. The ships were undoubtedly sighted, but not challenged as *Jervis* led the way between Scarpento and Rhodes, then round the easterly point of Kos via the narrows which separate the island from Turkey, up the east coast of Kalymnos to Leros. The night was full of the sound of aircraft seeking the destroyers, flares fell in long lines across their route in an endeavour to silhouette them for the bombers. Both ships used a ruse developed by *Petard* (Commander Rupert Egan) and dropped canisters which gave off dense white smoke that clung to the surface of the sea which in moonlight or light of the flares misled the aircraft to bomb while the ships stole away.

Flares were falling in profusion from several planes as *Jervis* nosed her way into the confines of Alinda Bay, but several canisters dropped outside the bay had distracted the Ju88's. In one hour the two ships unloaded their stores for the Anglo-Italian garrison into barges manned by very jittery islanders, *Jervis* also disembarked 40 naval and military personnel. Daniel Geluyckens has recalled the general astonishment of his new ship at the sight of the officer landing to be the Royal Navy Liaison Officer, going ashore to an island already under continuous air and sea attack, plus an imminent threat of invasion, *carrying his golf clubs!*.

Unloading was completed by 2230 and the destroyers left at high speed, steaming south close to the coast-line of Kos and as they went bombarding the island's airfield and other nominated targets. *Penn* collected a few splinter holes from the return fire but no casualties. In their headlong dash *Jervis* nearly collided with a ferry barge and a schooner in company. The searchlight flashed on, showed both to be wearing the German ensign; a hurricane of main armament, pom-pom and oerlikon fire from both ships as they dashed past destroyed the small vessels. At dawn, south of Scarpento, *Aurora* and her attendants waited and, together, the force made Alexandria 1800/18th.

Twenty-four hours later *Jervis* was again alongside No 43 Shed but this time with *Pathfinder* loading jeeps and their trailers, anti-tank guns and 2 tons each of crated petrol. They also each embarked 8 tons of food and 50 soldiers. This time when the fleet destroyers entered the Aegean they were accompanied by two Hunts, *Hurworth* and the Greek *Adrias*, whose purpose was to cause a diversion while the larger destroyers tried to make Leros unobserved. The Hunts made a great display firing starshell and with their searchlights so much so that they were comprehensively flared and bombed.

The fleet destroyers entered Alinda Bay undetected and without anchoring started to unload into the lighters, taking rather longer this time as the destroyers had only their torpedo davits for off-loading the jeeps, trailers and anti-tank guns. The job was finally done with nothing more alarming than one or two planes flying low over the anchorage but without making any aggressive moves.

The Hunts turned for home as soon as they estimated that the unloading had been completed. *Jervis* and *Pathfinder* departed at high speed down the east side of the islands without drawing attention to themselves but the two Hunts ran into disaster; a minefield laid by the German layer *Drache*. *Adrias* lost her bow back to the bridge with the fore twin 4″ mounting blown back onto the bridge; *Hurworth*, coming to her flotilla ship's assistance, hit another mine, broke in two and sank in 7 minutes. Both crews suffered heavy casualties. The Greek ship succeeded in reaching Turkish waters where she beached. Over the next few weeks the crew of *Adrias*, helped by experts smuggled in from Alexandria, worked feverishly to make the mangled hull capable of being steamed to Alexandria.

Jervis and *Penn* returned to base late in the evening of the 23rd and after landing expatriates from Leros, refuelled then berthed on No 43 Shed and stood-by for another run. Disastrous news came cascading in, the first came as *Jervis* was having her fore tubes lifted out for the second time to be replaced by a 4" HA gun. Commodore (D) had embarked in *Eclipse* for the next supply run to Alinda Bay, to see for himself the 'facts of life and death' of an operation, the futility and hopelessness of which his destroyer captains were commenting on with increasingly forceful terms in their reports of proceedings, frequently followed up by personal visits to protest at his headquarters.

Eclipse and *Petard* were each crowded with 200 Territorial Army members of the H/Q and A company of the 4th Battalion of the Buffs, withdrawn from their Egyptian re-training camp after a long spell garrisoning Malta under siege. In the narrows and neutral waters between Kos and the Turkish mainland, *Eclipse*, leading *Petard*, blew up in the minefield laid to trap the destroyers making their nightly passage to Leros.

Percy Todd died with many of the *Eclipse* ship's company – casualties amongst the heavily armed and accoutremented Territorial soldiers from Kent were very nearly total. *Petard* returned to Alexandria with a few survivors and her passengers, after the attempt to land them on Leros was abandoned.

The next blow came when *Aurora*, escorting *Petard* and *Belvoir* up to the island of Scarpento, was hit amidships during a heavy air attack on the ships. The cruiser lost many killed and wounded among the gun crews manning the ships 4" AA battery.

When *Jervis* completed her short refit on 14th November, the Dodecanese débâcle was drawing to a close. In the previous night the enemy had landed in Leros and on the same night *Dulverton* – one of three destroyers carrying reinforcements – was sunk by a glider bomb. On the 16th Leros had fallen. Two nights later the garrison in Samos was evacuated. The graveyard operation which had made no contribution to the Allied cause was over, it had a debit balance of six destroyers sunk, three destroyers and four cruisers damaged – one beyond repair. Two submarines and eight minor war vessels sunk. Two battalions of soldiers had been lost, many soldiers killed and hundreds made prisoners of war. For six weeks the Levant Command had been made, by the politicians, to conduct a useless operation without air support. Furthermore senior professional leaders and advisors from the armed services had made no effective opposition to this repetition of Norway, Dunkirk, Greece, Crete and

Tobruk (Operation Agreement) where ships were committed without air cover in support of the army.

Very much to the surprise of *Jervis* ship's company and the flotilla, Captain Crawford was relieved on the 16th by Captain H.P. Henderson. It would be difficult to find a greater contrast between two men, Crawford kindly, gentle in manner, small and dapper – Henderson large, abrupt, aggressive and unapproachable. The new Captain (D) must have caused problems for Peter Loasby who served both captains. He was the flotilla staff signals specialist Lieutenant (Flags) whose extra-mural duties were to take charge of the few social obligations that remained to a Captain (D) in wartime; they were all on a modest scale. Captain Henderson was very different from his predecessors – he was always first ashore whenever *Jervis* entered harbour for more than a refuelling stop, and he was the last to return. Loasby had the task of keeping tabs on the whereabouts of Captain (D).

On Saturday 28th November, *Jervis*, *Penn* and *Pathfinder* arrived off the small island of Kastellorizo situated a mile from the Turkish mainland. The task was to lift out a garrison of 450 infantrymen and replace them with 40 special commandos who had the task of making the island appear to be occupied in strength and to maintain a staging refuelling post for MTB's and ML's making sorties into the Dodecanese. Many of the relieved garrison had adopted the dress and attitude of freelance brigands, a fact recorded by a recently joined Leading Stoker Alex Wisely:

> . . . these troops dressed to look like the natives, complete with beards, knee length boots, bands of ammunition around chest and waist, daggers and knives of every description, shape and size. Only by getting them to speak did you get to know that behind the beard, dress and smell lurked a Scouse or Geordie.

December 3rd, *Jervis* and *Penn* made contact with *Adrias* after the Greek Hunt, minus her bow, had escaped observation from German posts on the islands of Nisero, Piskopi and Rhodes: *Adrias*, making 10 knots was escorted to Limassol and then on to Alexandria where she entered the port in triumph.

With *Penn* and *Pathfinder* in company *Jervis* returned to Malta on the 11th having escorted Prime Minister Churchill in the cruiser *Penelope* after he had attended conferences at Teheran and Cairo. There were many manning the escort ships, who wished that they could tell the PM what they felt about their recent experiences and losses in the Dodecanese. A few days in Malta then on to Algiers to collect a convoy of four troopships which the 14th DF escorted to Port Said where the troopers entered the Canal taking reinforcements to the Eastern war theatre. *Jervis* arrived back at Alexandria on 22nd December to find fifteen bags of mail waiting for the ship and similar quantities for other flotilla ships. In port for Christmas Eve and Day, Bill Skilling's black book has a note, 'What a day – went for a swim alongside – plenty of drink, some from the WR – big eats then head down.'

Also in December and while *Jervis* remained in Alexandria, the flotilla received back *Janus* (Lieutenant-Commander W.B.R. Morrison). Her refit following the acoustic mine damage had been completed on the Tyne in August; since then she had operated briefly with the Home Fleet as far north as Spitzbergen, now here she was again back in the East Mediterranean getting a warm welcome from the men in the leader – tempered with a little envy, for after all *Janus* had been in home waters for seven months. The third remaining 'J', *Javelin*, was still completing her refit in Portsmouth.

The two 'J's' sailed from Alexandria – fate was to dictate that this would be the last time that the Egyptian port would see *Jervis* in her role of a destroyer flotilla leader. Left behind were *Petard* and *Paladin* who were about to leave the 14th DF; within a few days they would pass through the Suez canal as part of the screen of capital ships deployed to join the Eastern Fleet. The two P's then became units of the 11th DF, based at Trincomalee.

Jervis and *Janus* arrived at Brindisi on New Year's Eve, passing through the boom soon after 2300. As D14 completed the berthing of his ship alongside a British-manned Liberty ship, the harbour and sky above exploded into a frenzy of rockets and coloured AA tracer fire to welcome in the New Year, 1944. One member of the ship's company turned the uproar and distraction by the lethal and undisciplined display to good effect. Leading Stoker Wisely, caterer of his stokers' mess, ever alert to improve the diet of his mess-mates and to achieve mess cash saving refunds, discovered that the Liberty ship was discharging foodstuffs onto a tightly guarded quay and that the ship's crew included a few fellow Scouses. The sharing of the leading stoker's hoarded and illicit 'one and one' grog to 'wet in' the New Year, produced, later in the remaining quiet and silent hour of the middle watch, generous gifts of tinned ham, chicken, sausages, potatoes and butter, luxuries beyond price in a period when dehydrated rations dominated the mess menus. For weeks to come the lavish diet of the stokers' mess, their zero spending of the mess allowance and large cash rebate became a cause of suspicion and gave rise to a number of snap searches for illicit food hoards – the bilges gave stokers a head start for the stowage of tinned food!

There was no time for rest or complacency, the Fifth (American) and Eighth Armies had been halted along the south banks of the Garigliano and Sangro rivers and a German defensive system they called the Gustav line. The drive to Rome was held up since 17th November. *Jervis* and *Janus* arrived for orders off the small Adriatic port of Manfredonia in the Gulf of the same name in the evening of 2nd January. These were not long in coming, the ships proceeded north deep behind the enemy lines to back up the harrying operations of four other pairs of destroyers – all had been bombarding road and rail lines of communication, coastal ports and sinking enemy supply shipping. In the night of the 3rd/4th *Jervis* and *Janus* bombarded the port and town of Pesaro under the light of their star shells. There was no opposition but after saturating the port area for an hour from 2230, Captain (D) withdrew seaward for a while in case enemy aircraft decided to appear, returning at 0100 to pour in more salvoes using fires, which had continued to burn from the first attack, as aiming points.

No shipping was encountered as the ships retired and returned to Bari, refuelling and topping up with ammunition. The destroyers departed again at midnight on the 5th and by nightfall on the 6th they were 150 miles north of where the Eighth Army – enduring appalling winter conditions and in the face of fierce enemy resistance – were still battling to breach the Sangro river line. It was to be a busy night, full of action in very rough seas and poor visibility. No doubt encouraged by the bad weather which they hoped would discourage the destroyers, the enemy along the coastline was more active. The J's found three schooners which they set on fire and sank without ceremony after the terrified crews had been ordered to abandon ship by an amplified loud-hailer voice coming out of the stormy darkness, behind merciless unblinking searchlight beams.

In succession, the lights of two trains were sighted moving along the coastal railway, *Jervis* with *Janus* hanging on astern like a terrier, carried out a deadly 'cat and mouse' action for two hours until both trains were brought to a halt with many fires and one locomotive blown up after systematic shelling. Captain Henderson then directed his attention to the coastal town of Civita Nova and commenced to bombard enemy concentrations of stores and transport on the outskirts, spotted below the drifting flares from star shells fired from the 4″ HA gun sited amidships. By 0130 the destroyers were off Ancona and shelling the rail junction. Here, for the first time, they were challenged in a long night of destruction – a battery ashore opened up with some accurate salvoes. *Janus* engaged with all three mountings, at the same time firing a torpedo which exploded and demolished a pier below the battery position and brought its activity to a close. While this was going on *Jervis* strayed into a minefield and for some very long and tense minutes Captain Henderson cautiously manoeuvred to extricate his ship from a highly dangerous and embarrassing situation – the minefield was British and clearly plotted on the chart!

The destroyers withdrew at 0430/7th and sailed south, steering into a strong southerly gale and rough sea. *Jervis* had expended 647 rounds, and *Janus* 500 rounds of HE ammunition and, when the ships arrived light with empty magazines, rolling badly, off Bari the conditions were too bad to allow the boom gate to be opened. As the ships had orders to proceed to Naples after re-ammunitioning D14 set off without waiting for the weather to moderate arriving in the early hours, 10th, and commenced re-ammunitioning and taking in fuel immediately. Before the task had been completed new orders arrived for D14 to take *Janus* and sail with all despatch for Malta. Not for the first or the last time the intentions and efficiency of officers serving on the staffs of Flag Officers ashore was pondered upon, and often cursed, when destroyers were made to chase their own tails on unproductive and fuel consuming sea passages. *Jervis* and her sister ship were forced to retrace their route over the circumvention of the southern part of the Italian peninsula.

While ammunitioning during her short stay in Naples, on the 10th, a new (the fifth) first lieutenant, Patrick Fletcher, arrived in the ship. He was immediately conscious of being very junior in a wardroom that contained a flotilla staff of senior lieutenants. His position and authority was made less than certain by his 'rather strange' captain who seemed reluctant to allow the man he had come to relieve, Thornycroft, to go. So for three weeks and until events were forced by enemy action, the ship had two first lieutenants.

Thirty-six hours after their arrival they set off again for Naples screening *Orion* and once there in the bay, the great muster of shipping which including many landing craft, cruisers and destroyers gave every indication that another landing was in the offing.

Jervis with some engine-room defects needed an alongside berth and as there was no space at Naples she went to Castellamare in the south-east corner of the Bay. Here the ship's company speculated on how much of the damage done to the harbour and town had been a contribution from their bombardments in 1943. The defects were soon cleared and *Jervis* returned to Naples where two libertymen – who had been adrift when the ship left suddenly for Castellamare – caused a minor sensation when army Red Caps returned them to the ship wearing *Italian naval uniform* after a night in a local jail. Their uniforms had been stolen when they had been mugged in a Naples brothel. Their escapade which could have cost them their lives went unpunished in the welter of events and administrative dislocation that ensued in the next few days.

Orion, Jervis, Janus, Faulknor and *Laforey* bombarded Gaeta and the bridge crossing the river Liri during the night of the 18th in support of the British X Corps whose forcing of the river Garigliano had come to a halt. The ships shelled positions ashore all night, at one stage *Jervis* – stopped and pointing at her river crossing targets – fired so many rapid salvoes from her Nos 1 and 2 mountings that the ship gathered considerable sternway speed and had to be constantly brought back and held by her screws at the datum firing point. The fire power from the sea forced the enemy to retire temporarily from their positions but the Gustav line still held on the sea flank.

Remaining within the Bay of Naples for just another day *Jervis* and *Janus* having refuelled and ammunitioned, stood by to take their part in the next Allied landing behind the enemy lines. Operation Shingle, a landing at Anzio was planned to break the deadlock ashore and to get the American Fifth Army into Rome within a few days. The objectives failed to mature and a four month slogging match developed which negated the highly successful joint American and British naval landing of the VI Corps on the Anzio beaches which took the enemy by surprise. *Jervis* and *Janus* were there until disaster struck both J's.

The ships arrived in company at 0001/22nd January at the lowering position off 'Peter' Beach north of Anzio, the landing area for the British 1st Division, having escorted the assault convoy from Salerno under cover of the night. The American 3rd Division was landing at the same time at 'X-ray' Beach, south of Nettuno.

Except for some light machine gun fire the landings were unopposed. In the morning that followed, between 1130 and 1215, the J's bombarded targets indicated to them by artillery FBO's

(Forward Bombardment Officers) ashore, between San Lorenzo and Sucastro; both ships fired between 65 and 80 rounds each, and receiving complimentary remarks from the FBO on their accuracy. The enemy had begun to recover from the initial surprise and sporadic air attacks developed mainly from low flying fighter bombers which were very hard to spot and shoot down. In anticipation that glider bombers might be launched at dusk when the ships off the beach-heads would be silhouetted against the evening sky, Captain Henderson took his destroyers to the north of the anchorage and masked it from the Dornier 217 bombers with funnel smoke, CSA and smoke floats. After dark they closed the anchorage to give it protection against E-boat attacks, but no incidents disturbed the night. By midnight 36,000 men, over 3000 vehicles and many tons of stores had been landed at the beach-heads.

At noon next day, the 23rd, a few isolated shells from an enemy mobile battery fell among the ships; *Janus* was near-missed but was undamaged. Twice during the afternoon D14 was called upon to fire on targets ashore, one was a suspected gun battery north of Ardea, both ships fired 50 rounds. Twenty minutes after cease-firing following the last call for fire from ashore, *Jervis* reverted to defence stations and was about to start the second night of anti E-boat patrolling when a Red alert aircraft warning was signalled to the ships off the Anzio beaches, Dornier 217's had been sighted.

After action stations had been stood down Bill Skilling had taken up his Defence watch station in the wheel house. He had been there for a short while when Captain Henderson's voice with sudden urgency came down the voice pipe as the action alarm rattlers called the ship back to action stations: 'Do what I tell you fast', followed by a rapid series of helm and telegraph orders. Bill left the wheel house at the double when Coxswain Stanislas and the action wheel house crew took over again, reaching his action station on No 2 mounting 'just as *Janus* blew up in thousands of colours.' Minutes later, while going full astern *Jervis*'s bow exploded in a tremendous crash of smoke and flame.

Both ships had been struck by radio controlled glider bombs, launched and guided by parent Dornier 217 aircraft. *Janus* – hit in No 2 magazine – exploded; the fo'c'sle and part of the bridge were blown away, the ship turned over leaving her keel above water before sinking six minutes later. *Jervis* had a miraculous escape. Her bow had been blown off back to number 9 frame and the fxle breakwater. The chain-locker, freshwater tanks, paint petrol and lower stores were all gone and a fierce fire raged, but the bulkhead to the lower messdeck held. Not a man was killed or injured.

Moving at slow speed dealing with the fires and shoring up the bulkhead, *Jervis* lowered boats and scrambling nets to rescue her flotilla mates. 82 were picked up, including 5 officers, 11 more were picked up by other craft but the losses were awful; the captain, 5 other officers and 152 men died. Leading Stoker Wisely's diary recalls the incident:

> My action station was in the engine-room, I took my throttle and the CERA on the other, we had a telegraph order from the bridge for EMERGENCY FULL ASTERN, we went full astern in *no* minutes flat but not quick enough to escape getting hit in the bows but if we hadn't been so quick we could possibly have ended up like *Janus*. These 'Chase me Charlies' zone onto the electric system of the ship . . . going for the dynamo compartment – by our crash stop the bomb almost missed ahead. We had a hell of a fire in the paint store, our fire party did a great job . . . my mate Ron Sutton was one, he got a mention in despatches – not long before the action the first lieutenant had informed him that he had lost all his family in an air raid. I used to think he was crazy trying to get himself killed; his work in the fire deserved more than a mention. The Chief Stoker got a DSM.

Underway, stern first, Captain Henderson set course for Naples escorted by the tug *Weasel*, the destroyer *Grenville* and others. Not long afterwards, the First Lieutenant Fletcher and the Commander (E) reported that shoring was well advanced and pumps were coping with a small intake of water, so Captain (D) turned his ship and worked up to 10 knots with *Jervis* pushing a foam-crested wave before her blunted hull. Weaving her way into Naples harbour and round the stranded wrecks, unaided by tugs Henderson berthed his damaged ship.

Lucky *Jervis* was indeed living up to her reputation, again the flotilla leader had survived without sustaining casualties, she was indeed 'Lucky *Jervis*'. The lower-deck had no doubts about the source of their good fortune – Snowball's grubby coat said it all, patted, stroked, touched and fondled by his devoted admirers – he revelled in every minute of his pampering. Unknown to his devotees the morning marked the moves to end their ship's career as a flotilla leader, and not even Snowball's luck could do anything to prevent the inevitable.

Captain Henderson had sent a signal to Admiralty and then went ashore to see the Commander-in-Chief, Admiral Sir John Cunningham, to state his intention of continuing the command of the 14th Flotilla from the destroyer *Grenville*, whose current commanding officer should then take *Jervis* to a suitable port for repairs.

Grenville although operating as a private ship, had been laid down and constructed as a flotilla leader for the *Ulster* or 'U' class destroyers of the 7th Emergency Flotilla. Since commissioning in May 1943 the new destroyer had seen exciting and demanding service in the English Channel, the Atlantic and, more recently, in the Adriatic. *Grenville*, after entering Naples with *Jervis*, had drydocked a short distance from where *Jervis* had berthed; she was having adjustments made to her propellers. Her commanding officer (Lieutenant-Commander Roger Hill, DSO) was mildly puzzled when a hand message was delivered ordering him to report to Captain (D) in *Jervis*. Walking across to the flotilla leader, Hill mulled over in his mind on the latest escape of the ship known to the fleet as 'Lucky *Jervis*' and her tremendous reputation in the 'Man's end' of the Mediterranean commanded by a series of men who were renowned leaders.

Roger Hill was shown down to the wardroom where Captain Henderson sat surrounded by members of the flotilla staff; he was asked to take a seat and with no preliminaries Captain (D) brusquely said, 'I've got to take over your bloody ship.'

This statement set the tone of the transfer and take-over – it was to take place on the following day – no time for the formal hand-over and checking of confidential books, accounts and stores. The first lieutenant, Fletcher, was to remain in *Jervis* and, as head of the naval, victualling and armament departments, he could ensure accountability to the new commanding officer. Henderson informed Hill that he was going to take with him to *Grenville* the entire signal department, W/T and V/S as well as his cook and stewards. Hill was to arrange that his telegraphists and signalmen were to follow him to *Jervis*; he could also have his seaman servant Charley and take two officers, Lieutenant Anthony Casswell RN and Lieutenant Peter Boissier RNVR.

Hill walked back to *Grenville* in a semi-daze bracing himself to announce the shattering news to *Grenville* that she was to become a flotilla leader with Captain (D) and his entourage arriving next day. He was having to come to terms that he would leave a ship's company which he had welded into an effective fighting unit, but he could see the logic of the change. *Grenville* had been built for the job as a flotilla leader. At the same time he enjoyed a glimmer of pleasure that he was to occupy the quiet, spacious, lavishly appointed commanding officer's day and night cabin suite aft in the *Jervis*, while the overbearing Henderson was to take over his more austere functional quarters located amidships, always noisy and lacking privacy.

The transfer took place on Thursday, 25th January; from noon *Jervis* became a private ship and, as such, was to gain new laurels for her role in the Normandy landings, Operation Neptune – the naval part of the Allied storming of the European mainland, Operation Overlord.

Jervis had established a record and unchallengeable reputation as a flotilla leader; with her destroyers the flotilla had been a keystone of the final victory in the Western desert, constantly in support of the desert's sea flank, supplying Tobruk and Malta against all odds; taking the army into Greece and Crete; out again in the subsequent evacuations in spite of overwhelming Axis air power and challenges by the Italian fleet. Her tally of destruction of enemy shipping was formidable. With her flotilla, *Jervis* had been responsible for the sinking of eight cruisers and destroyers, and sixteen supply ships. Ashore her bombardments had destroyed innumerable vehicles and ammunition dumps, railway tracks and rolling stock. Many coastal batteries were silenced. She was present when her destroyers sank submarines but was unable to claim her own sinking of a U-boat. At least two dozen enemy aircraft had been brought down by her guns.

In January 1944 only one other 'J' class, *Javelin*, had survived and of the 'K's' who had come to the 14th DF after the early demise of *Kelly* and the 5th flotilla, only *Kelvin* and *Kimberley* remained. *Jervis* had survived 3½ years of conflict in the Eastern Mediterranean, throughout that time not one of her men had died from enemy action.

CHAPTER SEVEN

Private Ship

The ship's company's self-respect had evaporated virtually overnight, to be supplanted by a turmoil of mixed emotions: first they had to come to terms with the fact that their proud ship was no longer a flotilla leader – at a stroke they were just another 'canteen boat' and a 'tail-end Charlie'. Painting out the leader's broad black funnel-band was a traumatic experience, symbolising their personal fall in status. Secondly, they all faced an uncertain future – the missing 28 feet of a trawler bow indicated a long period in dockyard hands – but where? In the Mediterranean, Alexandria, Malta or Gibraltar? Or could it be a home port? The long-serving east Mediterranean veterans should have been certain now of a draft chit, but there was no information, the end of the war was still in the mists of an uncertain future, would death come to some of them before getting home?

Then there were the unknown qualities of a junior commanding officer to be faced; they had known only 'four ringed' Captains (D). He was a big handsome bearded, two and-a-half striper, a seemingly pleasant and vigorous personality, but none of his new crew could guess at the professional and domestic problems hidden by a slightly flamboyant façade. Roger Hill made no bid for instant popularity with the men who manned the ship whose name and record he had so admired. He later wrote 'I felt both humble and proud to command this famous flotilla-leader'. He gave no indication of such feelings when he introduced himself to the ship's company cleared from the lower deck and mustered before him. He was probably still smarting from his rough handling by Captain Henderson, for he took a tough line on the appearance of the ship and her men, turning his audience into an instant tooth-sucking body of resentful sailors. This feeling was fuelled by Charley, the captain's seaman servant, imported from *Grenville* who was less than tactful, grumbling to his new messmates that it had taken him two days to scrub out the pantry, day and night cabin to bring it up to his master's standards.

Fortunately for *Jervis* – her new commanding officer and a ship's company which had momentarily lost direction and faith in themselves – she still had Snowball, an infallible symbol of good fortune.

Roger Hill had brought with him a small canine pet which had lived with him in his previous command. Named Skerki after the shoal-bank at the western entrance to the Sicilian Channel, the small bitch had good Mediterranean connections. With his usual sense of the occasion, and to the huge Rabelaisian delight of his ship-mates, Snowball discovered Skerki, cornered her and then comprehensively served the less-than-willing bitch in full view of both watches of the hands fallen in to be detailed off for work. The ship's good humour was restored in a flash as the news, accompanied by lurid detail, went round the ship, 'Snowball is screwing the captain's bitch'. Within the hour, the coupling had wiped the slate clean of all resentments, replaced by a firm acceptance and rapport between Hill and his men. It was to be a trust and admiration that would be repaid in later months off the Normandy beaches by his brilliant ship-handling and combat professionalism.

Jervis escorted by the minesweeper *Cadmus* left Naples on 30th January 1944 and at 8 knots made for Bizerta where she joined the columns of a slow convoy for Gibraltar, arriving there in the evening of 5th February. There was no going home for repairs; *Jervis* entered a drydock shared by the headquarters ship *Largs*. The bottom of the dock was smelly and claustrophobic so the officers and most of the ship's company were given accommodation in *Warspite* which lay alongside the dockyard undergoing repairs to her shattered boiler rooms.

Roger Hill obtained permission from Gibraltar's Captain (D) to take compassionate leave and fly back to the UK to deal with his domestic problems; before he departed he learned that he had been awarded the Distinguished Service Cross for his time commanding *Grenville* in operations based on Plymouth. After some delay he succeeded in getting a place on an RAF flight home but his young First Lieutenant Pat Fletcher and Wardroom had to cope with a mass of problems in his absence.

There was the rebuilding of the bow and a general refit to oversee and of more urgency, a ship full of men hoping to get drafts home. An overworked first lieutenant had a ship 'stiff with regular long service ratings and survivors of many ships dying to get home'. He was also having a hard task in seeking replacements and facing the facts of a virtually complete change of crew plus all the problems of shaking down a new ship's company. To complicate matters, during the last call at Malta, all the Maltese wardroom stewards had been changed: . . . 'they were a rough lot and went for each other with knives'; they had to be sorted out and some sent back to the island. To use Roger Hill's own words before he left for the UK, 'morale fell to rock bottom, the ship was full of gloom'.

The priority was to get the 'old' ship's company away and Fletcher succeeded in this by early March; most went as passengers in a cruiser going home, a few had left earlier in ships of a United Kingdom-bound convoy. Bill Skilling and some of his friends obtained berths in a collier, ss *Borde* (2014 tons), and worked their passage *shifting coal in the holds!* The ship was left with a nucleus of officers and men who had joined in the last months and weeks of 1943; these included Pat Fletcher, Daniel Geluyckens, the two ex-*Grenville*s Anthony Casswell and Peter Boissier, the Engineer D.W. Walker and Mr Cooke Gunner (T). There were a number of ratings remaining, including the coxswain, Chief Petty Officer Stanislas, Chief Yeoman of Signals Moult, Petty Officer Telegraphist Roberts, the 'Buffer', Chief Petty Officer Lewin, Chief Stoker Gabey and Leading Stoker Alex Wisely. In addition there was also the longest-serving member of the ship's establishment with nearly four years in the ship since joining in Alexandria, July 1940, the white Egyptian mongrel, Snowball.

Jervis with a new bow, her refit completed and a fresh crew sailed from Gibraltar on 17th April after trials and arrived at Plymouth for a 36-hour stop before proceeding to Scapa Flow where she arrived on the 24th to a complete change of environment: from brilliant sunshine, calm warm blue seas the ship was thrown straight into a situation of gale following gale and constant anchor-watches when in harbour. This period of the *Jervis* saga – the five months until the ship withdrew from her place in the Normandy landings and Operation Neptune – have been covered in depth in Roger Hill's classic autobiographical book *Destroyer Captain* so this work on the ship's career will only touch upon the main events of the period.

At Scapa Flow *Jervis*, in company with many other destroyers exercised their skills of naval bombardment, working closely with embarked Royal Artillery Bombarding Liaison Officers (BLO) and Bombarding Observation Officers (BOO). With Daniel Geluyckens retained in the ship as her GCO, the new gun crews and control team soon regained the old Mediterranean expertise in this form of naval gun support for the army ashore. On 3rd May *Jervis* left Scapa Flow for a short boiler-cleaning break at Rosyth; on passage Skerki gave birth to her puppies on the captain's bunk in his cabin aft. Snowball's offspring were all adopted with affectionate enthusiasm by several of the messes. Exercising and training continued at Scapa Flow in preparation for the Operation Neptune landings until the ship departed for Portsmouth arriving to anchor in a great concentration of shipping in the Solent on 24th May.

Jervis was in the van of the invasion armada, steaming towards the British Assault Area and the Sword landing beaches in the night of 5th/6th June and there she was to remain except for short withdrawals for refuelling and ammunitioning until 18th July. At 0625/6th June, D-day, *Jervis* with the other destroyers off the Sword Beaches opened fire on their nominated beach defence targets as landing craft surged in to land the first troops and tanks. Daniel Geluyckens and his gun crews engaged with all six 4.7″ guns, using a deadly cocktail of SAP and DA high explosive shells, a pill-box that enfiladed Green beach with 88mm gun fire. The position was effectively silenced and over the remainder of a very long day and the days that followed the accuracy of the ship's supporting fire received many enthusiastic and flattering reports over the gun R/T net from unseen BOOs. *Jervis* continued her charmed life, always in the thick of the action but surviving enemy battery fire, air and E-boat attacks where less fortunate ships suffered many casualties, were damaged or sunk.

Unfortunately for Roger Hill, he fell foul of Captain Henderson who in *Grenville* was Captain (D) off the beaches. He escaped for a while from the immediate consequences of this uncharismatic senior officer's displeasure because Captain (D) ran *Grenville* aground and was forced to retire from the Normandy beaches for several weeks. After the initial days occupied in establishing the beach-heads, *Jervis* with MTBs carried out night patrols to defend the assault fleet anchorages from E-boat attacks. On 19th June, in a north east-gale which lashed the exposed anchorages and brought to a stop, all unloading onto the beaches. *Jervis* at anchor, was struck at 0825 by an American-manned Liberty ship running amok in the gale. The 10,000 ton ship rammed the destroyer from ahead, bending back 6ft of the bow, then bumped down the starboard side wrecking a portion of the bridge structure outside the chart-house, continued along the ship aft, tearing away guardrails, boats and davits and finally the scuttle to No 1's cabin, disappearing astern into the murk and spume of the gale without a sign of a wave or signal of regret from the rogue merchantship. *Jervis* incurred no casualties and her ability to operate remained unimpaired.

Bombarding went on day after day from anchorages that were frequently under attack by enemy fighter bombers and glider bombs. The destroyers were, from time to time, supported by cruisers and battleships firing over them from seaward. Roger Hill used all the skills he had acquired in the Adriatic to anticipate and avoid the enemy return salvoes while Daniel 'G' in a new role, continued to receive verbal bouquets from the BOO for success in knocking out German mortar crews, a few hundred yards ahead of pinned down British troops.

Lieutenant-Commander Roger Hill, decorated with a DSO and DSC for his achievements while commanding three destroyers in a hard and bloody war, learned on 30th June that he had been passed over for promotion to commander in the half yearly promotion lists. This news which must have a blow to his pride, arriving while his ship was hotly engaging the enemy, did not crush this hard-pressed officer whom many considered was not getting a fair deal from the senior establishment within the regular naval service.

Neither did the spirit of the wardroom flag, as recalled by Robin McGarel-Groves, Captain Royal Marines, serving off the British assault beaches in the cruiser *Enterprise*. The two ships were in the Solent together for a night but no shore leave permitted. The cruiser's wardroom received a RPC from the destroyer. McGarel-Groves was one of the team which accepted the *Jervis* invitation and found themselves in a company and a ship where the drinks were not slow in coming or sluggish in being recharged. But, he found something indefinably odd when trying to make small talk to whom he thought was his opposite number in the BLO field. Overhearing his companions, he found that they too seemed to be also having problems getting through to their apparent professional equals. Holding the centre of the stage was a large, genial, bearded gunner. The gaffe was finally blown when a signalman obviously not briefed, entered the wardroom, approached the gunner with a signal and addressed the Warrant Officer as, 'Captain Sir'. It then became clear that their hosts had changed uniforms! The RA Army BLO was masquerading as the first lieutenant, the gunner and commanding officer had changed places and so on. It was apparently a popular *Jervis* party trick which on this occasion had not been detected by puzzled guests.

From 22nd July, after days of bomb, guided missile, E-boat and shell salvo dodging *Jervis* was deployed to operate off the Western Assault Area defending and protecting minesweeping flotillas with smoke screens and gun-fire. Here again *Jervis* experienced a charmed life moving slowly on one engine over acoustic and pressure mines that were sinking and damaging other ships.

Between 28th July and 11th August, the ship was having a boiler clean and gave leave to both watches and was back in action on the 12th with *Faulknor* and escorting *Rodney* which used her 16″, in three triple turrets, to knock out a powerful enemy battery on Alderney. That night *Jervis* had a skirmish with E-boats without positive evidence of damage or sinkings of the enemy. Next day *Jervis* entered the captured port of Cherbourg and fuelled from a French tanker in Grande Rade, leaving immediately on completion for a three-day patrol off the Brest peninsula and round the Channel Islands which were still in enemy hands, returning to Cherbourg on the 17th. To satisfy the whim of the American Admiral commanding the area, *Faulknor* and *Jervis* were ordered to patrol the straits of Alderney in range of three powerful German radar-assisted coastal batteries, to seek for non-existent inter-island shipping.

Jervis entered the tide rip of the straits after dark, the 17th, while *Faulknor* stood-off to the west to make a demonstration and draw the enemy fire. At 2245 *Jervis* was nearly through the straits when the three enemy batteries opened up with extremely accurate fire; salvoes falling in her wake swept the ship with splinters. Using smoke and at the same time releasing a floating fire decoy, Roger Hill with superb seamanship and his sixth sense to avoid fall-of-shot, helped by Anthony Casswell's navigation skills escaped significant damage or casualties and rejoined *Faulknor*. Joined by Captain (D) in *Grenville* and *Saumarez* the destroyers then spent three days bombarding targets in the Brest peninsula and on 31st August were supported by the battleships.

On 3rd September, the fifth anniversary of the outbreak of the war, *Jervis* set off in very bad weather for her last patrol north of Alderney, signals had arrived in the ship ordering her to Belfast for a major refit which would include stripping-down and repairing the turbines and the destroyer was to pay off. On 6th, three months after D-day *Jervis* berthed on an oiler at Spithead, departing from the Solent next day, passing up the Irish sea in very dirty weather to arrive at Belfast flying her paying off pennant in the afternoon of the 8th.

It was here that Snowball left the ship in the care of his current keeper, the PO/Tel. Snowball's four years in the ship were probably unique for an animal mascot in war; there was no one left who had been in the ship when the small Egyptian mongrel puppy was given a floating home in Alexandria, July 1940. As a symbol of good luck Snowball had an unblemished record; in the countless actions and incidents where *Jervis* played a part not a single man had been killed or injured by the enemy.

Patrick Fletcher left the ship on 17th September for leave and a new appointment; the commanding officer Roger Hill and everyone else had already departed. *Jervis* paid off from her first commission. Only two stayed with the ship to oversee the refit, Lieutenant (E) D.W. Walker and the Gunner (T) Mr L.F. Cooke.

*

Jervis remained in dockyard hands at Belfast until after VE day 8th May 1945 – she was recommissioned in mid-May by a new commanding officer, Commander G. Ransome DSC (nicknamed predictably, Handsome Ransome), he was a very senior and in relative active service terms, a rather elderly commander. In complete contrast his No 1 was a young and madly enthusiastic lieutenant, a product of Britannia Naval college, Dartmouth, the son of a distinguished serving Admiral and brother of a successful and famous coastal forces leader of MTB and MGB flotillas. He was Lieutenant Claude Dickens, a young man dedicated to living up to the reputations of his father and brother. The engineer officer Walker and Mr Cooke rejoined the ship and so did Peter Boissier who had been to the gunnery school HMS *Excellent*, and qualified as a GCO. He had been appointed back to *Jervis* to take on Daniel Geluyckens' old job. Apart from these three officers *Jervis* had a completely new ship's company.

After trials and working-up, the ship was under orders to join the Mediterranean fleet and on 3rd June departed from the United Kingdom bound for Gibraltar – on passage Ransome was ordered to call into Lisbon to collect some U-boat crew prisoners. The ship berthed in Alcantara dock and embarked (from the Portuguese destroyer *Dão*) four officers and forty-three ratings who had scuttled their submarine off the northern port of Leixoes, being picked up by the *Dão*. *Jervis* arrived in Gibraltar on the 6th and landed her prisoners of war and then instead of sailing on to Malta remained in port for two weeks during which time Commander Ransome suddenly left the ship. A couple of days later he was replaced by

Commander D.H. Maitland-Makgill-Crichton DSO, DSC, a well known bon viveur who was known as Champagne Charley by his friends and equals, but soon became nick-named 'Uncle David' by his wardroom officers.

Rejoining the Mediterranean Fleet in a sea cleared of the menace of hostile submarines and aircraft created conditions that would be unrecognisable to the men of the first commission. The ship could now steam with scuttles and deadlights open; below-deck spaces were sweetened by air sucked in through wind scoops; deck-lighting at night was permitted which improved the safety of passage along the upper decks. The ship at sea worked on a four watch system so that a middle watch came only once in four nights; men no longer had to keep four hours on and four hours off watch and could expect six or more hours every night in their hammocks.

Jervis returned to Malta on 22nd June and rejoined the 14th Flotilla, still as a private ship, staying at the fleet base for three weeks. Captain (D) and most of his staff operated from shore headquarters. The ship then proceeded to Alexandria where the main units of the fleet had moved because of growing problems over the British mandate of Palestine. *Jervis* arrived back at her old wartime base on 13th July carrying mail for the fleet, which had been flown out to Malta.

For the next four months *Jervis* exercised with the fleet and visited Middle East ports to show a naval presence, often where there was now a menace of political terrorism. In Haifa there were particular dangers, libertymen could not be allowed ashore and a constant watch had to be kept for saboteurs. But much of the time was spent, in contrast to the experience of the years 1940 to 1944, doing little more than cruising in glorious weather, calling at ports where British ships were welcomed; the new crew enjoyed generous hospitality from liberated peoples grateful for the achievements of the long departed East Mediterranean veterans.

There were the occasional flurries of activity: at Trieste two platoons of seamen and stokers were landed for training in the arts of the infantry and commando-style combat; to be capable of dealing with violence in Greek or Palestinian ports. At sea on 19th November in the Gulf of Venice *Jervis* came across an abandoned American liberty ship, US *Jesse Billingsley*. A boarding party found that the ship had apparently been damaged by a mine but her bulkheads were holding and there was no danger of the vessel sinking. A tug summoned from Trieste towed the American into port.

Christmas 1945, bomb-battered Malta held a few more attractions than were available when the first commission ship's company endured a wet comfortless and half starved Christmas day in 1943. The weather however was the same, frequent rainstorms and gales, but beer was plentiful and the 'Gut' had regained some of its pre-war attractions. *Jervis* ammunitioning from a lighter on 5th January, dragged her anchor in a hurricane-strength squall and grounded, causing slight damage to one of her screws. Commander Maitland-Makgill-Crichton managed to put to sea with the lighter still secured alongside and with difficulty rode out the storm before returning to port and into drydock for underwater examination and repair to the propeller.

Bad weather persisted for the whole of January; on the 23rd with the destroyers *Chevron*, *Chequers* and *Chaplet*, *Jervis* was detailed to tow some motor torpedo boats to Alexandria for sale to the Egyptian Government. Each destroyer was to tow two MTBs with two seamen taking passage in each boat. *Jervis* was the senior ship of the group and Commander Maitland-Makgill-Crichton asked for a postponement of their departure because of the bad weather conditions, but permission was refused by Flag Officer Malta. The destroyers and their tows sailed on the 25th, and within 36 hours every torpedo boat had sunk in appalling seas and with immense difficulty the 16 men in the sinking craft were recovered.

In the same storm a commandeered Italian liner, the ex-Hospital ship, *Gradisca* carrying British troops to the Middle East went aground on Gavdo island, south of Crete. The cruiser *Orion* answered the ship's distress call and took off the troops and 106 of the crew, leaving the master and 140 of his men to try to salvage their ship. *Jervis* arrived on the scene in the evening of Tuesday 29th to take charge of the salvage operation while *Orion* left, returning to Malta with the troops and crew.

Three days of immense difficulty followed. The Italian master reported that his men had got out of hand, they had broached the liquor store, were refusing orders, had commenced looting, some had armed themselves. Peter Boissier was sent across in *Jervis*'s boats with a platoon of his commando-trained sailors and restored order. While this was taking place, two salvage tugs arrived, *Salventine* and *Marauder*; shortly afterwards a signal was received informing *Jervis* that a third tug had gone aground on a lee shore on the other side of the island.

Because *Jervis* had to stay guarding the *Gradisca* and its mutinous crew, Boissier was landed on Gavdo with a rescue party which made an over-night forced march across trackless, unknown and rough terrain. The stranded vessel was located next morning and the crew rescued with the exception of one man – drunk on rum – who died in the surf. The attempt to salvage the *Gradisca* failed and the ship eventually had to be abandoned.

In mid March *Jervis* left Haifa at high speed for Beirut to assist some small British Army units who were struggling to keep the peace between the civilian population and hated mainland French troops sent to garrison the city. Then followed a period of extraordinary complexity backing up the phlegmatic Army in its delicate task and at the same time enjoying the heady fruits which came with popularity expressions from the locals, particularly numerous and uninhibited Lebanese beauties.

This interlude came to a hasty end with a grim signal that a British destroyer at Rhodes was in a state of unrest. The saddest aspect of this traumatic information was that the ship in trouble was the only other surviving 'J' class, *Javelin*. When *Jervis* arrived, *Javelin* lay at anchor and appeared to be abandoned; there was no sign of life on the upper-deck and no response to light signals. After some delay and in response to orders issued over the loud-hailer, a boat manned by officers came across to report to Commander Maitland-Makgill-Crighton that there was indeed trouble in the ship – the crew refused to turn to for work or to steam the ship. The Commander sent the party of subdued and shamefaced officers back with orders that steam was to be raised immediately and that the ship under *Jervis*'s guns was to make for Malta. The wretched *Javelin* entered Sliema Creek and was boarded by an army Red Cap detachment and Royal Marines. A number of her ship's company were taken into custody. Valletta then became the setting for small groups of young sailors being marched, ignominiously, under armed escort to and from a court martial venue.

Javelin sailed from Malta 9th May and arrived in Portsmouth on the 17th. She was paid off into category B reserve and was broken up in Troon in 1946. *Jervis* was spared seeing the departure and sad collapse of an old flotilla mate with a proud war record, for she was back in the East Mediterranean on a task that was detested by all ships engaged in it. The flow of the surviving Jewish peoples fleeing from the holocaust and persecution in Europe and trying to enter Palestine was on the increase. Entry overland was well nigh impossible, so scores of often grossly overloaded ships with refugees were setting out from the Balkans and the Adriatic to break the British blockade of Palestine. British sailors were forced to restrain and turn back the very people which many in the fleet believed the long war had been fought to save.

The worst and final interception involving *Jervis* happened on 25th May in international waters. A ship, mv *Smyrni*, flying the Star of David as her ensign, was sighted and then stopped. A steel helmeted boarding party, armed with entrenching tools, found that the ship's master and twenty of his crew were Romanian, two others were Greek. The small ship was packed to the point of being unstable with 1760 refugee passengers, of which half were female, 220 were under twelve years of age, 8 were babies and 80 very elderly. The ship was in an appalling condition, short of everything including fresh water.

Smyrni with the boarding party still embarked was directed into Haifa where Palestine Police took charge of the passengers who had suffered so much to reach their goal and refuge.

Jervis remained based on Haifa for a further 12 days before sailing to Malta where she received orders to proceed to Chatham and to pay off. She left the 14th Flotilla and the Mediterranean on the last day of June and on arrival at Chatham paid off into the reserve, allocated for Sea Cadet training. *Jervis* never put to sea again under her own power, remaining in the Reserve Fleet for nine years until in 1954 it was approved that she should be scrapped. Later in the year *Jervis* was sold to Messrs Arnott Young & Co, and was broken up at Troon in the Firth of Forth. Thus ended the career of the first and, to date, the only ship to bear the name of one of England's most illustrious admirals. It was a fitting conclusion to a matchless career, that *Jervis* was the last of the J and K class to go to the breakers yard.

By any standard, *Jervis* had been a formidable and successful flotilla leader and no less so as a private ship. For the 5¾ years of World War 2, under six commanding officers and a long-serving ship's company, the ship had been responsible for an immense degree of damage to the enemy (Appendix 3 for shipping sunk), without losing a single man in action. Paradoxically, her record and that of many other highly successful fighting destroyers is unknown to the public at large who know only of her unfortunate sister flotilla-leader of the K class. *Kelly*, in her less-than-nine-months' active sea service, created no significant inconveniences for the enemy but became a legend because of the charismatic aura of her commanding officer.

This book is a belated attempt to record the achievements of 'lucky' *Jervis* and of those who served in her; in doing so, it names a few of the hardworking and successful fleet destroyers which – having never been accorded a place in history – are mentioned when they were in company with *Jervis* and the 14th Flotilla.

APPENDIX

Appendix 1

The letter written to his father by Ordinary Seaman Albert Stoker on arrival in Alexandria after witnessing the sinking of 'Lively', 'Kipling' and 'Jackal' on 11th May 1941.

> A Stoker Ord Sea
> C/JX 279145.
> 6 mess
> HMS JERVIS
> 13 May '41.

Dear Father,

Just a few lines hoping this finds you as it leaves me, sober I mean. One of my pals is coming back to England and is bringing this back with him. He is very lucky to be coming home because we nearly caught a packet in our last dust up. I suppose you heard about *Lively, Kipling* and *Jackal* being sunk in the Med: by enemy aircraft. Well we were the only ship to get out of it and not one of us even expected to. Four ships went out to intercept a convoy and about 3 oclock on Monday we were spotted by the Jerries reconnaissance plane. We turned for home and shortly after tea, brrrr, action stations.

I am in the rangefinder at the very top of the ship and I have a bird's eye view of everything. We were attacked for 4 hours and bombed all the time. When I got to my action station there was a Jerry overhead and he let a stick of bombs go. They missed us and I thought they had fallen in the hogswash but when I looked the *Lively* was just going under. Her skipper had her hard over and when they were hit on the foc'sle the ship turned turtle and went down in three minutes. Our guns were belting away all the time and a couple of Beaufighters chased the Jerries for a while.

We picked up the survivors and we had about 70 on board while the *Kipling* had about 150. I had the phones on and could hear all the orders coming through and about half an hour later a report came up 'Formation of planes approaching starboard quarter, angle of sight 80'. We trained round and could see them coming in out of the sun, 10 of them. We were banging away with everything we had, the pom poms and oerlikons did some great shooting and kept them a decent height up. Then they began to make their runs coming in in twos. The control were saying 'They're coming in! Long barrage, commence, commence, commence'. I couldn't hear anything but guns banging, bombs dropping and the fire gong ringing. They came at us first, they usually do as we are the flotilla leader. The first stick dropped well ahead of us but I thought she was all up with the next stick. Whoosh it dropped just astern and bomb splinters are flying all over.

They kept attacking, coming in from all directions and next time I looked at *Kipling* she was settling down by the stern. She caught a packet amidships and went down in about 20 minutes. That meant all the survivors from the *Lively* were in the water again. I looked at *Jackal* and saw she was lowering a boat, she seemed to be alright but she had been hit and the boiler-room was on fire. We kept dodging bombs and twisting and turning because if they had hit us it was the finish for all of us. When we thought the attack was over we went to the *Jackal* and told her we would come back to them after we had picked up the *Kipling* survivors. We went alongside the place where the survivors were swimming about and told them we'd pick them up after dark. We suddenly revved up and went full ahead, I looked up and there was the old Junkers overhead, he nearly caught us napping. It is good oh watching the bombs falling, they generally drop four at a time and they come down in a little cluster. This was our second near miss, they just missed us and fell on the starboard bow.

By this time I might tell you I had the old life belt blown up and my boot laces loose ready to jump if they got us. It was deadly leaving the chaps in the water until dark but we couldn't stop because we were the only ship left and if they got us! They were all shouting and we couldn't do anything. The 1st Lieutenant shouted through the megaphone and told them we would come back. They had thought it was all up when Jerry had just missed us. When we went back after dark, they were all shouting together, there were about 350 in the water and what a shout went up when they saw the *Jervis* back on the job. We lowered our whaler and put out to pick some up but there was that many trying to get they nearly pulled it under.

We had heaving lines over the side, scrambling nets, ladders, anything in fact. We could hardly haul them up they were so slippery with oil. We finally got them all inboard and what a mess. Everything was covered with oil. I was turning the whaler in with Lieut. Lacey and was on my knees practically as you couldn't stand up it was that slippery. The messdecks were crammed full of chaps, they just lay down and went to sleep no matter where they were. We were stripping them and rubbing them down and giving them our kit to put on. I was closed up all night with only my overalls on, I was a wee bit cold. Then we took half of *Jackal*'s crew on board and took her in tow. We were only doing about six knots and about three o'clock the tow rope parted. The *Jackal* was still on fire in the boiler room and the deck was white hot. We took the rest of the crew off then got underway, we made a run past *Jackal* and fired a fish at her. That fish missed so we fired another one and up she went. We had about five or six hundred survivors, oh what a state we were in, clothes soaked in oil all over, blokes dying and others that were hurt stretched out all over the place. Next morning we got an escort of destroyers that had come out and some aircraft. When we got back to Alex word had already got back and everybody in the fleet was watching the old *Jervis* come. We went alongside the jetty and ambulances were waiting for the wounded. We got them off and then had to clean ship and hanged if we hadn't to ammunition ship the same night. I borrowed 40 akkers and went ashore to get out of that. We have been washing down all the fore noon and today is a make and mend. It's just as well as everybody needed some sleep. I was closed up and had the phones on for 16 hours and the others were spent pulling survivors in and making tea for them.

There were any amount of my pals in the *Kipling* but they all got picked up. That just about finishes the 14th destroyer flotilla. We have the RAF out here, while the Jerries are overhead the Beaufighters are calmly circling around out of the way. Well thats all for now, so cheerio.

Albert.

Don't show my mother this.

Appendix 2

HMS JERVIS – Commanding Officers

Captain P.J. Mack DSO*   4th April 1939   23rd February 1942
(2nd June 1940, completion of collision damage repairs, Lieutenant-Commander A.F. Burnell Nugent DSC in command for trials and steaming out ot the Mediterranean where Captain P.J. Mack DSO* resumed command, 14th July 1940.)

Lt/Cdr J.B. Laing DSC   23rd February 1942   19th March 1942
(Temporary command while Captain Mack was ashore sick)

Captain A.L. Poland CB DSO* DSC	19th March 1942	8th January 1943
Captain A.F. Pugsley DSO	8th January 1943	21st June 1943
Captain J.S. Crawford DSO	21st June 1943	16th November 1943
Captain H.P. Henderson	16th November 1943	28th January 1944
Lt/Cdr R.P. Hill DSO DSC	28th January 1944	17th September 1944
Commander G. Ransome DSC	May 1945	June 1945
Commander D.H. Maitland-Makgill-Crichton DSO	June 1945	June 1946

HMS JERVIS – Battle Honours

Mediterranean	1940–1942
Libya	1940–1942
Matapan	1941
Sfax	1941
Crete	1941
Malta convoys	1941–1942
Sirte	1942
Sicily	1943
Salerno	1943
Aegean	1943
Adriatic	1944
Anzio	1944
Normandy	1944

Two other ships were also awarded thirteen World War Two Battle Honours, the cruiser *Orion* and destroyer *Nubian*. Only one ship was awarded more, fourteen, but from two World Wars, the veteran battleship *Warspite*.

Appendix 3

Enemy shipping sunk or captured by HMS *Jervis* with flotilla ships associated with the action.

Date	*Jervis* and ships in company.	Enemy warships.	Enemy merchantships captured or sunk.	Remarks
1939. 4th Sept.	*Jervis*		*Sunk – scuttled* Johannes-Molkenbuker 5294 tons.	North Sea
14th Oct.	*Jervis* *Janus* *Jackal* *Jersey*		*Prizes* *Bonde* 1570 tons. *Gustaf E Reuter* 6336 tons.	North Sea
1941 28/29 Mar.	*Jervis* *Nubian*	*Sunk* *Zara* *Pola* (10,000 ton 8×8" cruisers)	*Sunk*	Battle of Matapan after damage by battle squadron.
15/16 April	*Jervis* *Janus* *Nubian* *Mohawk**	*Tarigo* (1628 ton destroyer 6×4.7" guns + 4TT) *Lampo* *Baleno* (1220 ton destroyers 4×4.7" guns + 6TT's)	*Adna* 4205 tons *Arta* 2452 tons *Aegina* 3704 tons *Iserholm* 3704 tons *Sabaudia* 1590 tons	Malta strike Force. Action off Sfax.

* Sunk by two torpedoes from *Tarigo* (TT = Torpedo tubes.)

Date	Jervis and ships in company.	Enemy warships.	Enemy merchantships captured or sunk.	Remarks
24th April	Jervis Janus Juno Jaguar	Egeo (3110 ton armed auxiliary.)		Sicilian Channel.
1942 2nd Dec.	Jervis Kelvin Javelin Nubian	Lupo (679 ton destroyer 3×3.9" guns 4TT's)		Gulf of Gabes.
20/21st Dec.	Jervis Nubian		One unnamed merchantship.	Off Tripoli.
1943 20th Jan.	Jervis Nubian		Two unnamed merchantships.	Off Turgueness.
2nd June	Jervis Queen Olga	Castore (652 ton destroyer 3×3.9" guns, 4TT's)	Supply ships Vragnizza & Postumia	Off Cape Spartivento
18th Oct.	Jervis Penn		Ferry Barge & Schooner	Aegean off island of Kos.
1944 6/7th Jan.	Jervis Janus		3 schooners	Adriatic off Pesaro

Appendix 4

Demise of the J's and the K's, date order.

G72	*Jersey*	2nd May	1941	Mined in entrance to Grand Harbour, Malta.
G46	*Juno*	21st May	1941	Bombed and sunk by Italian S79's, Crete.
G85	*Jupiter*	27th February	1942	Mined in the Java Sea.
G34	*Jaguar*	26th March	1942	Sunk by U 652 off Tobruk.
G22	*Jackal*	12th May	1942	Dive bombed by Ju 87's in east Med.
G53	*Janus*	23rd January	1944	Sunk by glider bomb off Anzio.
G61	*Javelin*		1949	Broken up at Troon.
G00	*Jervis*		1954	Broken up at Troon.
G45	*Khartoum*	23rd June	1940	Lost in action with Italian submarine *Terricelli* in the Red Sea.
G01	*Kelly*	23rd May	1941	Sunk by dive bombers south of Crete.
G12	*Kashmir*	23rd May	1941	Sunk by dive bombers south of Crete.
G28	*Kandahar*	19th December	1941	Mined off Tripoli.
G64	*Kingston*	11th April	1942	Bombed in Malta drydock.
G91	*Kipling*	11th May	1942	Dive bombed by JU 87's in east Med.
G50	*Kimberley*		1949	Broken up at Troon.
G37	*Kelvin*		1949	Broken up at Troon.

Appendix 5

25th March 1942 – General Signal sent to the ships in Admiral Vian's force following the 2nd Battle of Sirte.

General   from C-in-C.

It gives me the greatest of pleasure to pass the following message which has been received by me from the Prime Minister.

I shall be glad if you will convey to Admiral Vian and all who sailed with him the admiration which I feel at this resolute and brilliant action by which the Malta convoy was saved. That one of the most powerfully modern battleships afloat attended by two heavy and four light cruisers and a destroyer flotilla should have been routed and put to flight with severe torpedo and gunfire injury in broad daylight by a force of 5 British cruisers and destroyers constitutes a naval episode of the highest distinction and entitles all ranks concerned and above all their commander, the compliments of the British Nation.

1930/25/3/1942.

24th December 1942– Signal to the Force K strike force based on Malta.

To Force K.   from C S 15.

The news from all the theatres of war is very good indeed, and in our homes throughout the British Empire this Christmas will be happy in the certain knowledge that, after three years of anxieties the Axis powers are now facing defeat and Annihilation, whilst the Allied Nations are looking forward to Victory and Reconstruction.

(2) In our own theatre of war, the last four weeks have witnessed two very important happenings. Firstly, Malta has been provisioned and stored for some months ahead. Secondly the sea routes used by the enemy to Tripoli have been dislocated, and the traffic probably reduced below that required to sustain the Axis efforts in Tripolitania. Force K has played a very large part in accomplishing these two successes, and will continue to do so, silently and in the traditional manner of our service.

(3) Should the Italian fleet decide to dispute our control of the waters in the Eastern Mediterranean, they shall have a Battle.

(4) In all Sincerity, I wish everyone a very Happy Christmas, and Victory in 1943.

1134A/24/1942.

Some Daily Orders.

Daily Orders
for Saturday 8th May 1943.

Saturday Routine.

Dress of the Day: No 3's Negative Jumpers.

0630	Port Watch fall in (Dress night clothing). Down FX clothes lines. Reeve M.C. and M.D. falls. Secure for sea. Sweep down the upper deck.
0715	Port Watch to breakfast.
0800	Both watches fall in (dress of the day). Magazine Party (6)
PM	Make and Mend.

Notes: We are at two hours notice from 0600.
The Magazine Party detailed will, as far as possible carry on with the job until it is finished.
During April we did 17 days at sea, steaming 4,997 miles, and cleaned our own boilers and painted ship.
Mileage since 1st January, 19,026
Mileage since the war started, 175,534.
White uniform will be worn as from Sunday 16th May.

(Sd) C.E.M. Thornycroft
FIRST LIEUTENANT.

....

NOTICE
HIS MAJESTY THE KING is travelling to Malta onboard HMS AURORA escorted by HMS ESKIMO, JERVIS, LOOKOUT and NUBIAN. Routine as far as JERVIS is concerned is as follows.

19th June 1943 (Today)

1800	Hands to clean
1835	Divisions (Tropical Rig).
1845	HIS MAJESTY THE KING leaves shore to go onboard *Aurora*.
2100	Port Watch fall in (Night clothing, negative jumpers).
2130	Weigh. Exercise Action Stations – then 3rd degree.

20th June 1943

0630	Call the Starboard watch. Clean into No 6's or No 5's with collars.
0715	Starboard watch close up in the vicinity of 3rd Degree stations. Phones to be kept manned. Suits to be kept clean. Prepare for going alongside, starboard side to. Port watch to clean into No 6's or No 5's with collars.
0800	Both watches of the hands fall in for entering harbour.
0815	Enter harbour. Secure alongside *Plumleaf.* Lower motor dinghy. *Nubian* secures on *Jervis.*
0855	Divisions. HIS MAJESTY THE KING goes ashore to Custom's House. Malta bells will ring a welcome.
0915	Landing party fall in on the jetty. (Dress: Long whites). After going ashore, HIS MAJESTY THE KING will return the Governor's call, then proceed on a tour of the Dockyard. Parties from all the ships and shore establishments will cheer him as he passes. *Jervis* party marches up to Corradino Ground and joins up with other parties from the fleet under command of the Captain of the *Nubian.* *Jervis* party will be formed as follows:–

FX Division	2 P.O.'s	2 Lg.Sea	+ 10
QD Division	2 P.O.'s	2 Lg.Sea	+ 10
ER DIVISION	/P.O.'s	2 Lg.Sea	+ 8
Torp division	1 P.O.	1 LG.Sea	+ 6
Comm Division	1 P.O.	2 Lg.sig	+ 6
Misc Division	G.M.	+ 4	

First Lieutenant in charge.

Remainder of the routine will be promulgated later.

> (Sd) C.E.M. Thorny-
> croft
> First Lieutenant.

(Later additional orders were posted)

ROUTINE FOR TONIGHT – 20th JUNE 1943.

2115	Port Watch fall in. Out brows. Single up. Secure for sea.
2135	Special Sea Dutymen.

2145	Slip. Sail for Tripoli with HIS MAJESTY THE KING in *Aurora*.
2155	Exercise Action Stations

MONDAY 21st JUNE 1943

About 0900	Arrive Tripoli. Forenoon Watchmen are to close up in clean tropical rig. Remainder of the ship's company is to be cleaned by 0900.
0905	Clear Lower Deck. All hands muster on the F.X. Petty Officers on No 2 Gun Deck. Cheer HIS MAJESTY THE KING into harbour.

NOTE

1.	If weather is bad *Jervis* will go alongside *Aurora* to take HIS MAJESTY into the inner harbour.
2.	We expect to sail for Malta at about 1000.

C. THORNYCROFT
FIRST LIEUTENANT.

....

BULLETIN 13/8/1943

We are to bombard the harbour of VALENTIA MARINA, the same place visited by *Euryalus* and *Pathfinder* the night we blew up the bridge! It is on the toe of Italy, some 25 miles south of the bridge, and we hope to find some landing craft and coasters in it.

Bombardment is due to start at 0115 (approx.).

C.E.M. Thornycroft.

....

Sources

(1) *Contributors*

P. Aylwin, J. Baston, D.F. Bates, B. Blowers, Heather Bone, P. Boissier, G.H. Boosey, W.J. Burch, R.D. Butt, A. Casswell, J. Clifton, P. Coney, R. Congdon, G. Cooke, J. Copper, J. Cowan, F.C. Dance, J. Dare, A.S. Donnett, D. Dykes, C.B. Featherstone Dilke DL, J.R.C. Edmunds, J.L. Ellis DSM, J.R.C. Engledue, T. Fanagher, P. Fletcher, R.S. Gibbs (deceased), A.E. Gore, D. Geluyckens, D.W. Hague, F. Hall, H.R. Hayes, M.A. Hemans DSC*, G. Hesford, R.P. Hill DSO DSC, E.A. Hutchinson, G. Jago, C. Parker Jervis, E. Johnson, W.R. Jones, H.G. Keen, A. Lee, E.H. Lee, W. Manners, V.G. Merry BEM, G. Morel, J.P. Mosse DSC, H. H.H. Mulleneux DSC, N. Myers, L. Pirie, A.F. Pugsley CB DSO**, A. Shirley, W. Skilling, W. Snape, A. Stoker, A. Stonehewer, R.T. Taylor, L.F. Waters, E. Wheeler, R. Wells DSC, V.C. Whitlock, D.R. Wilks, A. Willis, A. Wisely.

(2) *Naval Historical Section – Ministry of Defence*

Battle Summaries

BR 1736 (2) Battle of Crete.
       (35) 1950. Battle of Matapan.
       (19) Tobruk run and bombarding Mersa Matruh.
       (30) Landing at Salerno.
       (38) Selected bombardments.
       (49) (2) Naval Staff Histories Vol II, November 1940–December 1941.
          First Battle of Sirte.
          Page 187. Operation Glencoe.
          Page 90. Malta Strike Force. April/June 1941.
          Page 99. Kelly and 5th Flotilla bombard Benghazi.

Summary of Service

S 3543	HMS *Panther*		S 7114	HMS *Jaguar*
S 3667	HMS *Kashmir*		S 7470	HMS *Kelvin*
S 5698	HMS *Mohawk*		S 8002	HMS *Kingston*
S 6149	HMS *Nubian*		S 8978	HMS *Jersey*

S 6233   HMS *Jervis*   S 9333   HMS *Janus*
S 6349   HMS *Khartoum*   S 9557   HMS *Javelin*
S 6390   HMS *Kelly*   S 9943   HMS *Kimberley*

Admiralty War Diaries 1939 to 1945.

Public Records Office – Kew

ADM 53   109400–7.   *Jervis* Log Books (May to December 1939)
ADM 199 781   Battle of Matapan
         787 to 798   Mediterranean operations reports
         1367   Operation Retribution
         1244   Operation Vigorous
ADM 1   (31)
         200027   Despatches and reports of C-in-C Levant. Naval
         operations in the Aegean.

Navy Lists, 1938 to 1946.
Navy Retired List 1986.

Commander Anthony Casswell RN (Rtd)
Jervis Log. 1944 February to September.

Bibliography

The Italian Navy in WW 2., Cdr (R) Marc' Antonio Bragdini., A Naval
Institute Publication.
Sicily, Martin Blumensen, Macdonald.
Destroyer, Ewart Brooks, Jarrolds Publishing Ltd.
The Fall of Crete, Allan Clark, Four Square.
A Sailor's Odyssey, Admiral of the Fleet, Viscount Cunningham of
Hyndhope, Hutchinson & Co.
Western Mediterranean 1942–1945, Captain Taprell Dorling DSO, Hodder &
Stoughton.
Destroyers at War, Gregory Haines, Book Club Associates.
Anzio, Christopher Hibbert, Macdonald.
Destroyer Captain, Roger Hill, William Kimber.
British Destroyers, Edgar J. March, Seeley Service & Co.
Salerno, Foothold in Europe, David Mason, Pan/Ballantyne.
Night Action off Cape Matapan, S.W.C. Parker, Ian Allan.
HMS Kelly, Kenneth Poolman, William Kimber.
The Mediterranean and Middle East Vol III, I.S.O. Playfair, HMSO.
Destroyer Man, A.F. Pugsley, Weidenfeld & Nicolson.
Chronology of the War at Sea 1939 to 1945, J. Rohwer & G. Hummelchen, Arco
Publishing & Co.
War at Sea Vols I, II & III, Roskill, HMSO.
Ravenstein, Rowland Ryder, Hamish Hamilton.
Malta Strike Forces, P.C. Smith & Edwin Walker, Ian Allan.
A Dictionary of Ships of the Royal Navy of the Second World War, John Young,
Patrick Stephens & Co.
World Ship Society, Warship Supplement No 19.

Index

ABBREVIATIONS:-

Nationality. Aus – Australian. Br – British. Du – Dutch. Fr – French.
Gr – German. Gk – Greek. It – Italian. No – Norway. Ph – Polish. Po
– Portuguese.
Type/Class of warship. ac – aircraft carrier. bs – battleship. bcs –
battlecruiser. cv – corvette. ds – destroyer. gb – gun-boat. ml –
minelayer. mo – moniter. ms – minesweeper. sb – submarine. sl –
sloop. tr – trawler.
HM ships are identified by Type/Class abbreviations.